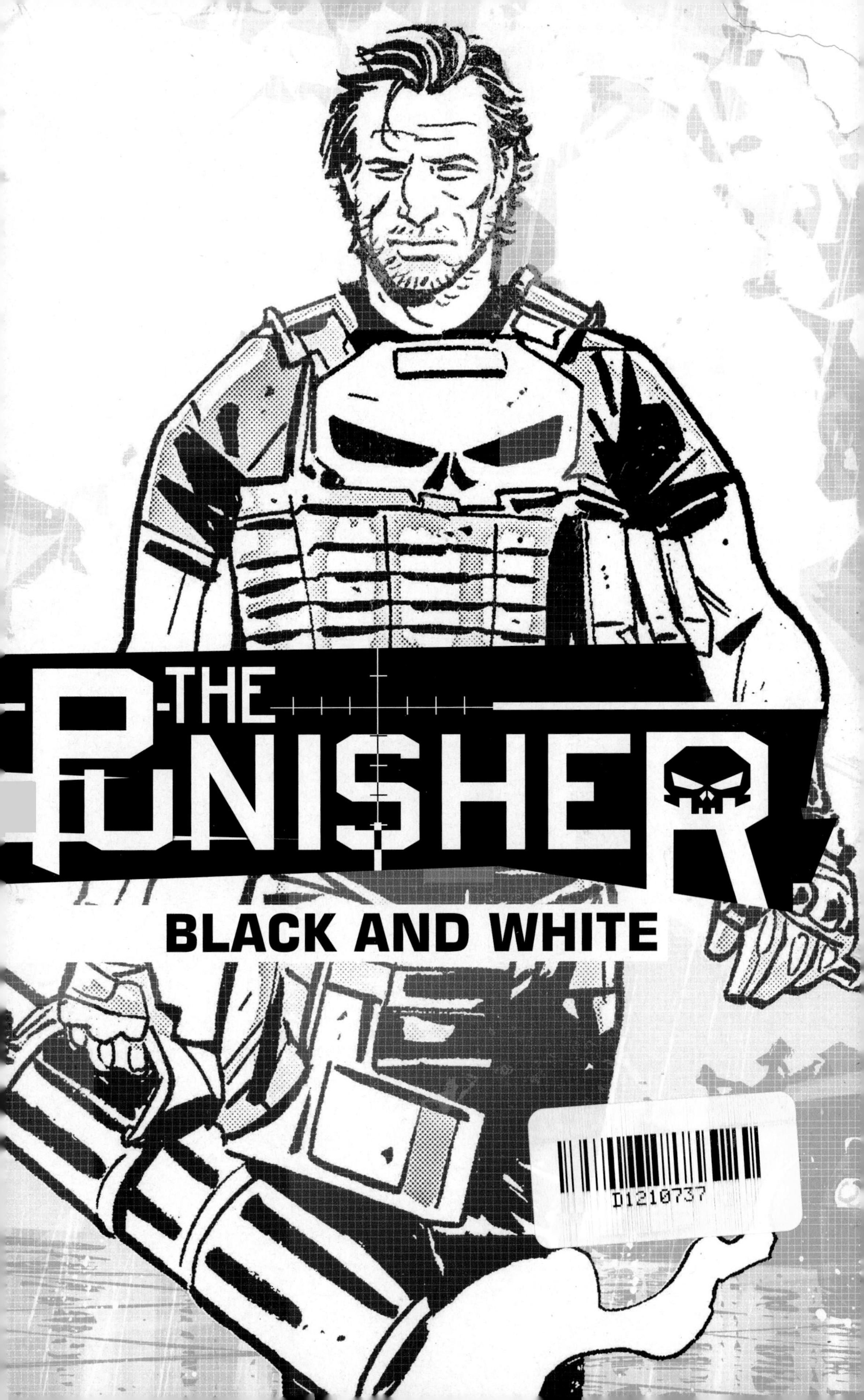
THE PUNISHER
BLACK AND WHITE

THE PUNISHER
BLACK AND WHITE

WRITER:
NATHAN EDMONDSON

ARTIST:
MITCH GERADS

LETTERER:
VC'S CORY PETIT

COVER ART:
MITCH GERADS

EDITOR:
JAKE THOMAS

COLLECTION EDITOR:
SARAH BRUNSTAD

ASSOCIATE MANAGING EDITOR:
ALEX STARBUCK

EDITORS, SPECIAL PROJECTS:
**JENNIFER GRÜNWALD
& MARK D. BEAZLEY**

SENIOR EDITOR, SPECIAL PROJECTS:
JEFF YOUNGQUIST

BOOK DESIGNER:
RODOLFO MURAGUCHI

SVP PRINT, SALES & MARKETING:
DAVID GABRIEL

EDITOR IN CHIEF:
AXEL ALONSO

CHIEF CREATIVE OFFICER:
JOE QUESADA

PUBLISHER:
DAN BUCKLEY

EXECUTIVE PRODUCER:
ALAN FINE

THE PUNISHER VOL. 1: BLACK AND WHITE. Contains material originally published in magazine form as THE PUNISHER #1-6. Second printing 2016. ISBN# 978-0-7851-5443-3. Published by MARVEL WORLDWIDE, INC., a subsidiary of MARVEL ENTERTAINMENT, LLC. OFFICE OF PUBLICATION: 135 West 50th Street, New York, NY 10020. Copyright © 2014 MARVEL No similarity between any of the names, characters, persons, and/or institutions in this magazine with those of any living or dead person or institution is intended, and any such similarity which may exist is purely coincidental. **Printed in the U.S.A.** ALAN FINE, President, Marvel Entertainment; DAN BUCKLEY, President, TV, Publishing and Brand Management; JOE QUESADA, Chief Creative Officer; TOM BREVOORT, SVP of Publishing; DAVID BOGART, SVP of Operations & Procurement, Publishing; C.B. CEBULSKI, VP of International Development & Brand Management; DAVID GABRIEL, SVP Print, Sales & Marketing; JIM O'KEEFE, VP of Operations & Logistics; DAN CARR, Executive Director of Publishing Technology; SUSAN CRESPI, Editorial Operations Manager; ALEX MORALES, Publishing Operations Manager; STAN LEE, Chairman Emeritus. For information regarding advertising in Marvel Comics or on Marvel.com, please contact Jonathan Rheingold, VP of Custom Solutions & Ad Sales, at jrheingold@marvel.com. For Marvel subscription inquiries, please call 800-217-9158. **Manufactured between 12/9/2015 and 1/11/16 by HESS PRINT SOLUTIONS, A DIVISION OF RANG PRINTING, BRIMFIELD, OH, USA.**

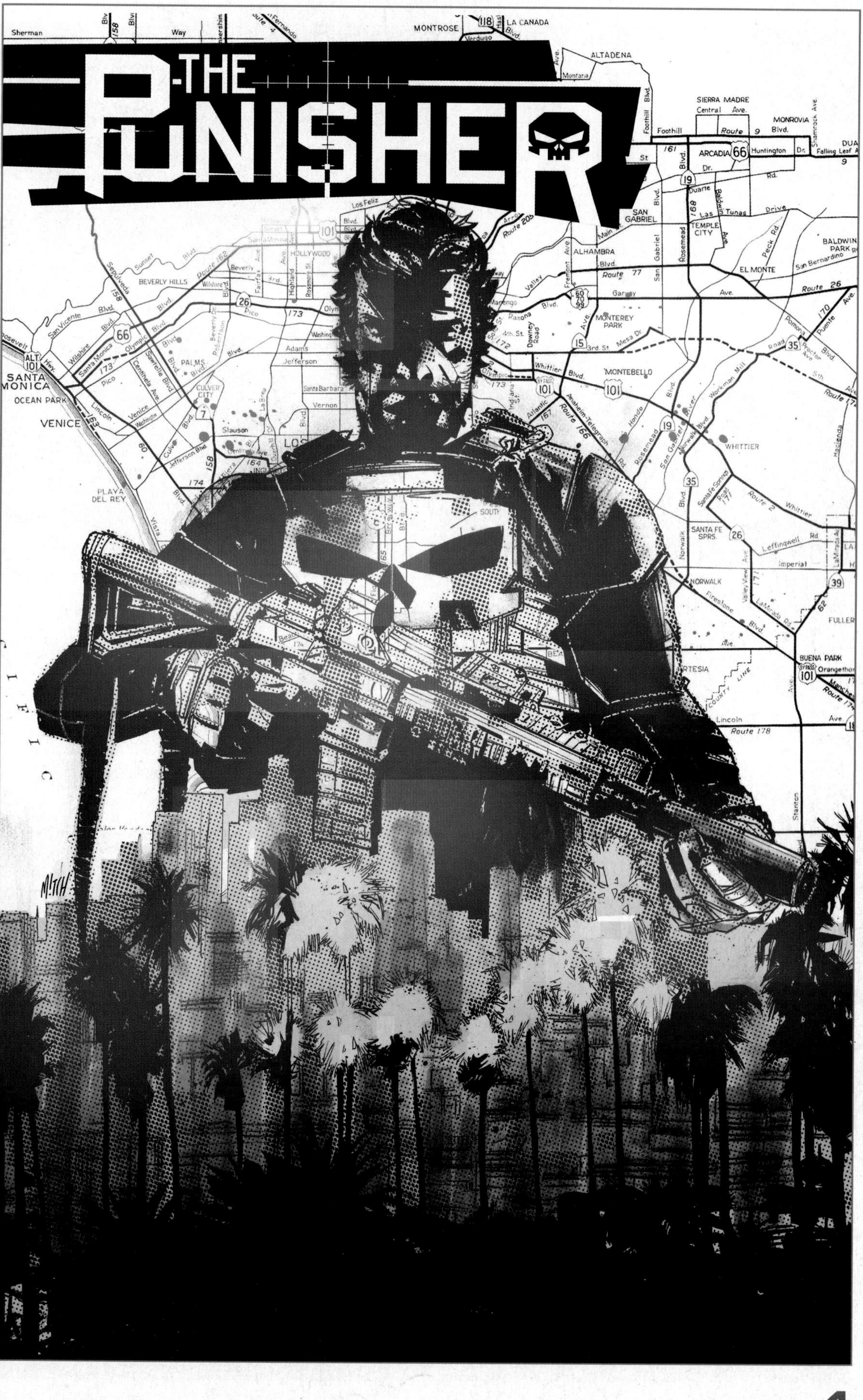
THE PUNISHER
MITCH
MONTROSE
LA CANADA
ALTADENA
SIERRA MADRE
MONROVIA
ARCADIA
SAN GABRIEL
TEMPLE CITY
ALHAMBRA
EL MONTE
BALDWIN PARK
HOLLYWOOD
BEVERLY HILLS
MONTEREY PARK
MONTEBELLO
SANTA MONICA
OCEAN PARK
VENICE
PALMS
CULVER CITY
PLAYA DEL REY
WHITTIER
SANTA FE SPRS.
NORWALK
BUENA PARK
ARTESIA

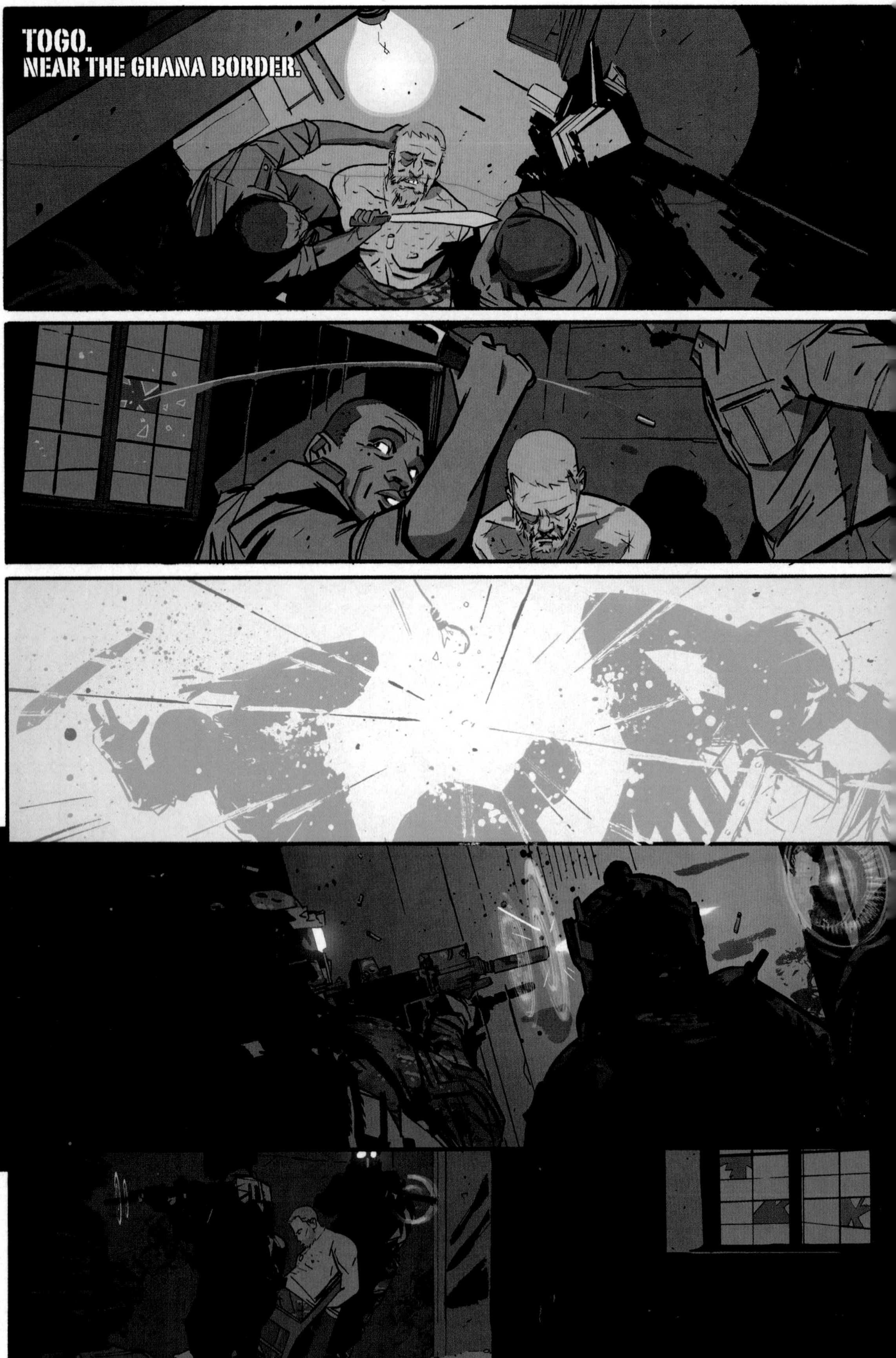
TOGO.
NEAR THE GHANA BORDER.

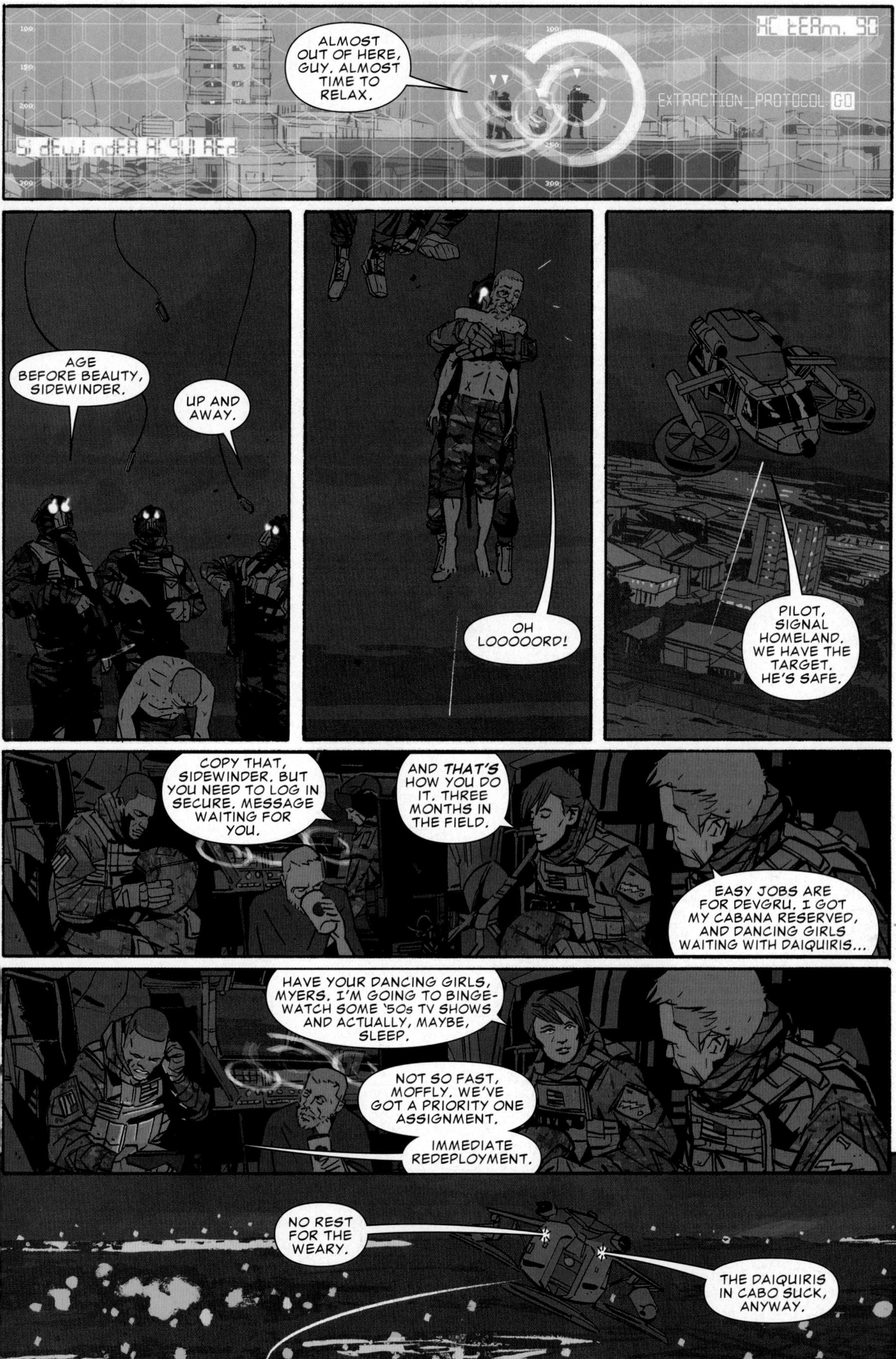
ALMOST OUT OF HERE, GUY. ALMOST TIME TO RELAX.
EXTRACTION_PROTOCOL GO
SIDEWINDER ACQUIRED
AGE BEFORE BEAUTY, SIDEWINDER.
UP AND AWAY.
OH LOOOOORD!
PILOT, SIGNAL HOMELAND. WE HAVE THE TARGET. HE'S SAFE.
COPY THAT, SIDEWINDER. BUT YOU NEED TO LOG IN SECURE. MESSAGE WAITING FOR YOU.
AND THAT'S HOW YOU DO IT. THREE MONTHS IN THE FIELD.
EASY JOBS ARE FOR DEVGRU. I GOT MY CABANA RESERVED, AND DANCING GIRLS WAITING WITH DAIQUIRIS...
HAVE YOUR DANCING GIRLS, MYERS. I'M GOING TO BINGE-WATCH SOME '50s TV SHOWS AND ACTUALLY, MAYBE, SLEEP.
NOT SO FAST, MOFFLY. WE'VE GOT A PRIORITY ONE ASSIGNMENT.
IMMEDIATE REDEPLOYMENT.
NO REST FOR THE WEARY.
THE DAIQUIRIS IN CABO SUCK, ANYWAY.

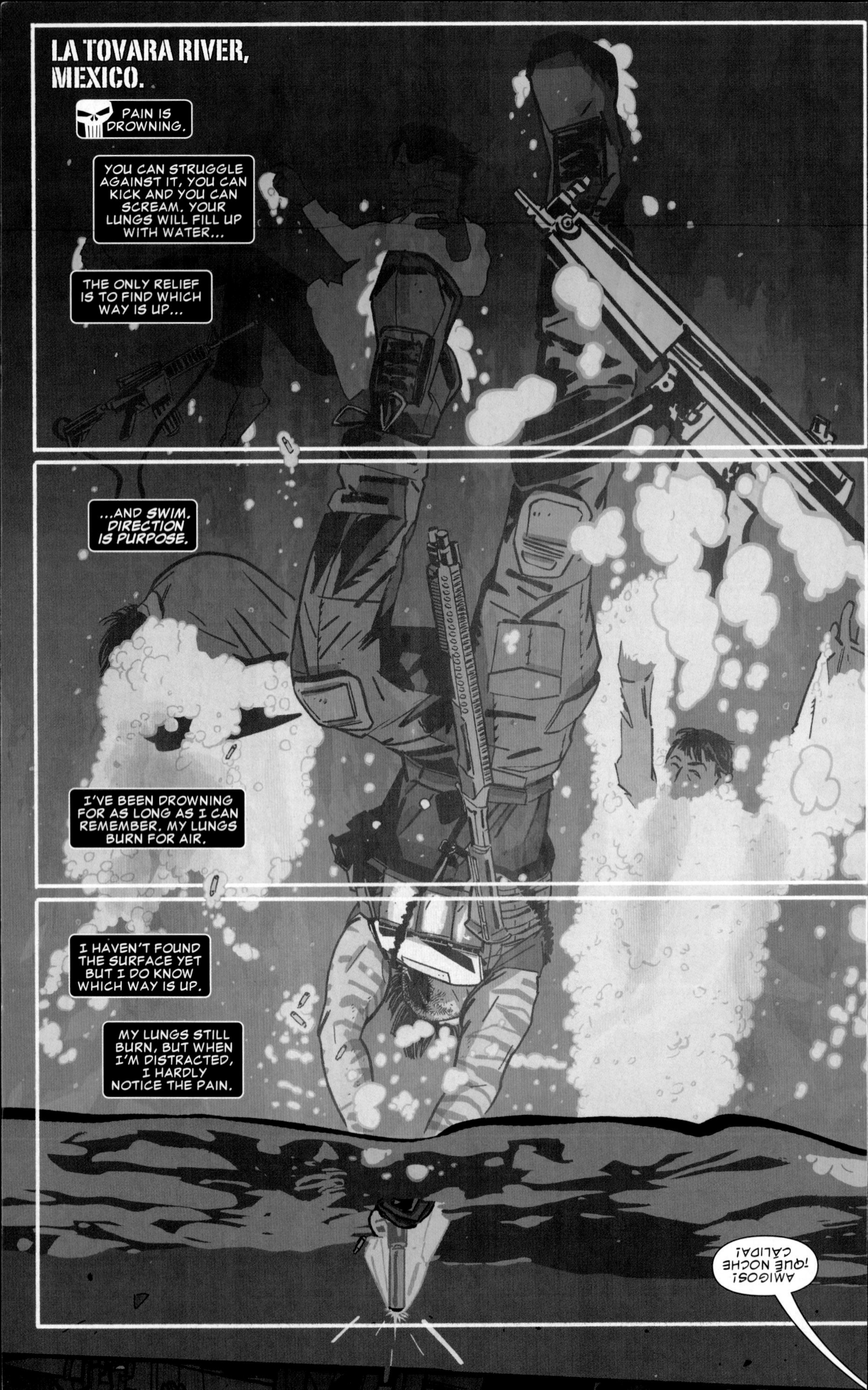
LA TOVARA RIVER, MEXICO.
PAIN IS DROWNING.
YOU CAN STRUGGLE AGAINST IT, YOU CAN KICK AND YOU CAN SCREAM. YOUR LUNGS WILL FILL UP WITH WATER...
THE ONLY RELIEF IS TO FIND WHICH WAY IS UP...
...AND SWIM. DIRECTION IS PURPOSE.
I'VE BEEN DROWNING FOR AS LONG AS I CAN REMEMBER. MY LUNGS BURN FOR AIR.
I HAVEN'T FOUND THE SURFACE YET BUT I DO KNOW WHICH WAY IS UP.
MY LUNGS STILL BURN, BUT WHEN I'M DISTRACTED, I HARDLY NOTICE THE PAIN.
AMIGOS! ¡QUE NOCHE CÁLIDA!

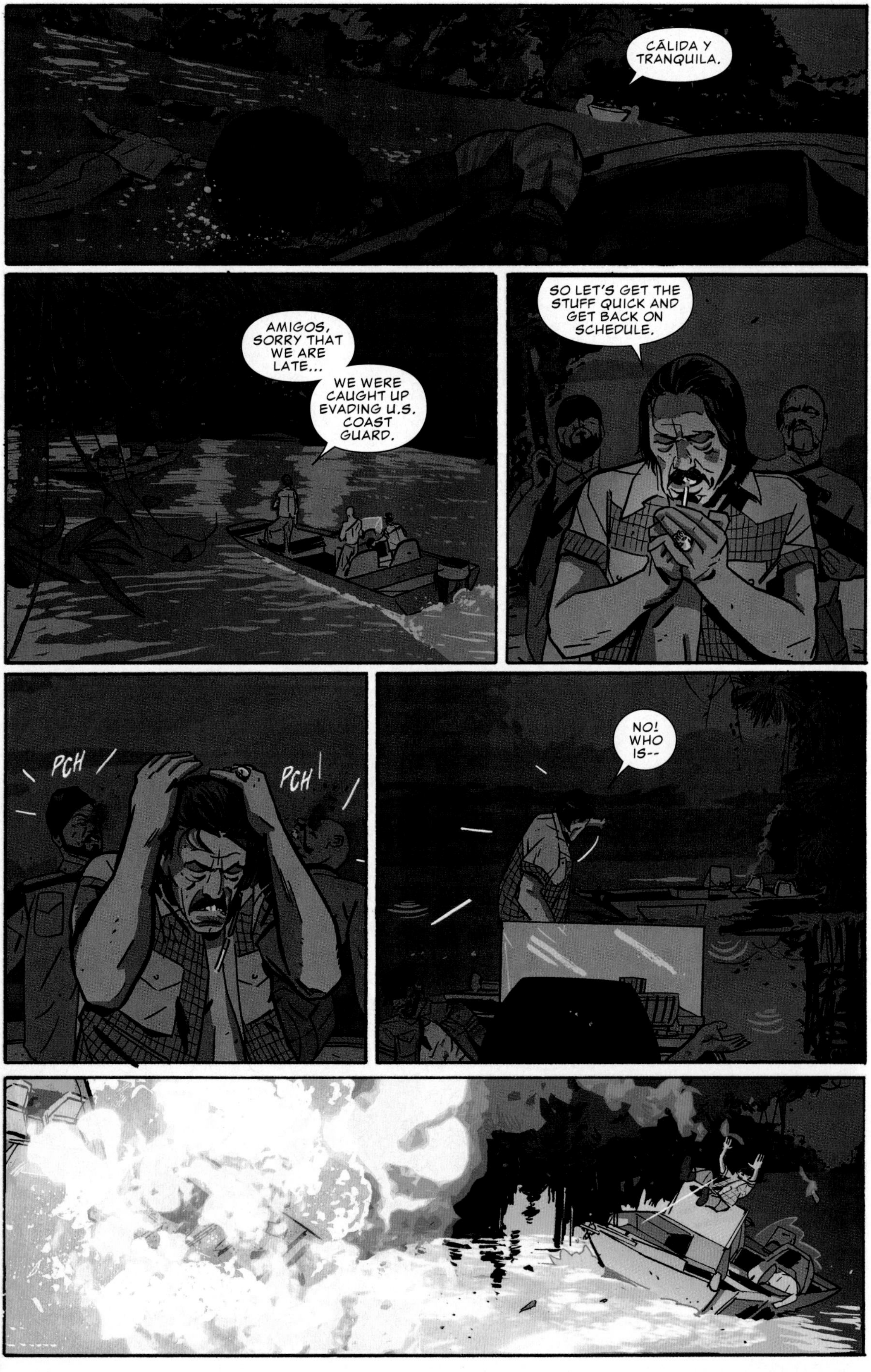

CĀLIDA Y TRANQUILA.
AMIGOS, SORRY THAT WE ARE LATE...
WE WERE CAUGHT UP EVADING U.S. COAST GUARD.
SO LET'S GET THE STUFF QUICK AND GET BACK ON SCHEDULE.
PCH
PCH
NO! WHO IS--

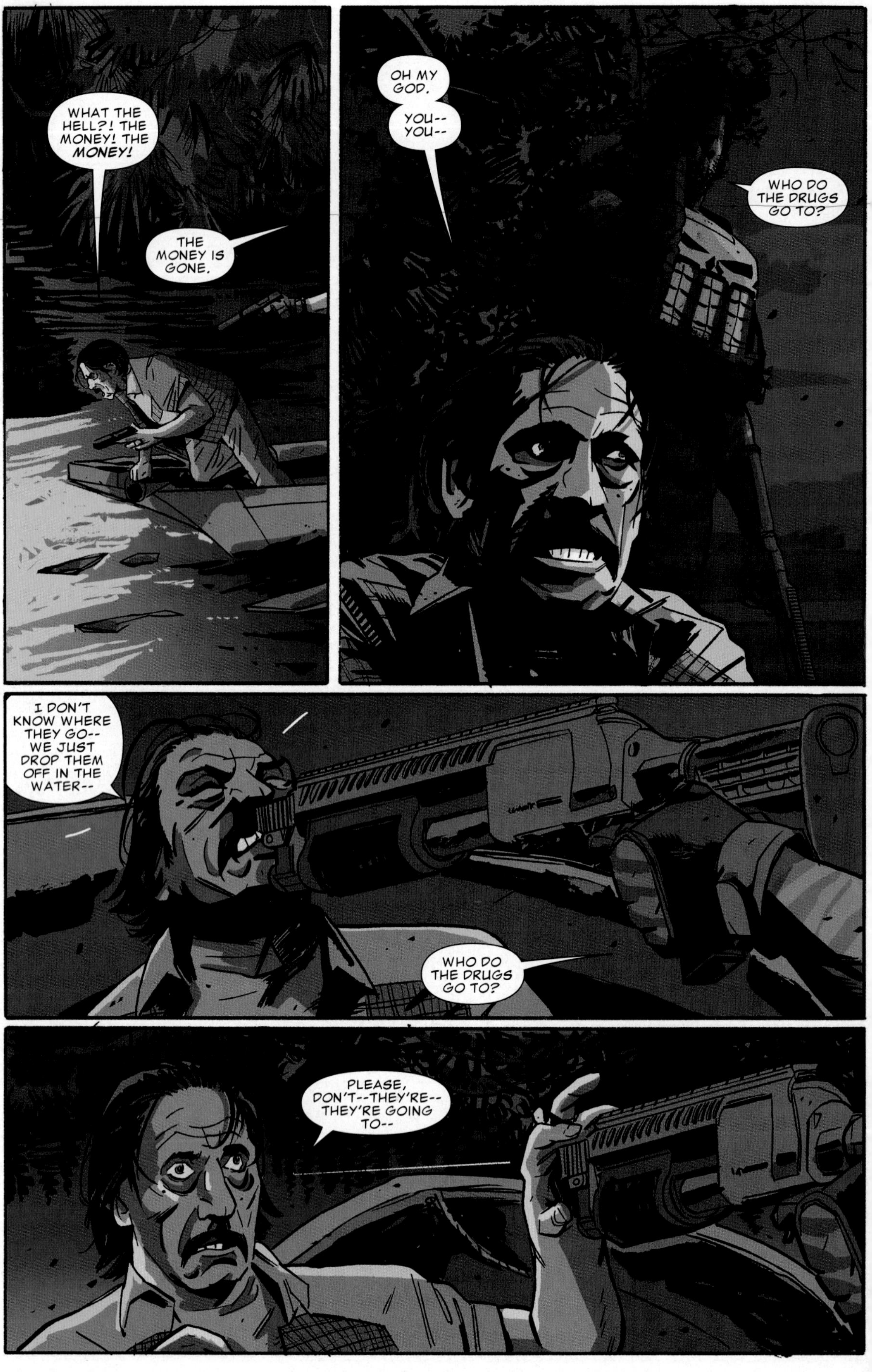
WHAT THE HELL?! THE MONEY! THE MONEY!
THE MONEY IS GONE.
OH MY GOD.
YOU-- YOU--
WHO DO THE DRUGS GO TO?
I DON'T KNOW WHERE THEY GO-- WE JUST DROP THEM OFF IN THE WATER--
WHO DO THE DRUGS GO TO?
PLEASE, DON'T--THEY'RE-- THEY'RE GOING TO--

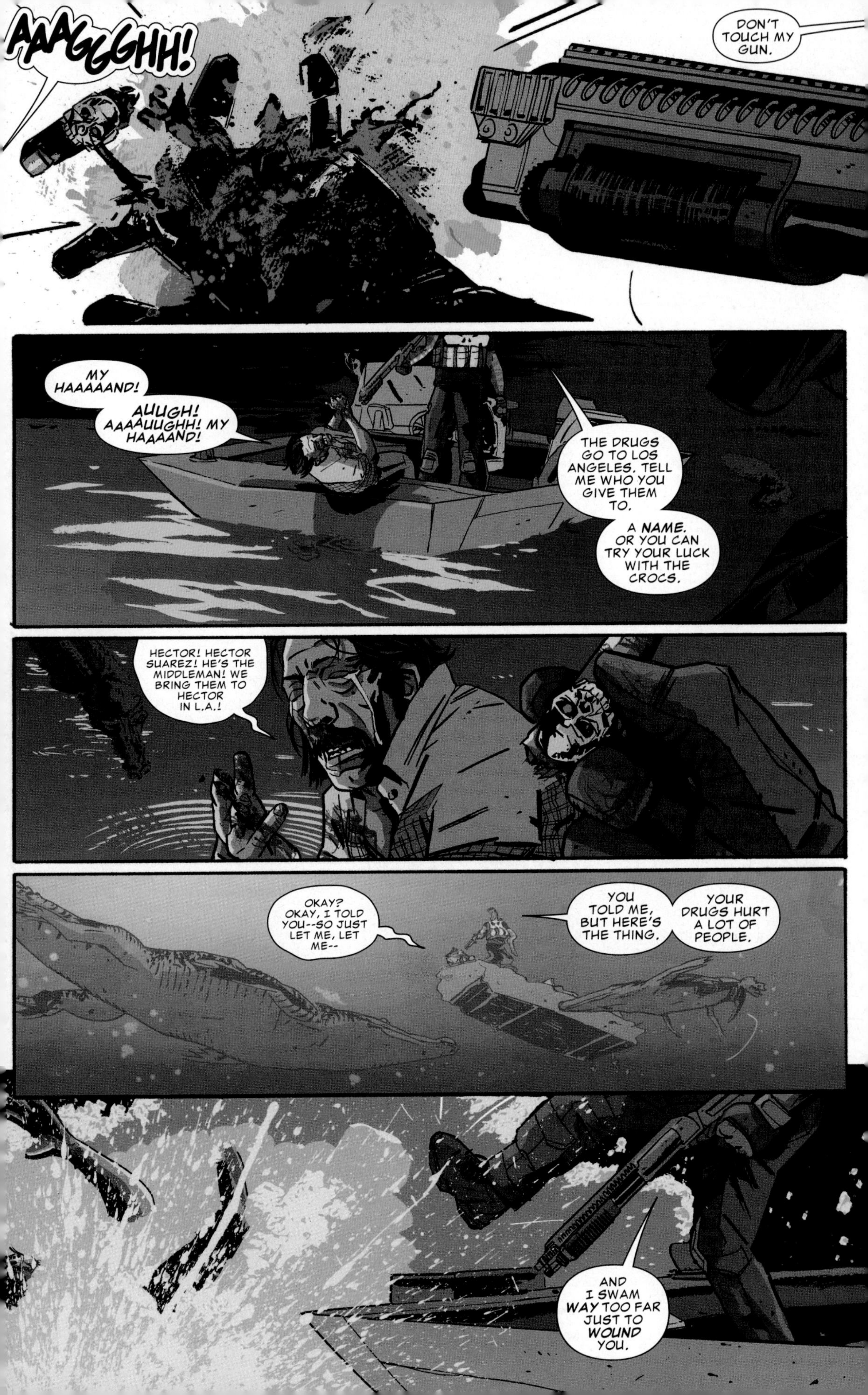
AAAGGGHH!
DON'T TOUCH MY GUN.
MY HAAAAAND!
AUUGH! AAAAUUGHH! MY HAAAAND!
THE DRUGS GO TO LOS ANGELES. TELL ME WHO YOU GIVE THEM TO.
A NAME. OR YOU CAN TRY YOUR LUCK WITH THE CROCS.
HECTOR! HECTOR SUAREZ! HE'S THE MIDDLEMAN! WE BRING THEM TO HECTOR IN L.A.!
OKAY? OKAY, I TOLD YOU--SO JUST LET ME, LET ME--
YOU TOLD ME, BUT HERE'S THE THING.
YOUR DRUGS HURT A LOT OF PEOPLE.
AND I SWAM WAY TOO FAR JUST TO WOUND YOU.

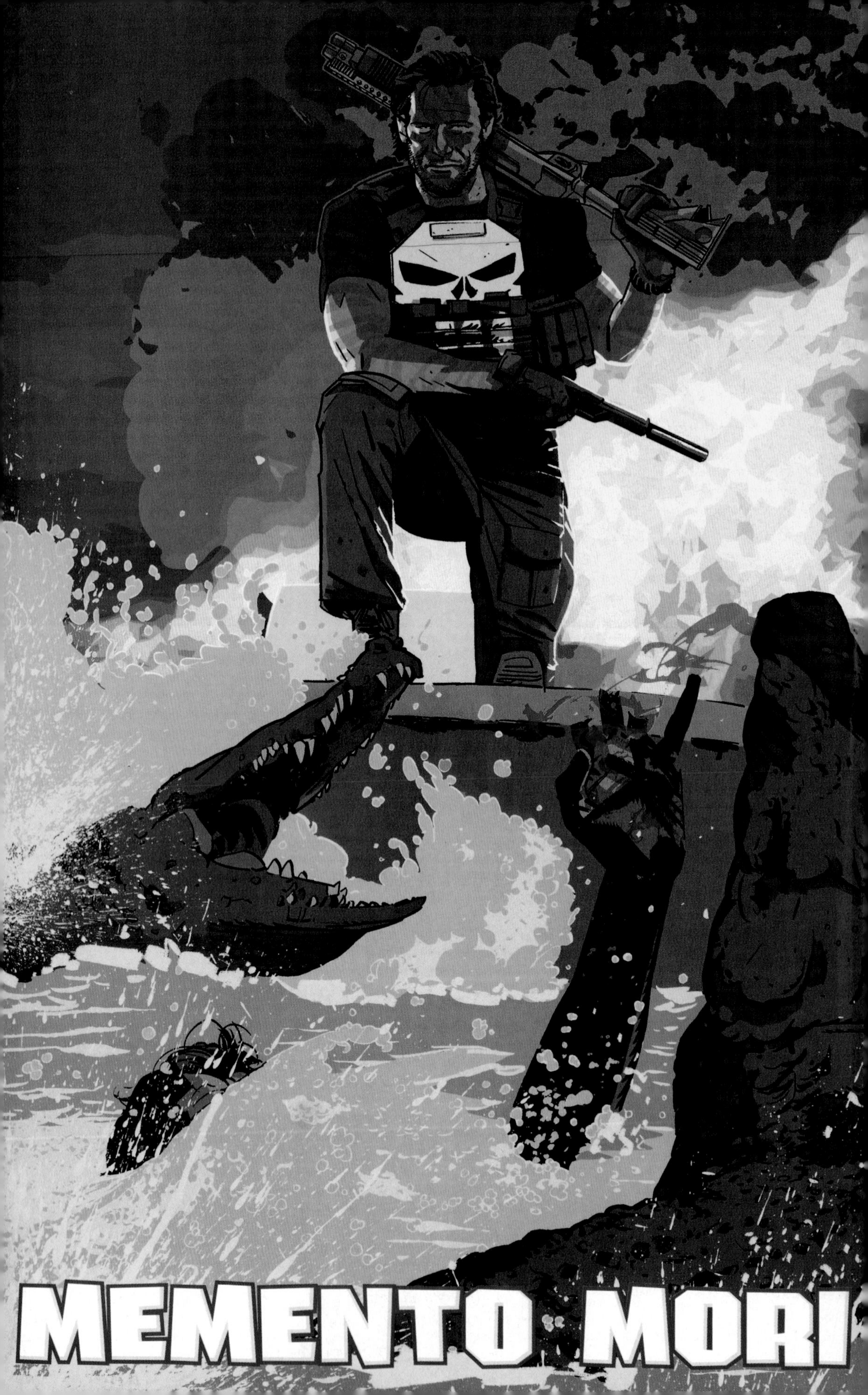
MEMENTO MORI

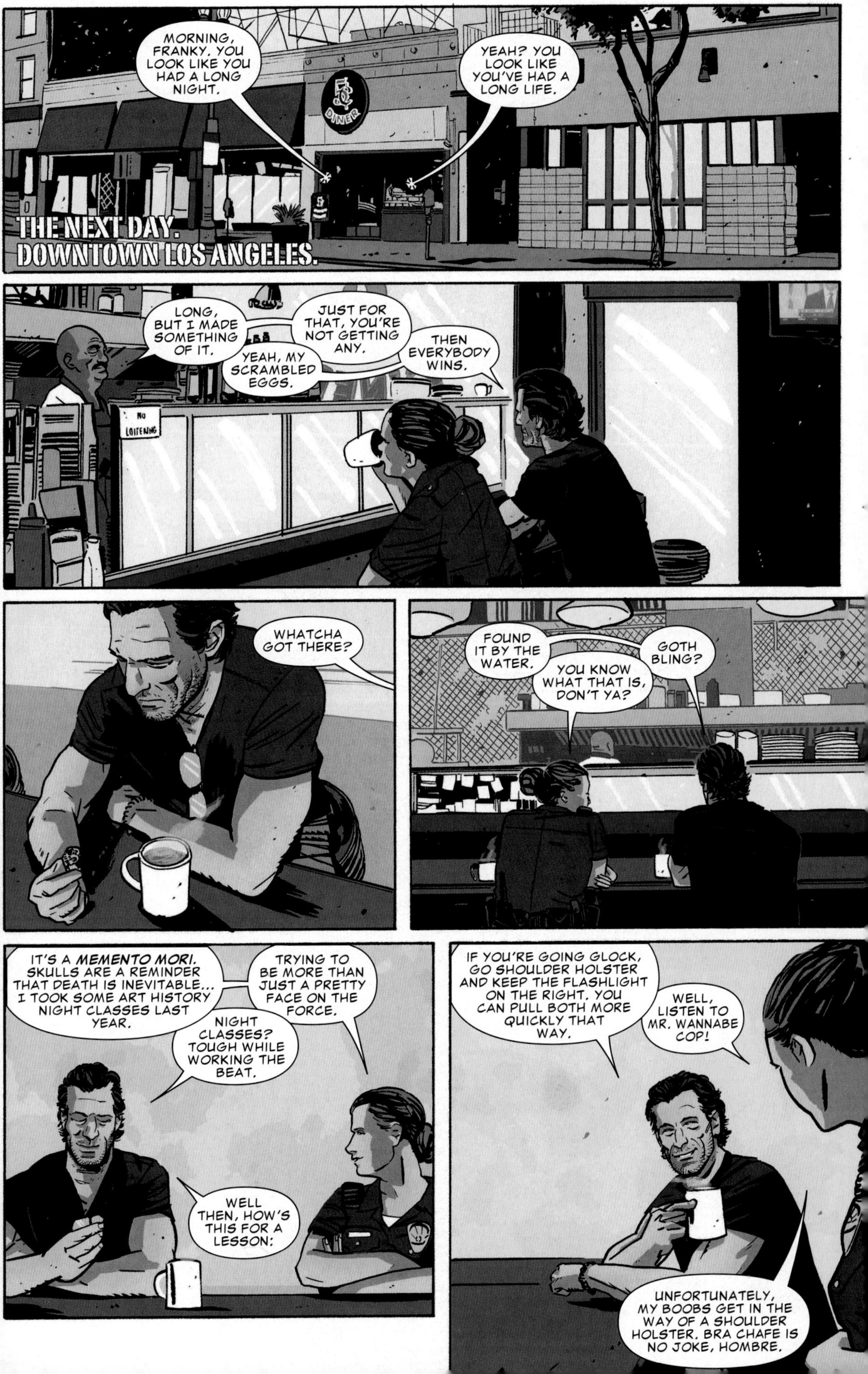
THE NEXT DAY. DOWNTOWN LOS ANGELES.
MORNING, FRANKY. YOU LOOK LIKE YOU HAD A LONG NIGHT.
YEAH? YOU LOOK LIKE YOU'VE HAD A LONG LIFE.
DINER
LONG, BUT I MADE SOMETHING OF IT.
JUST FOR THAT, YOU'RE NOT GETTING ANY.
YEAH, MY SCRAMBLED EGGS.
THEN EVERYBODY WINS.
NO LOITERING
WHATCHA GOT THERE?
FOUND IT BY THE WATER.
GOTH BLING?
YOU KNOW WHAT THAT IS, DON'T YA?
IT'S A *MEMENTO MORI.* SKULLS ARE A REMINDER THAT DEATH IS INEVITABLE... I TOOK SOME ART HISTORY NIGHT CLASSES LAST YEAR.
TRYING TO BE MORE THAN JUST A PRETTY FACE ON THE FORCE.
NIGHT CLASSES? TOUGH WHILE WORKING THE BEAT.
WELL THEN, HOW'S THIS FOR A LESSON:
IF YOU'RE GOING GLOCK, GO SHOULDER HOLSTER AND KEEP THE FLASHLIGHT ON THE RIGHT. YOU CAN PULL BOTH MORE QUICKLY THAT WAY.
WELL, LISTEN TO MR. WANNABE COP!
UNFORTUNATELY, MY BOOBS GET IN THE WAY OF A SHOULDER HOLSTER. BRA CHAFE IS NO JOKE, HOMBRE.

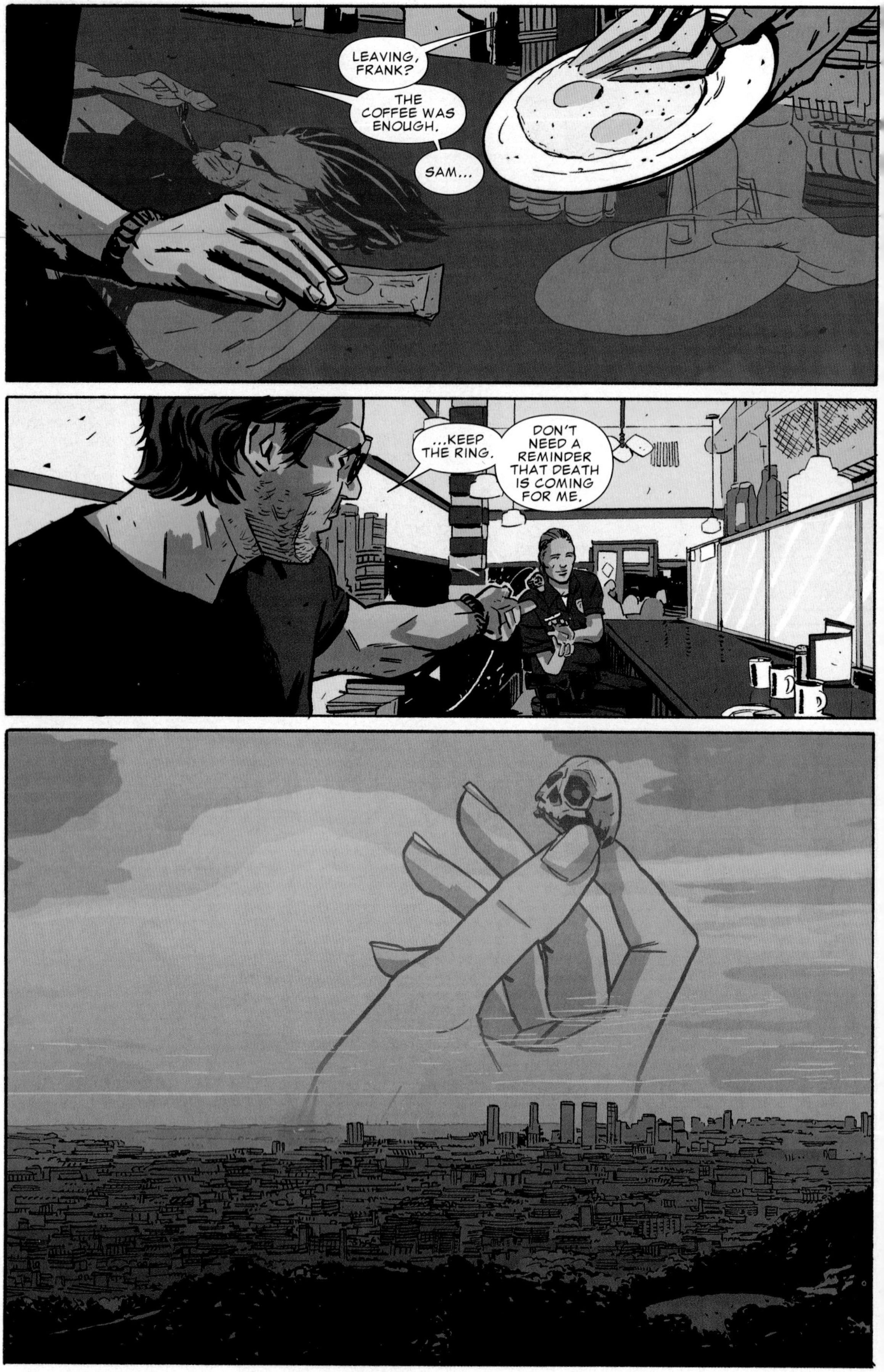
LEAVING, FRANK?
THE COFFEE WAS ENOUGH.
SAM...
...KEEP THE RING.
DON'T NEED A REMINDER THAT DEATH IS COMING FOR ME.

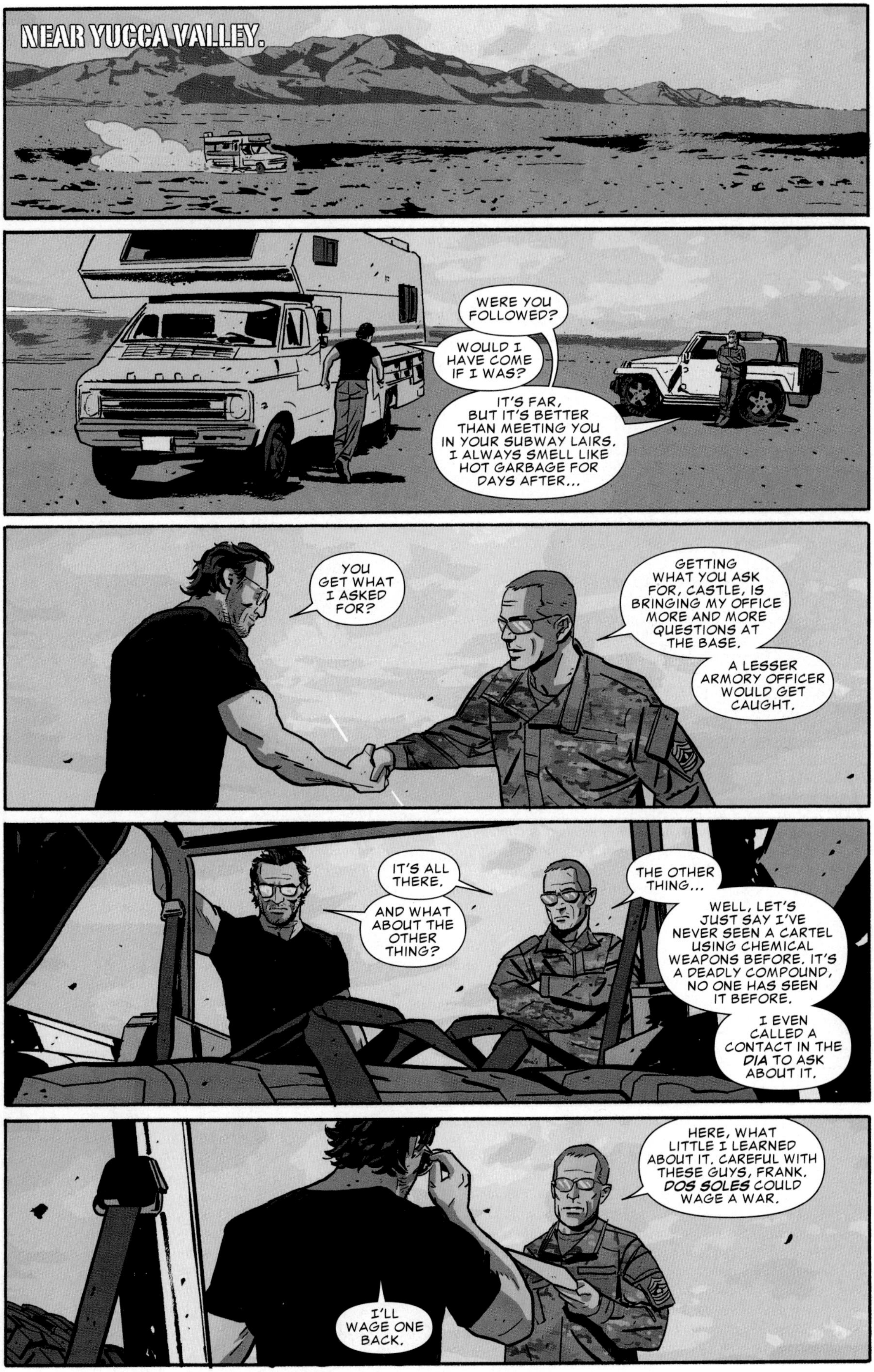
NEAR YUCCA VALLEY.
WERE YOU FOLLOWED?
WOULD I HAVE COME IF I WAS?
IT'S FAR, BUT IT'S BETTER THAN MEETING YOU IN YOUR SUBWAY LAIRS. I ALWAYS SMELL LIKE HOT GARBAGE FOR DAYS AFTER...
YOU GET WHAT I ASKED FOR?
GETTING WHAT YOU ASK FOR, CASTLE, IS BRINGING MY OFFICE MORE AND MORE QUESTIONS AT THE BASE.
A LESSER ARMORY OFFICER WOULD GET CAUGHT.
IT'S ALL THERE.
AND WHAT ABOUT THE OTHER THING?
THE OTHER THING...
WELL, LET'S JUST SAY I'VE NEVER SEEN A CARTEL USING CHEMICAL WEAPONS BEFORE. IT'S A DEADLY COMPOUND, NO ONE HAS SEEN IT BEFORE.
I EVEN CALLED A CONTACT IN THE *DIA* TO ASK ABOUT IT.
HERE, WHAT LITTLE I LEARNED ABOUT IT. CAREFUL WITH THESE GUYS, FRANK. *DOS SOLES* COULD WAGE A WAR.
I'LL WAGE ONE BACK.

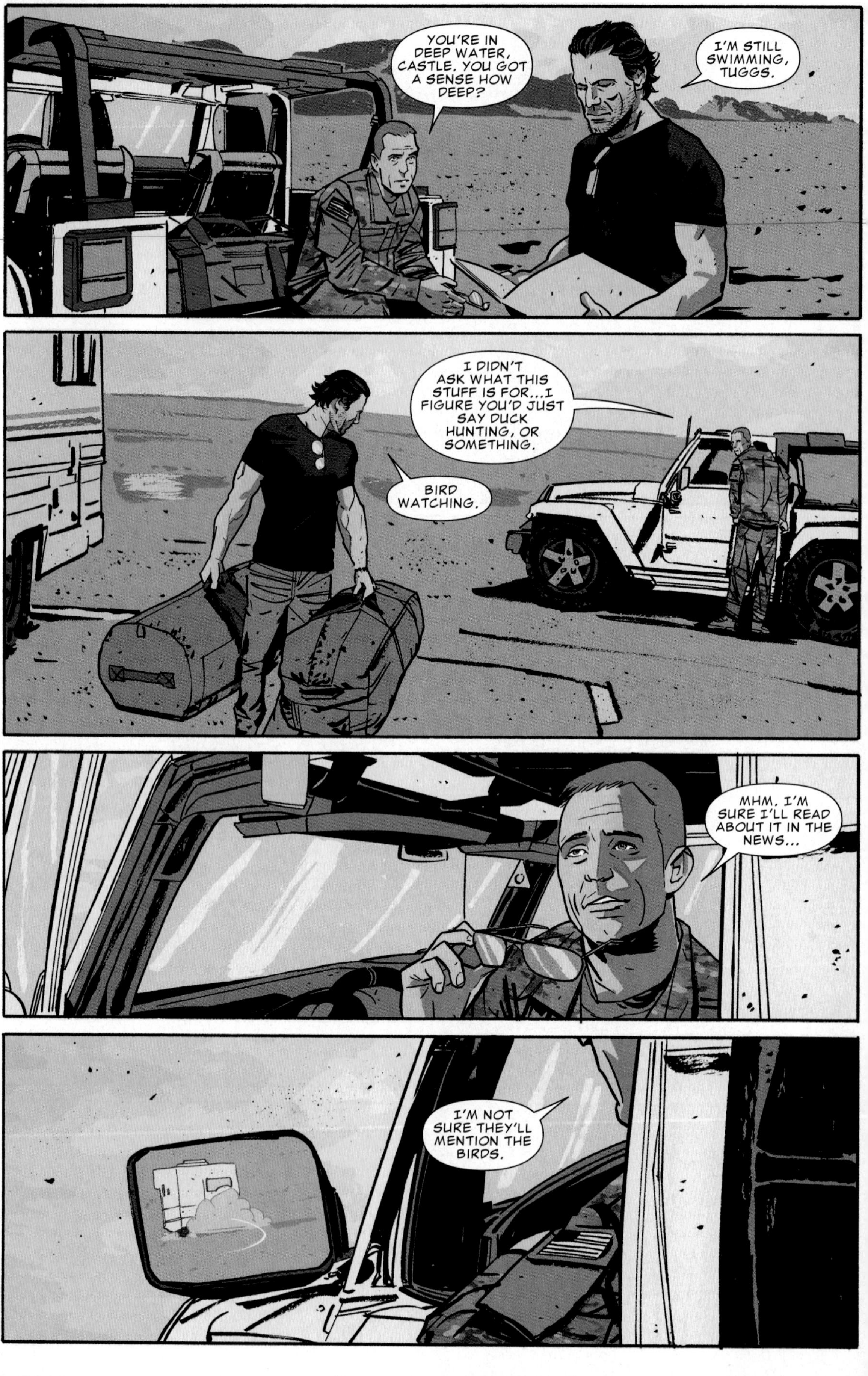
YOU'RE IN DEEP WATER, CASTLE. YOU GOT A SENSE HOW DEEP?
I'M STILL SWIMMING, TUGGS.
I DIDN'T ASK WHAT THIS STUFF IS FOR...I FIGURE YOU'D JUST SAY DUCK HUNTING, OR SOMETHING.
BIRD WATCHING.
MHM. I'M SURE I'LL READ ABOUT IT IN THE NEWS...
I'M NOT SURE THEY'LL MENTION THE BIRDS.

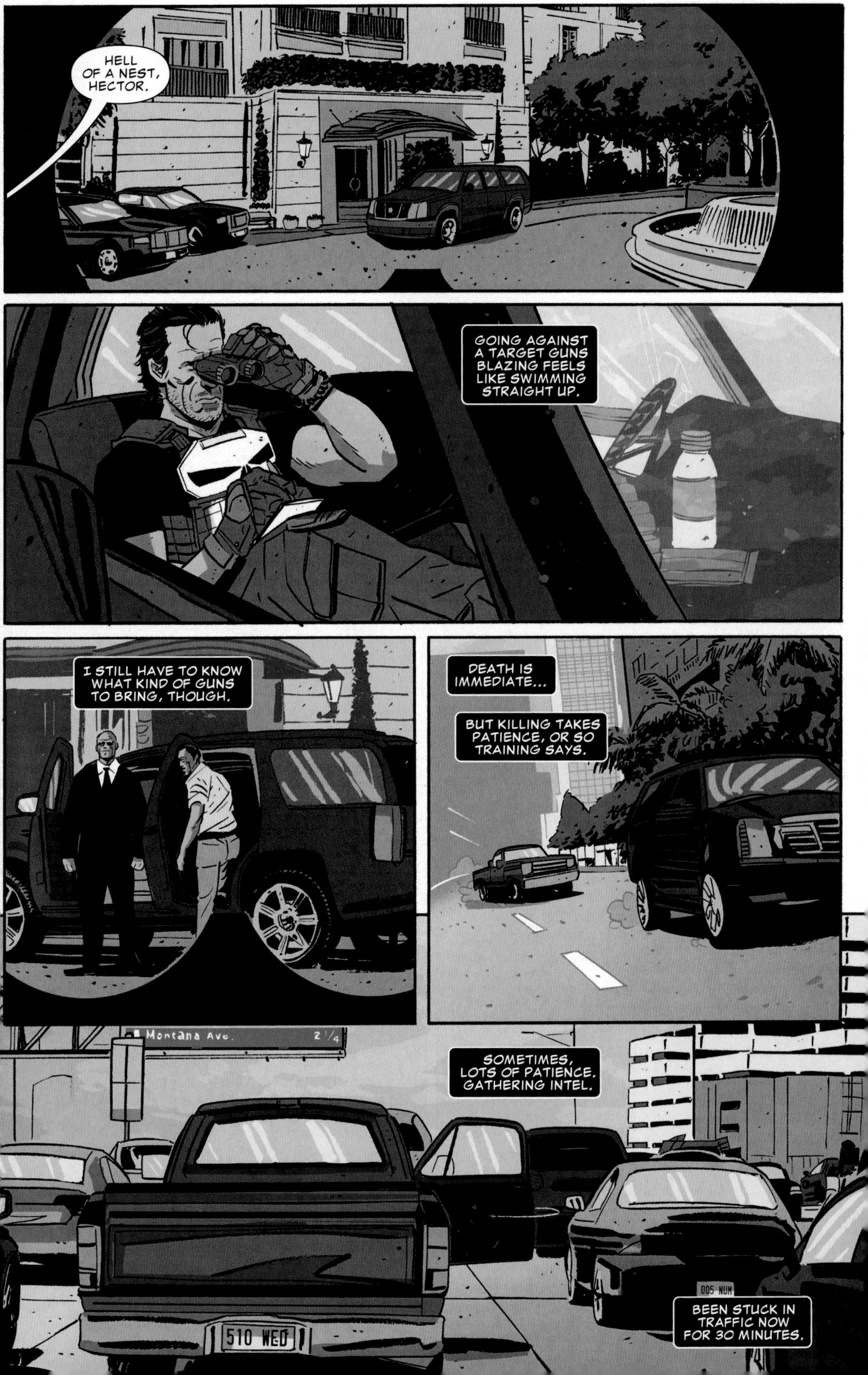
HELL OF A NEST, HECTOR.
GOING AGAINST A TARGET GUNS BLAZING FEELS LIKE SWIMMING STRAIGHT UP.
I STILL HAVE TO KNOW WHAT KIND OF GUNS TO BRING, THOUGH.
DEATH IS IMMEDIATE...
BUT KILLING TAKES PATIENCE, OR SO TRAINING SAYS.
Montana Ave. 2 1/4
SOMETIMES, LOTS OF PATIENCE. GATHERING INTEL.
005 NUM
510 WED
BEEN STUCK IN TRAFFIC NOW FOR 30 MINUTES.

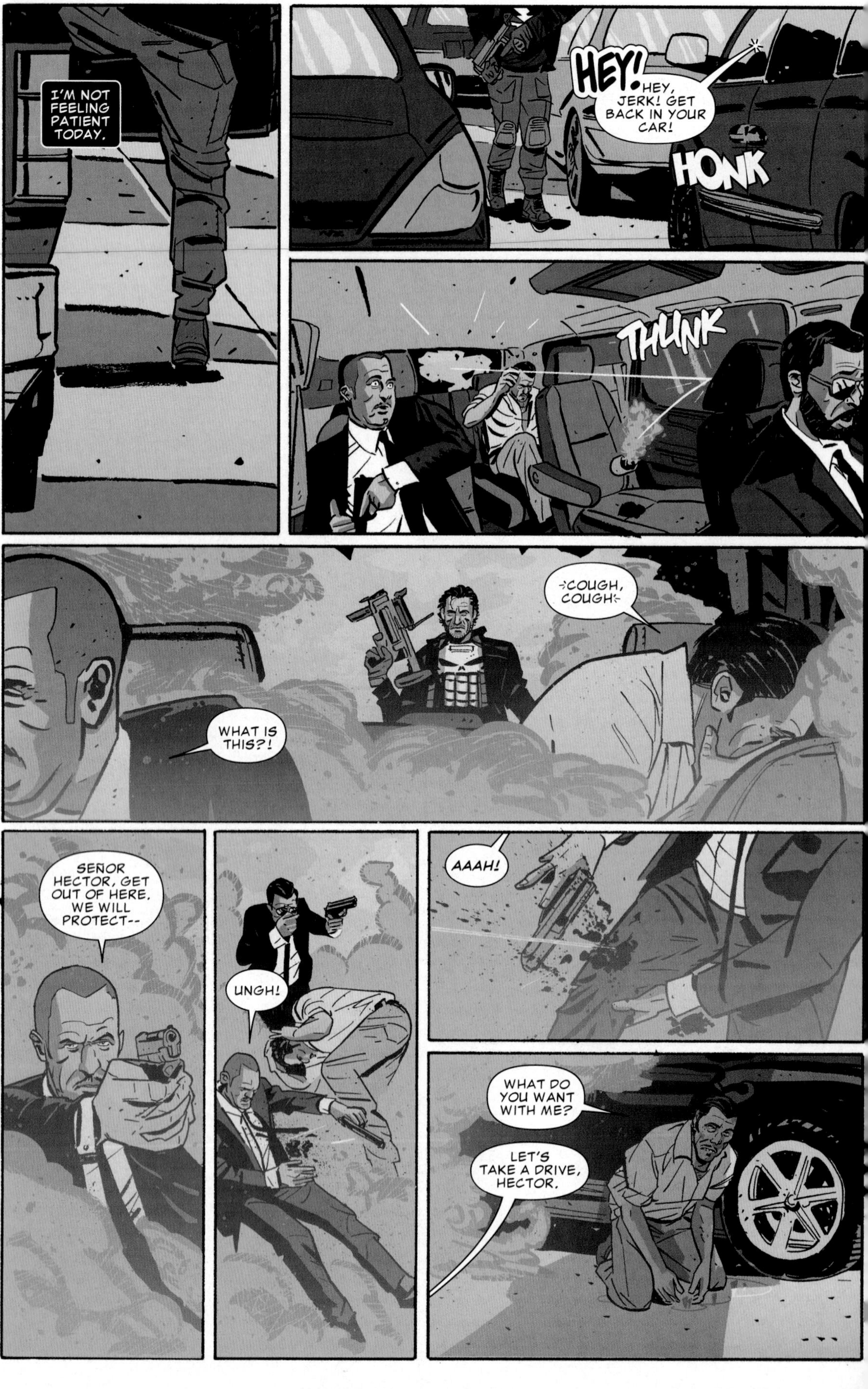
I'M NOT FEELING PATIENT TODAY.
HEY!
HEY, JERK! GET BACK IN YOUR CAR!
HONK
THUNK
WHAT IS THIS?!
COUGH, COUGH
SEÑOR HECTOR, GET OUT OF HERE. WE WILL PROTECT--
UNGH!
AAAH!
WHAT DO YOU WANT WITH ME?
LET'S TAKE A DRIVE, HECTOR.

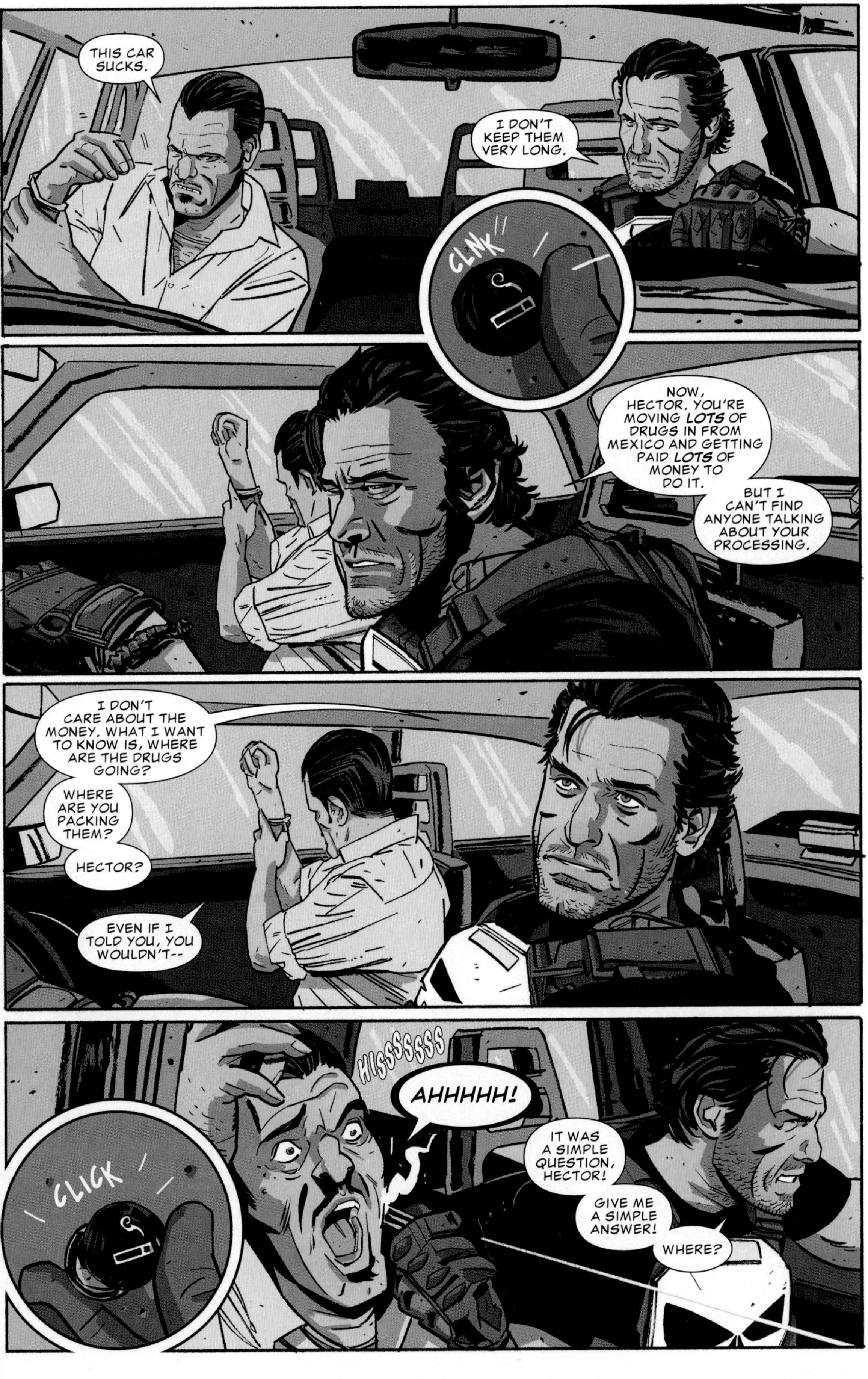
THIS CAR SUCKS.
I DON'T KEEP THEM VERY LONG.
CLNK
NOW, HECTOR. YOU'RE MOVING LOTS OF DRUGS IN FROM MEXICO AND GETTING PAID LOTS OF MONEY TO DO IT.
BUT I CAN'T FIND ANYONE TALKING ABOUT YOUR PROCESSING.
I DON'T CARE ABOUT THE MONEY. WHAT I WANT TO KNOW IS, WHERE ARE THE DRUGS GOING?
WHERE ARE YOU PACKING THEM?
HECTOR?
EVEN IF I TOLD YOU, YOU WOULDN'T--
HISSSSSSS
AHHHHH!
CLICK
IT WAS A SIMPLE QUESTION, HECTOR!
GIVE ME A SIMPLE ANSWER!
WHERE?

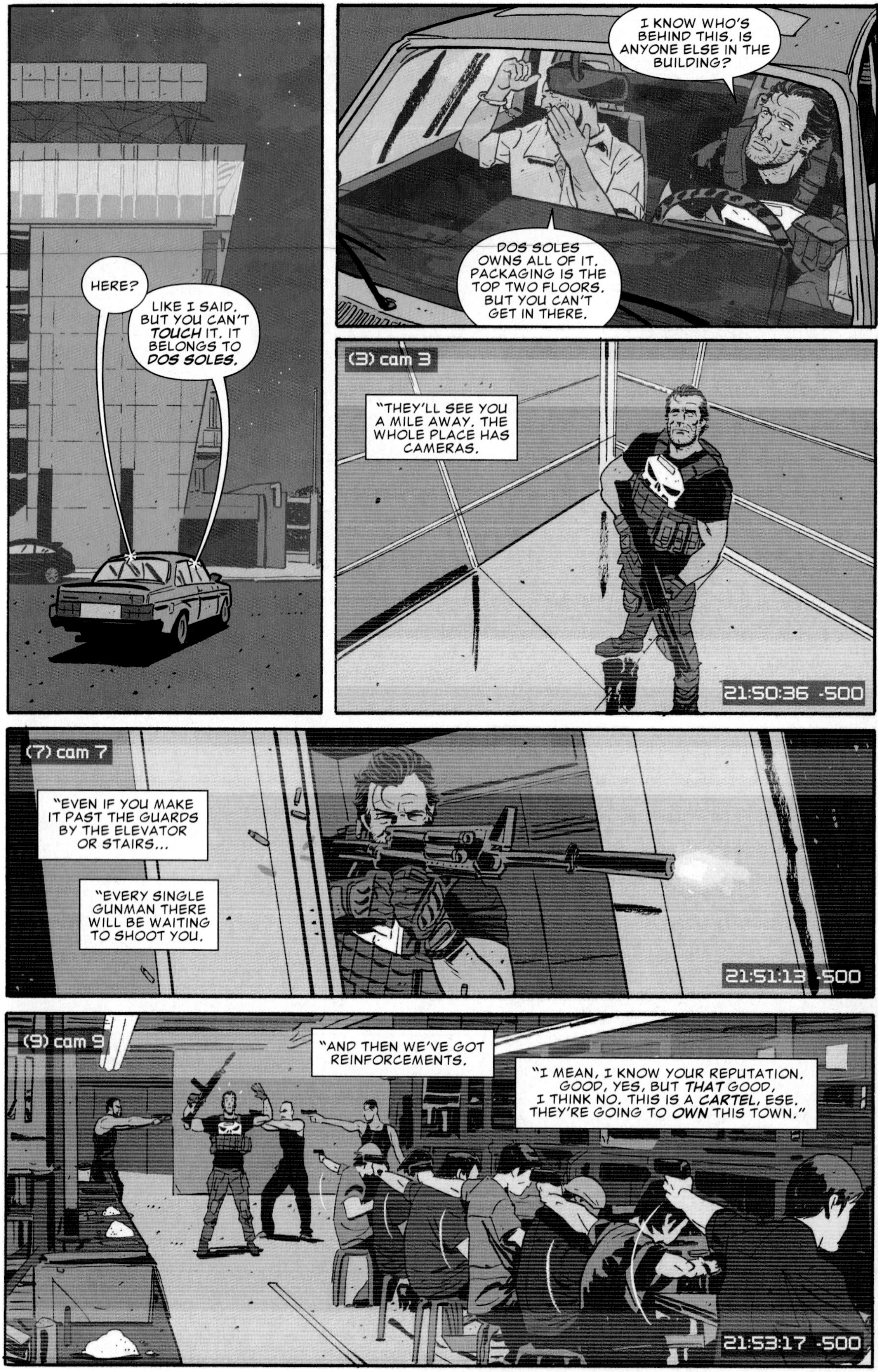
HERE?
LIKE I SAID. BUT YOU CAN'T *TOUCH* IT. IT BELONGS TO *DOS SOLES.*
I KNOW WHO'S BEHIND THIS. IS ANYONE ELSE IN THE BUILDING?
DOS SOLES OWNS ALL OF IT. PACKAGING IS THE TOP TWO FLOORS. BUT YOU CAN'T GET IN THERE.
(3) cam 3
"THEY'LL SEE YOU A MILE AWAY. THE WHOLE PLACE HAS CAMERAS.
21:50:36 -500
(7) cam 7
"EVEN IF YOU MAKE IT PAST THE GUARDS BY THE ELEVATOR OR STAIRS...
"EVERY SINGLE GUNMAN THERE WILL BE WAITING TO SHOOT YOU.
21:51:13 -500
(9) cam 9
"AND THEN WE'VE GOT REINFORCEMENTS.
"I MEAN, I KNOW YOUR REPUTATION. GOOD, YES, BUT *THAT* GOOD, I THINK NO. THIS IS A *CARTEL*, ESE. THEY'RE GOING TO *OWN* THIS TOWN."
21:53:17 -500

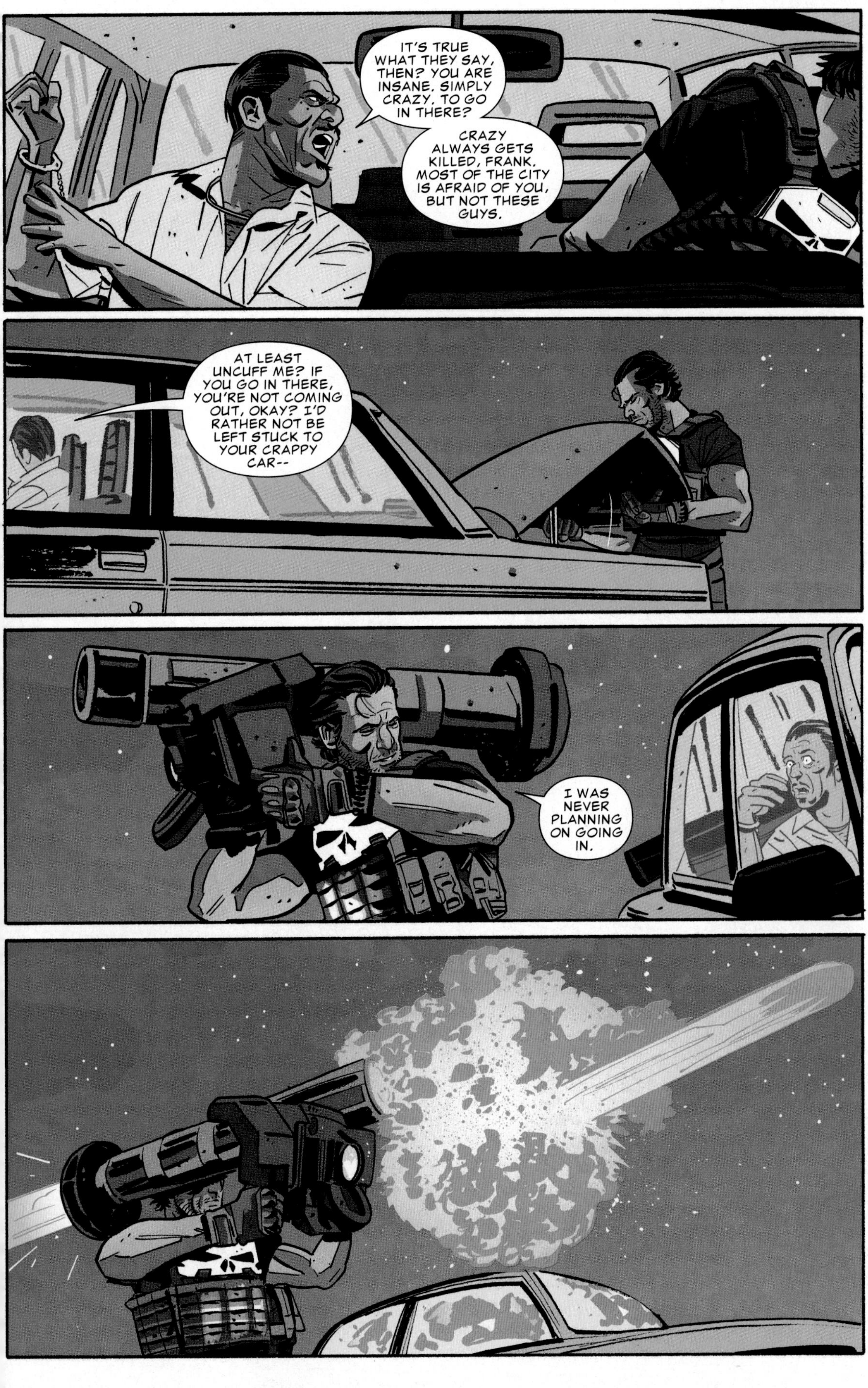
IT'S TRUE WHAT THEY SAY, THEN? YOU ARE INSANE. SIMPLY CRAZY. TO GO IN THERE?
CRAZY ALWAYS GETS KILLED, FRANK. MOST OF THE CITY IS AFRAID OF YOU, BUT NOT THESE GUYS.
AT LEAST UNCUFF ME? IF YOU GO IN THERE, YOU'RE NOT COMING OUT, OKAY? I'D RATHER NOT BE LEFT STUCK TO YOUR CRAPPY CAR--
I WAS NEVER PLANNING ON GOING IN.

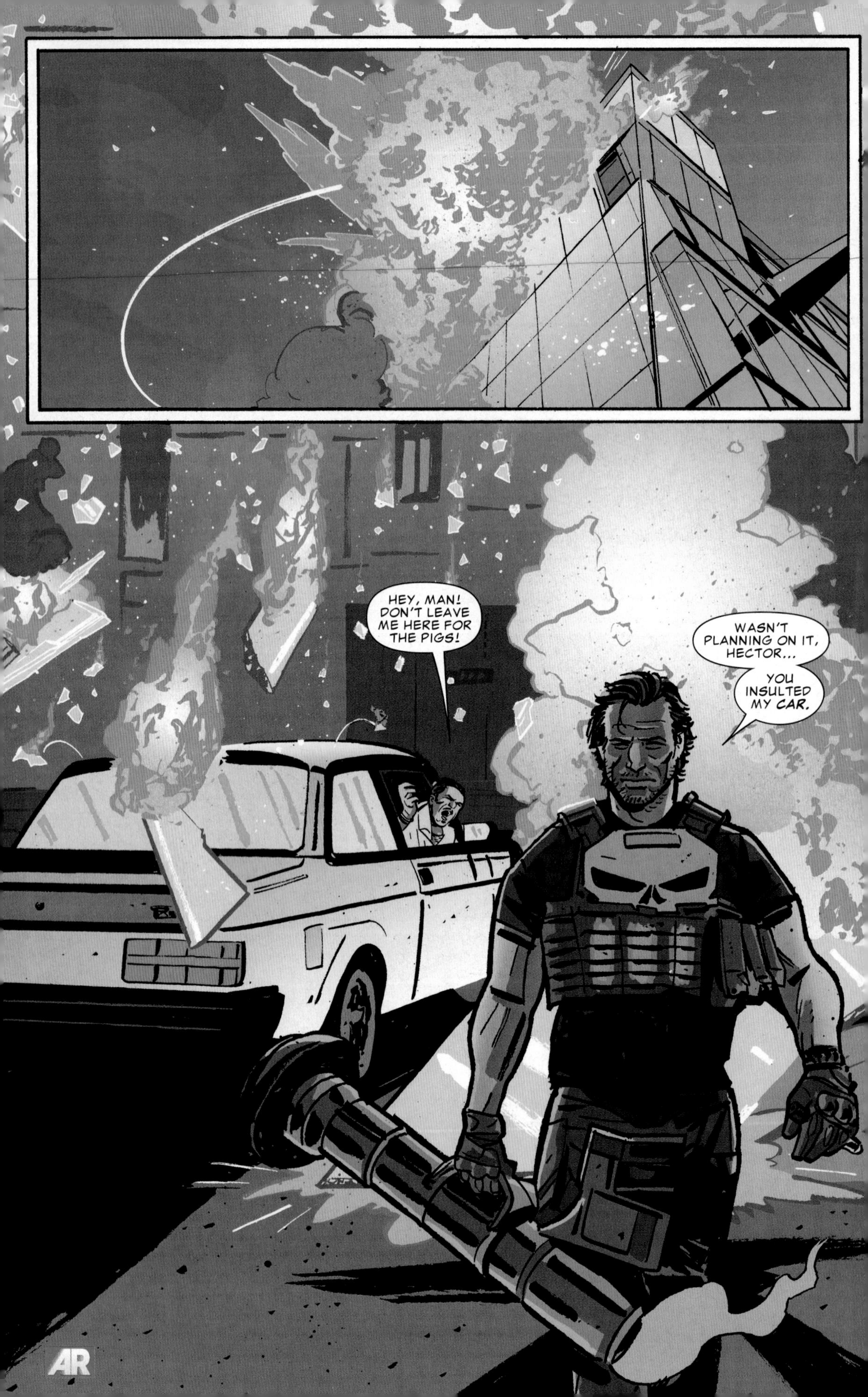
HEY, MAN! DON'T LEAVE ME HERE FOR THE PIGS!
WASN'T PLANNING ON IT, HECTOR...
YOU INSULTED MY **CAR.**

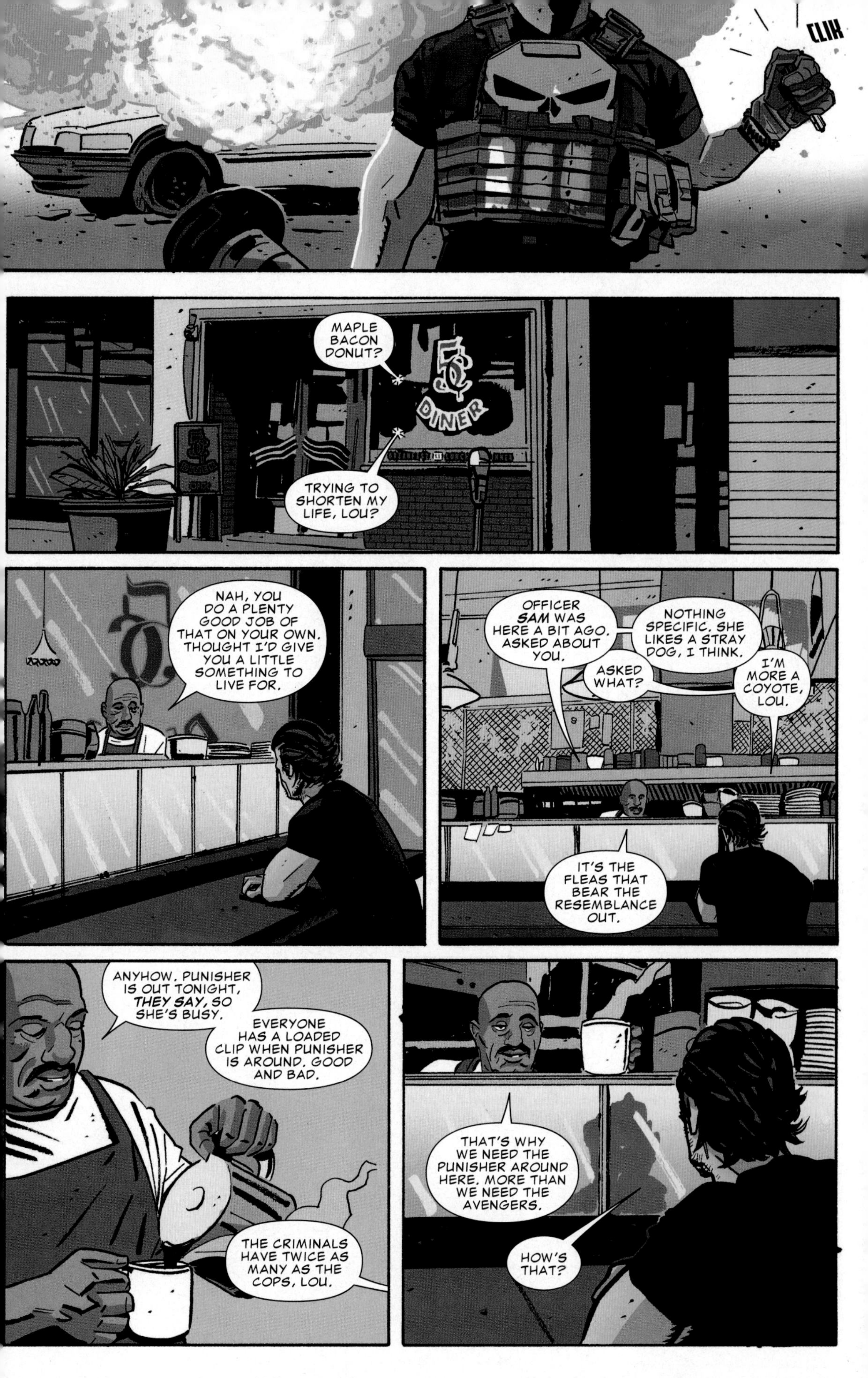
CLIK
MAPLE BACON DONUT?
TRYING TO SHORTEN MY LIFE, LOU?
NAH, YOU DO A PLENTY GOOD JOB OF THAT ON YOUR OWN. THOUGHT I'D GIVE YOU A LITTLE SOMETHING TO LIVE FOR.
OFFICER SAM WAS HERE A BIT AGO. ASKED ABOUT YOU.
ASKED WHAT?
NOTHING SPECIFIC. SHE LIKES A STRAY DOG, I THINK.
I'M MORE A COYOTE, LOU.
IT'S THE FLEAS THAT BEAR THE RESEMBLANCE OUT.
ANYHOW. PUNISHER IS OUT TONIGHT, THEY SAY, SO SHE'S BUSY.
EVERYONE HAS A LOADED CLIP WHEN PUNISHER IS AROUND, GOOD AND BAD.
THE CRIMINALS HAVE TWICE AS MANY AS THE COPS, LOU.
THAT'S WHY WE NEED THE PUNISHER AROUND HERE, MORE THAN WE NEED THE AVENGERS.
HOW'S THAT?

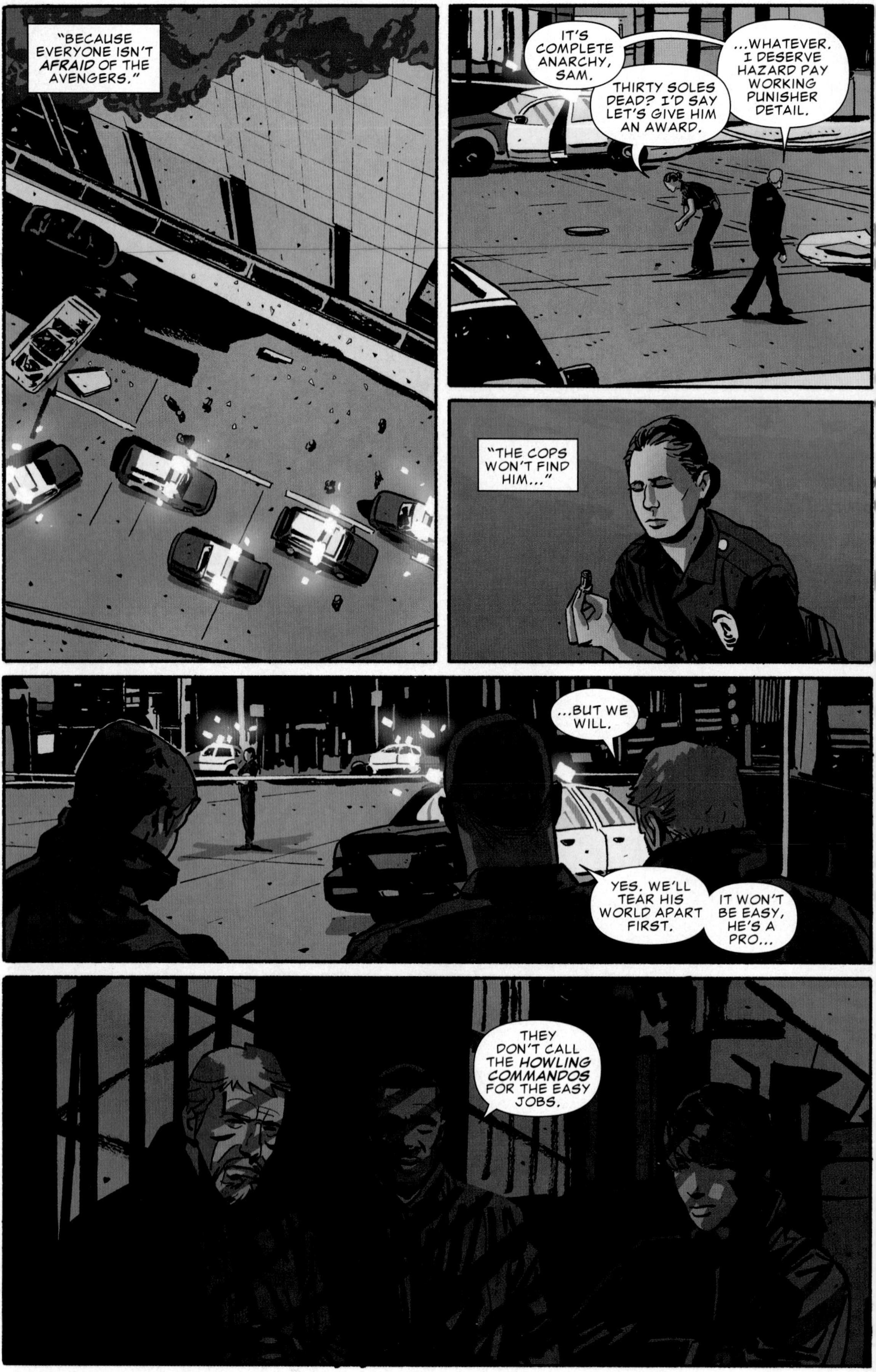
"BECAUSE EVERYONE ISN'T *AFRAID* OF THE AVENGERS."
IT'S COMPLETE ANARCHY, SAM.
THIRTY SOLES DEAD? I'D SAY LET'S GIVE HIM AN AWARD.
...WHATEVER. I DESERVE HAZARD PAY WORKING PUNISHER DETAIL.
"THE COPS WON'T FIND HIM..."
...BUT WE WILL.
YES. WE'LL TEAR HIS WORLD APART FIRST.
IT WON'T BE EASY, HE'S A PRO...
THEY DON'T CALL THE *HOWLING COMMANDOS* FOR THE EASY JOBS.

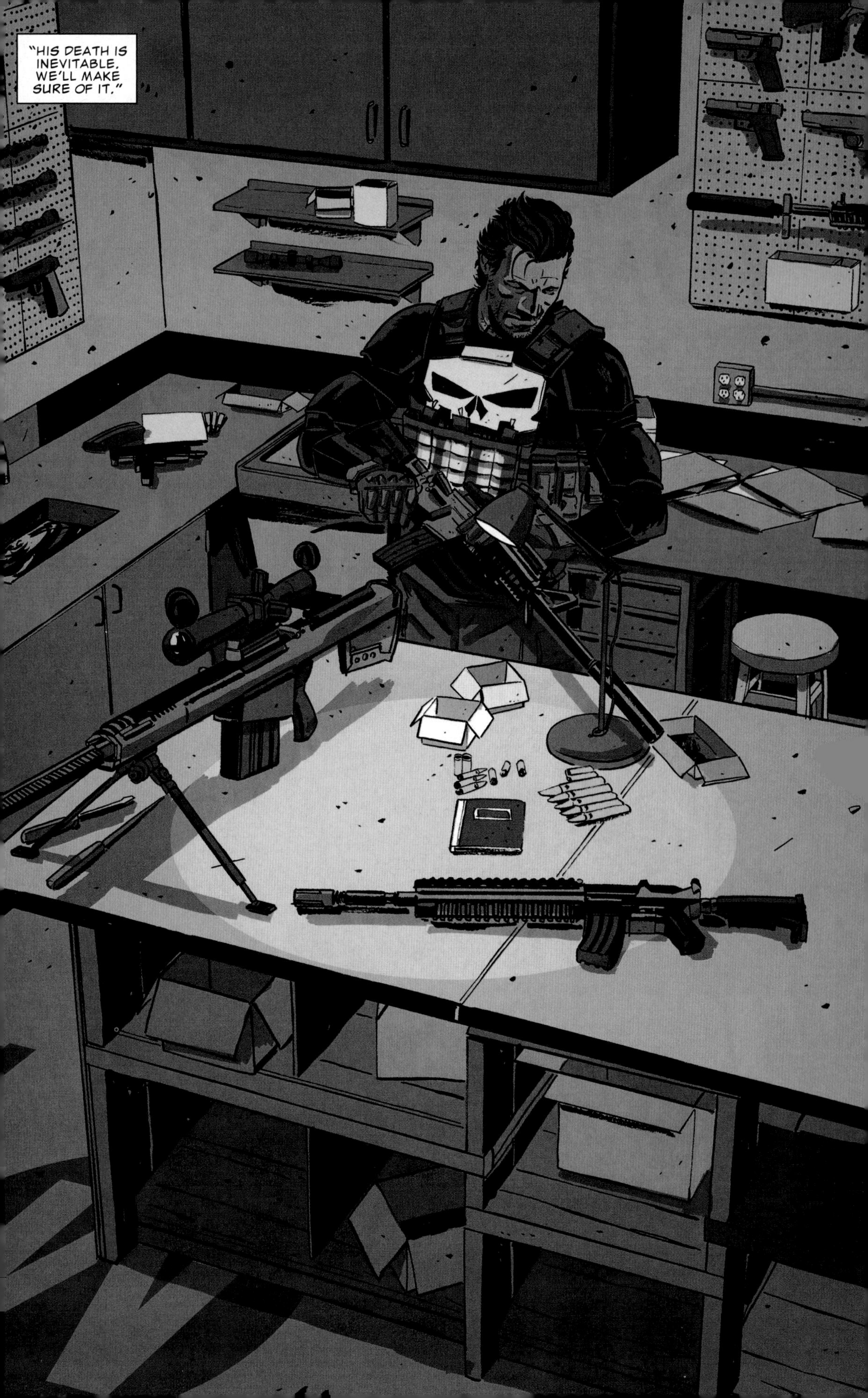
"HIS DEATH IS INEVITABLE. WE'LL MAKE SURE OF IT."

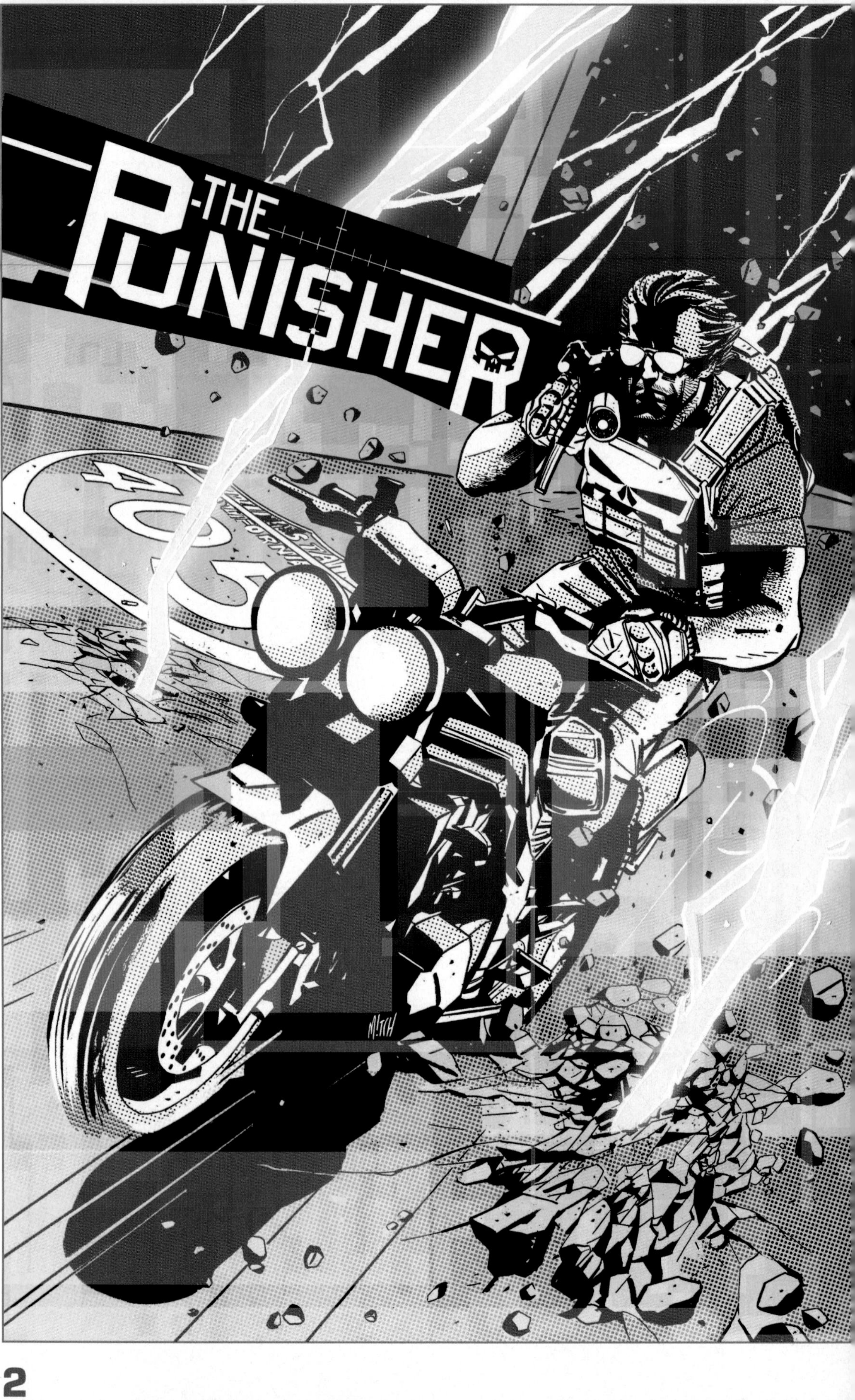
THE PUNISHER
40
MITCH

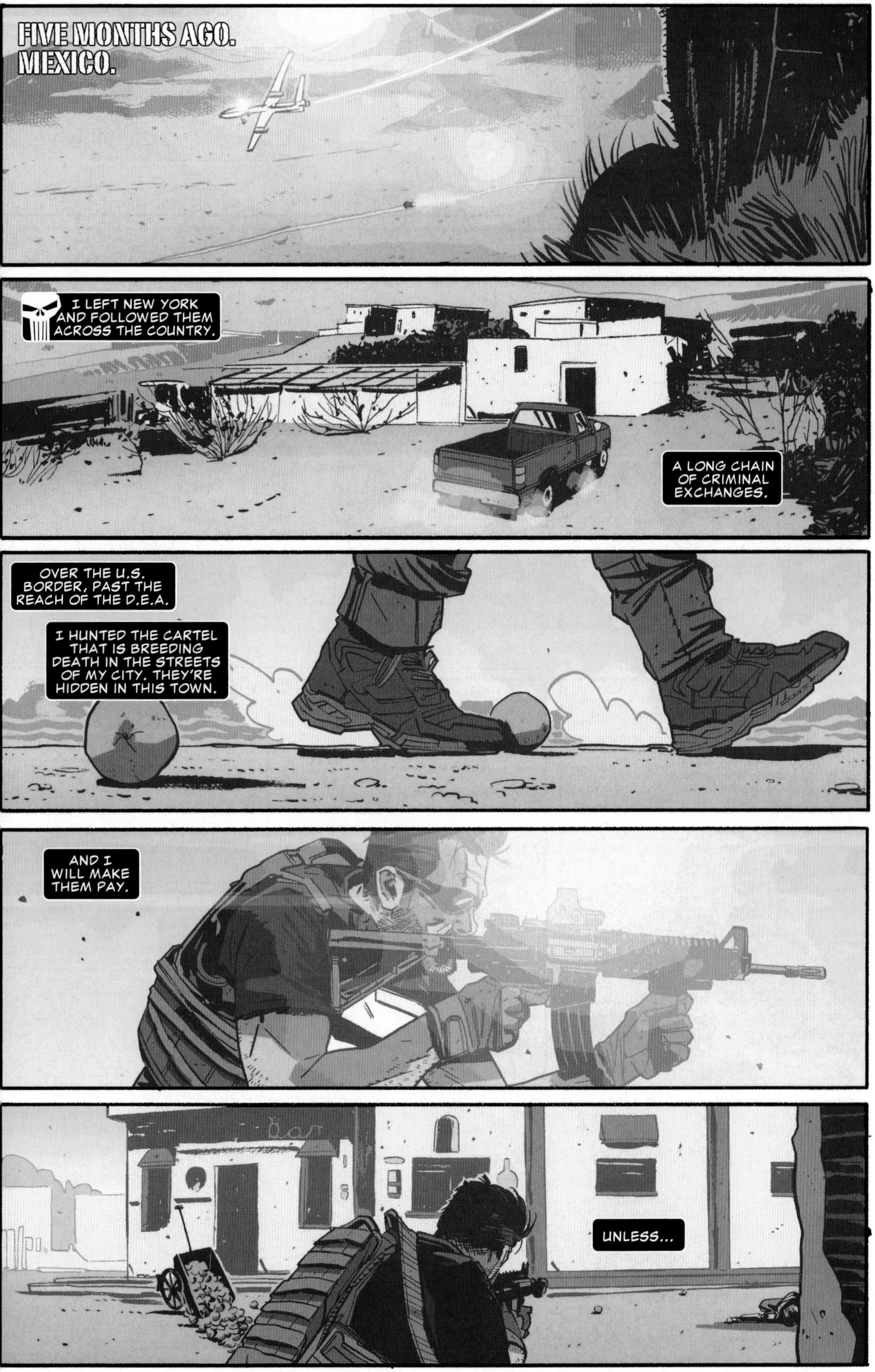

FIVE MONTHS AGO. MEXICO.
I LEFT NEW YORK AND FOLLOWED THEM ACROSS THE COUNTRY.
A LONG CHAIN OF CRIMINAL EXCHANGES.
OVER THE U.S. BORDER, PAST THE REACH OF THE D.E.A.
I HUNTED THE CARTEL THAT IS BREEDING DEATH IN THE STREETS OF MY CITY. THEY'RE HIDDEN IN THIS TOWN.
AND I WILL MAKE THEM PAY.
UNLESS...

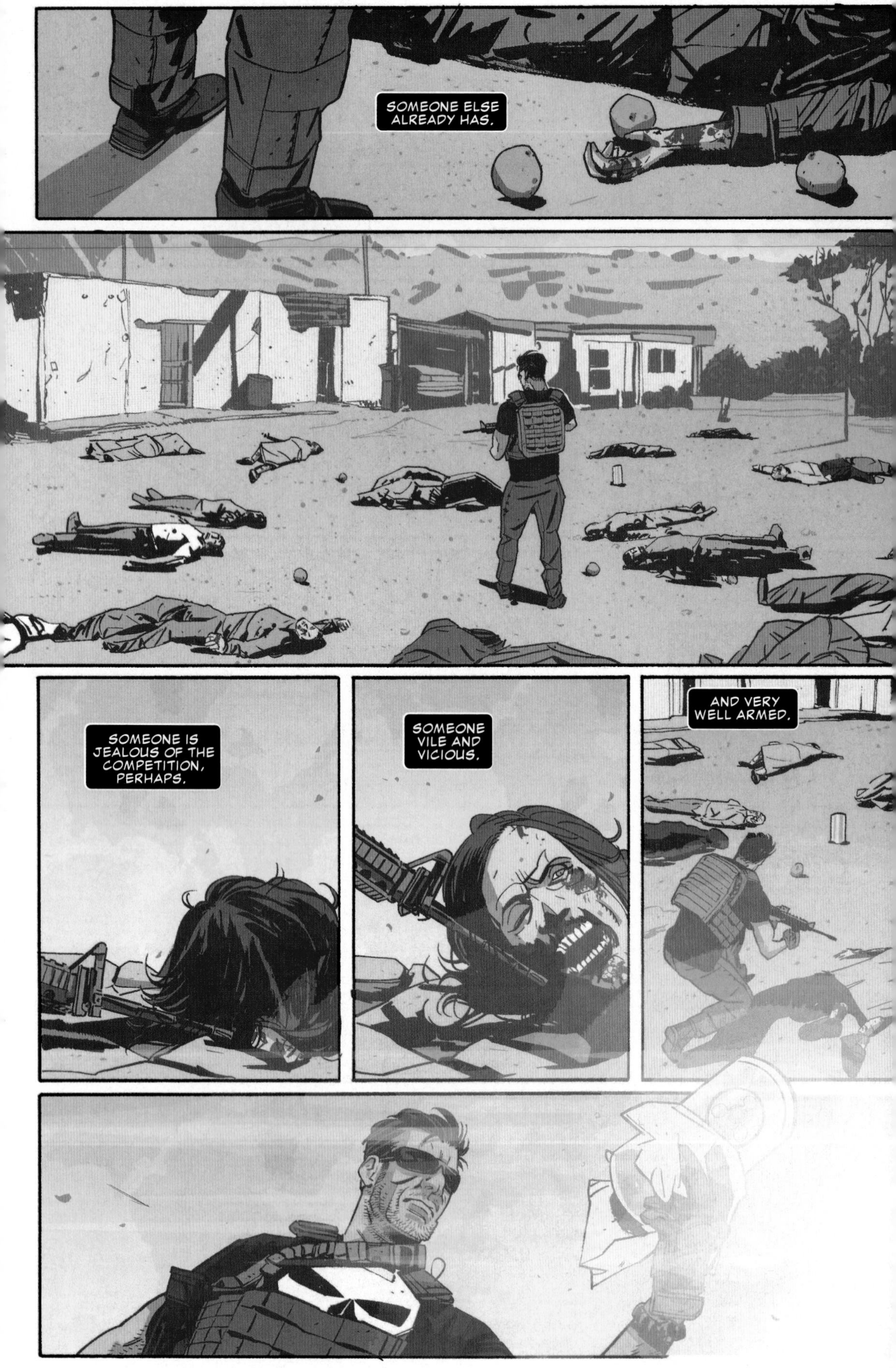
SOMEONE ELSE ALREADY HAS.
SOMEONE IS JEALOUS OF THE COMPETITION, PERHAPS.
SOMEONE VILE AND VICIOUS.
AND VERY WELL ARMED.

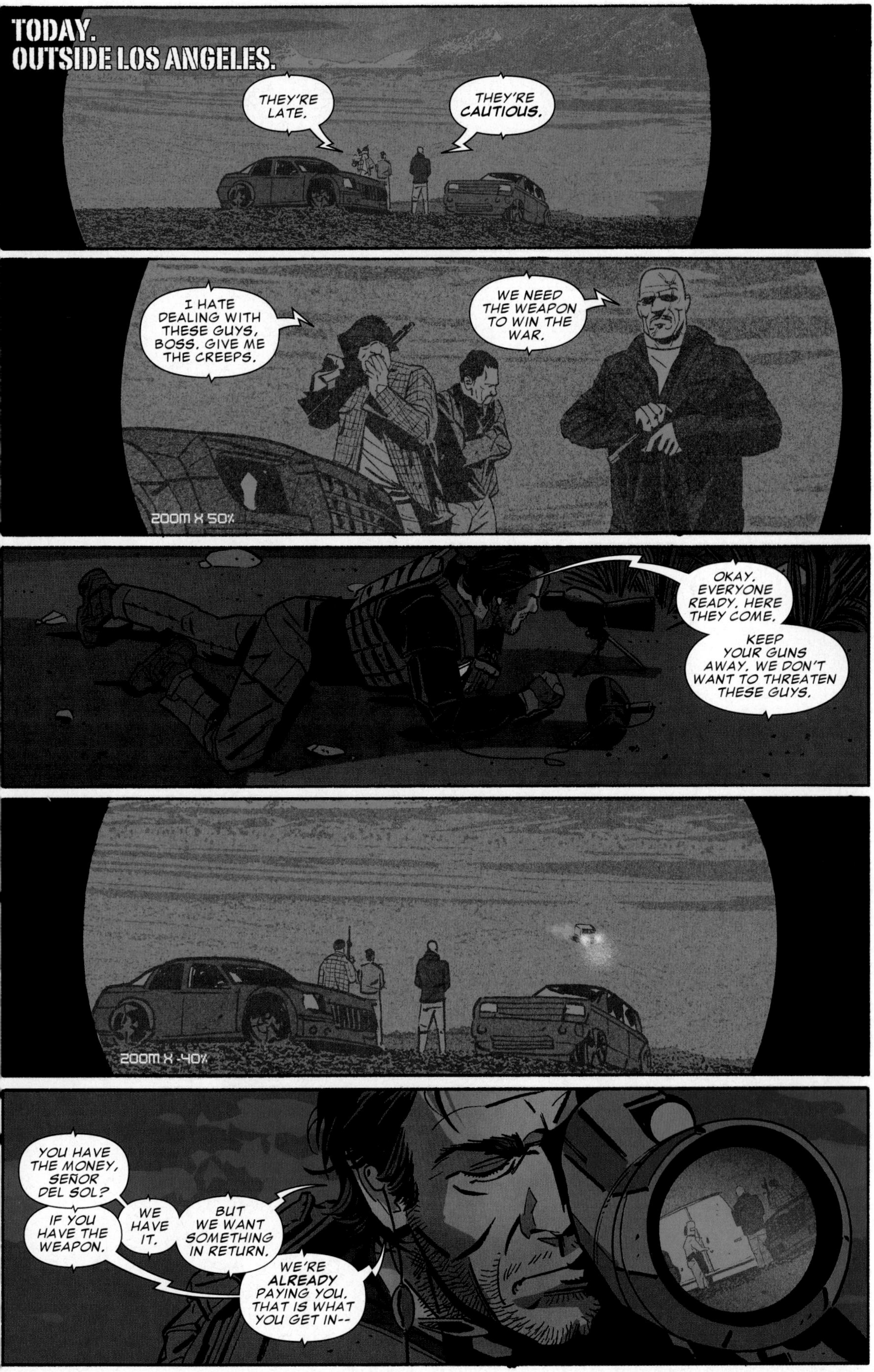
TODAY.
OUTSIDE LOS ANGELES.
THEY'RE LATE.
THEY'RE CAUTIOUS.
I HATE DEALING WITH THESE GUYS, BOSS. GIVE ME THE CREEPS.
WE NEED THE WEAPON TO WIN THE WAR.
ZOOM X 50%
OKAY. EVERYONE READY. HERE THEY COME.
KEEP YOUR GUNS AWAY. WE DON'T WANT TO THREATEN THESE GUYS.
ZOOM X -40%
YOU HAVE THE MONEY, SEÑOR DEL SOL?
IF YOU HAVE THE WEAPON.
WE HAVE IT.
BUT WE WANT SOMETHING IN RETURN.
WE'RE ALREADY PAYING YOU. THAT IS WHAT YOU GET IN--

THIS WON'T COST YOU ANYTHING. WE JUST NEED YOU TO LET US KNOW BEFORE YOU TAKE THE CITY. DAY AND HOUR.

...FINE, WE CAN DO THAT.

GOOD.

NOW AS FOR THE WEAPON...

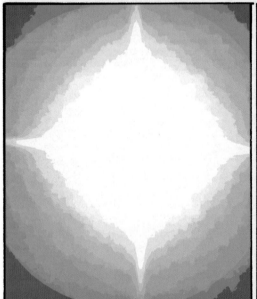

AH.

THNK

GO CHECK IT OUT.

LET THEM TAKE CARE OF THIS. I'LL LEAD YOU TO OUR L.A. FACILITY.

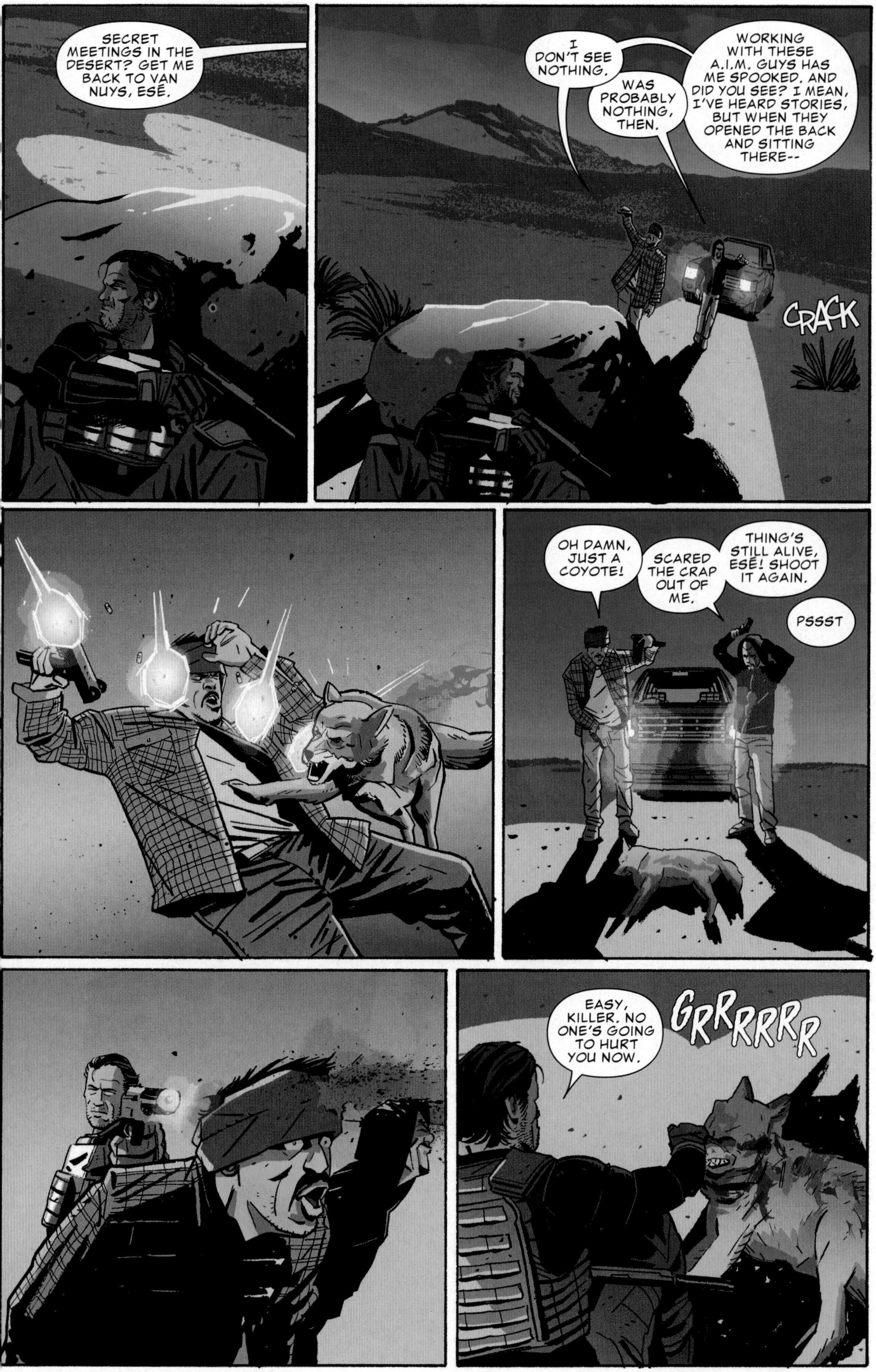

SECRET MEETINGS IN THE DESERT? GET ME BACK TO VAN NUYS, ESÉ.
I DON'T SEE NOTHING.
WORKING WITH THESE A.I.M. GUYS HAS ME SPOOKED. AND DID YOU SEE? I MEAN, I'VE HEARD STORIES, BUT WHEN THEY OPENED THE BACK AND SITTING THERE--
WAS PROBABLY NOTHING, THEN.
CRACK
OH DAMN, JUST A COYOTE!
SCARED THE CRAP OUT OF ME.
THING'S STILL ALIVE, ESÉ! SHOOT IT AGAIN.
PSSST
EASY, KILLER. NO ONE'S GOING TO HURT YOU NOW.
GRRRRRR

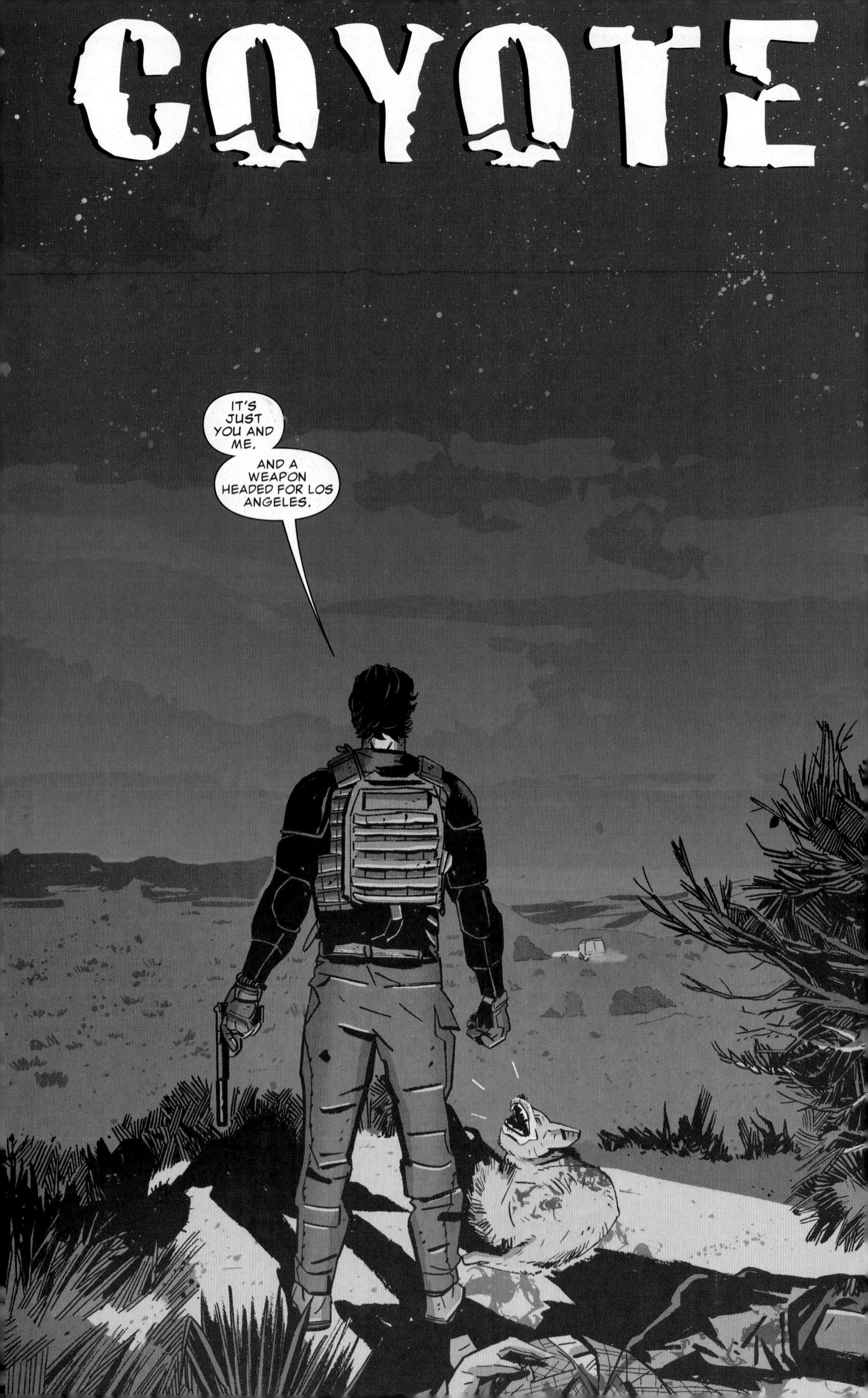
COYOTE
IT'S JUST YOU AND ME.
AND A WEAPON HEADED FOR LOS ANGELES.

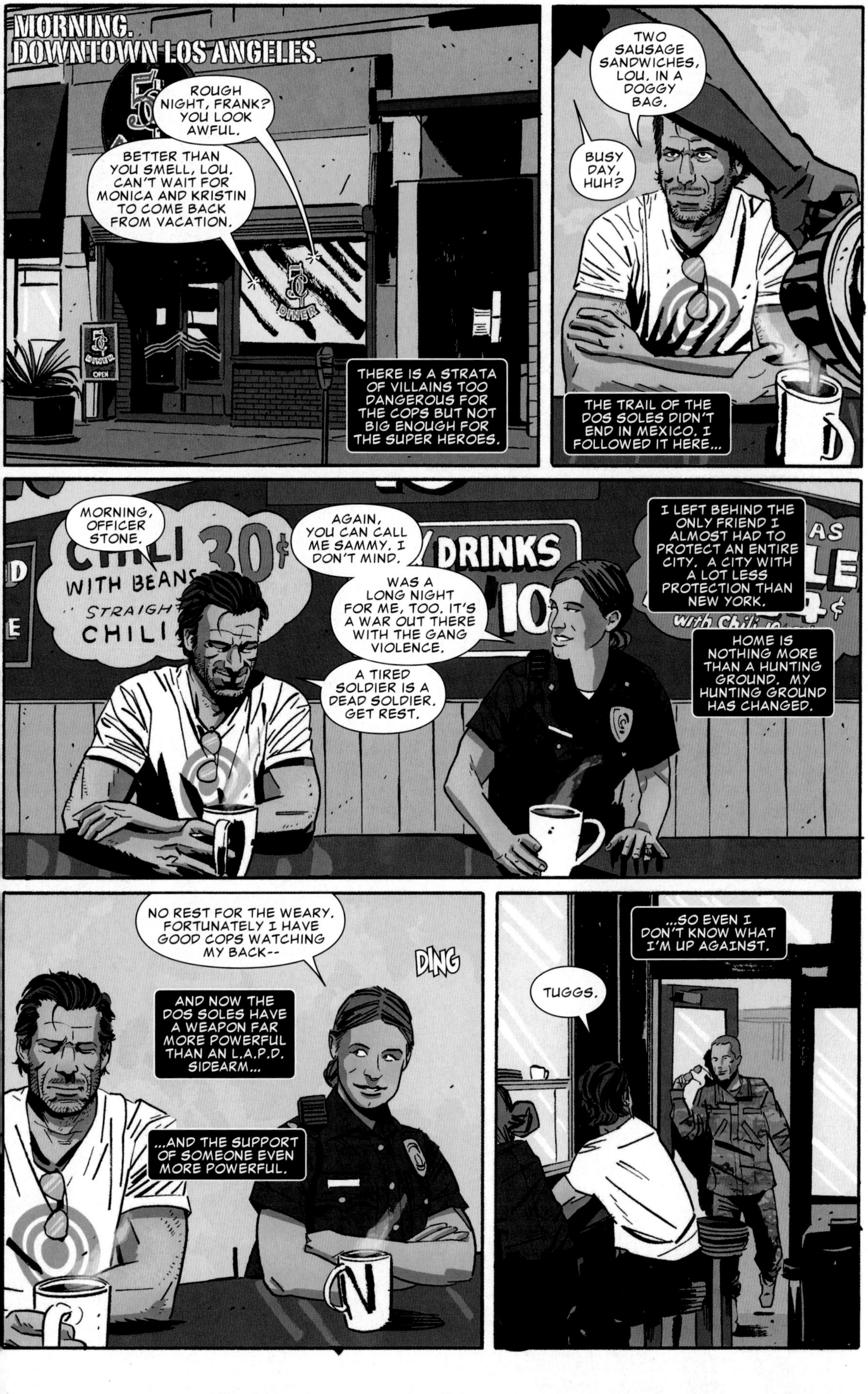
MORNING. DOWNTOWN LOS ANGELES.
ROUGH NIGHT, FRANK? YOU LOOK AWFUL.
BETTER THAN YOU SMELL, LOU. CAN'T WAIT FOR MONICA AND KRISTIN TO COME BACK FROM VACATION.
THERE IS A STRATA OF VILLAINS TOO DANGEROUS FOR THE COPS BUT NOT BIG ENOUGH FOR THE SUPER HEROES.
TWO SAUSAGE SANDWICHES, LOU. IN A DOGGY BAG.
BUSY DAY, HUH?
THE TRAIL OF THE DOS SOLES DIDN'T END IN MEXICO. I FOLLOWED IT HERE...
MORNING, OFFICER STONE.
AGAIN, YOU CAN CALL ME SAMMY. I DON'T MIND.
WAS A LONG NIGHT FOR ME, TOO. IT'S A WAR OUT THERE WITH THE GANG VIOLENCE.
A TIRED SOLDIER IS A DEAD SOLDIER. GET REST.
I LEFT BEHIND THE ONLY FRIEND I ALMOST HAD TO PROTECT AN ENTIRE CITY. A CITY WITH A LOT LESS PROTECTION THAN NEW YORK.
HOME IS NOTHING MORE THAN A HUNTING GROUND. MY HUNTING GROUND HAS CHANGED.
NO REST FOR THE WEARY. FORTUNATELY I HAVE GOOD COPS WATCHING MY BACK--
DING
AND NOW THE DOS SOLES HAVE A WEAPON FAR MORE POWERFUL THAN AN L.A.P.D. SIDEARM...
...AND THE SUPPORT OF SOMEONE EVEN MORE POWERFUL.
...SO EVEN I DON'T KNOW WHAT I'M UP AGAINST.
TUGGS.

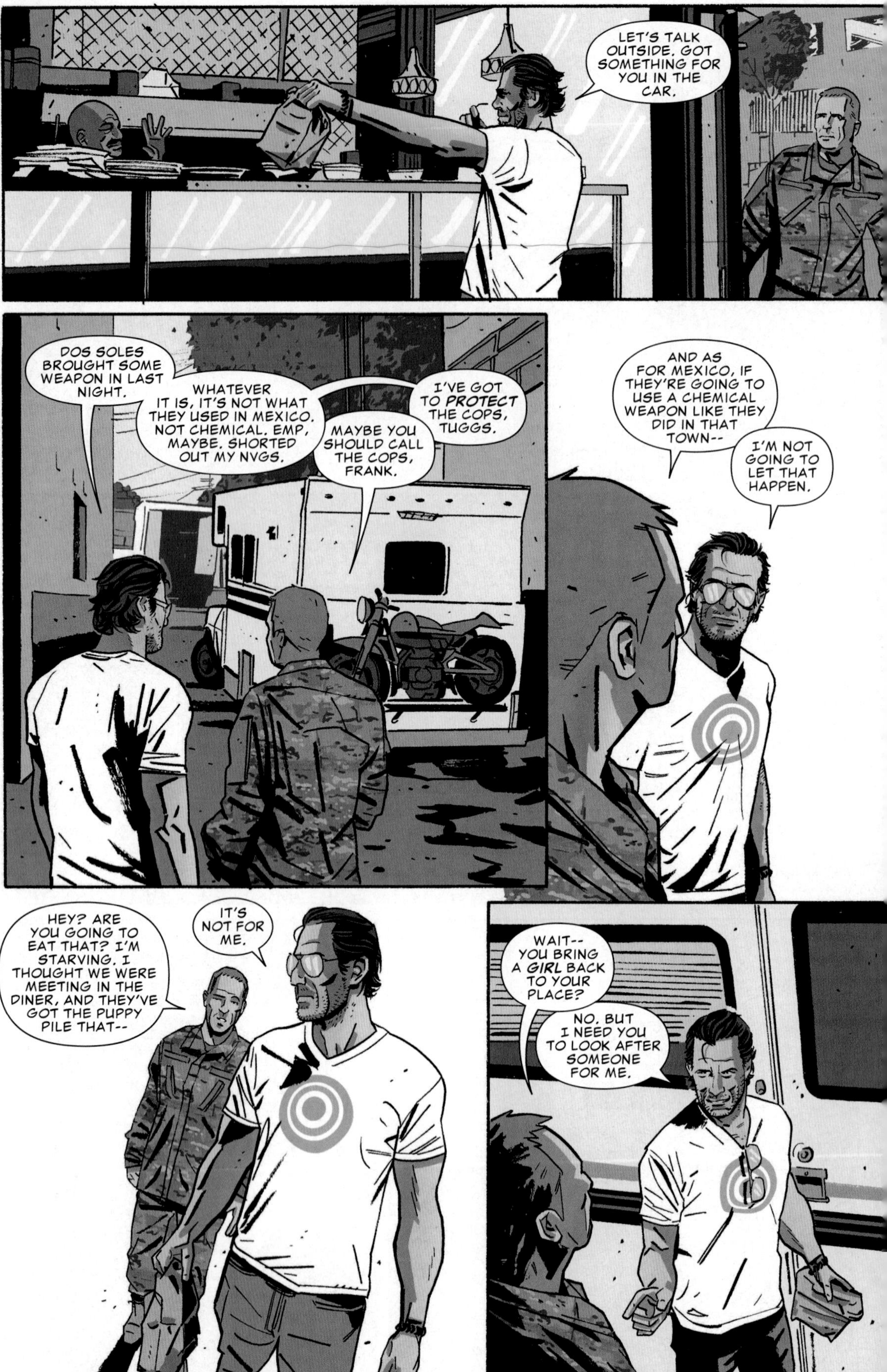
LET'S TALK OUTSIDE. GOT SOMETHING FOR YOU IN THE CAR.
DOS SOLES BROUGHT SOME WEAPON IN LAST NIGHT.
WHATEVER IT IS, IT'S NOT WHAT THEY USED IN MEXICO. NOT CHEMICAL. EMP, MAYBE. SHORTED OUT MY NVGS.
MAYBE YOU SHOULD CALL THE COPS, FRANK.
I'VE GOT TO *PROTECT* THE COPS, TUGGS.
AND AS FOR MEXICO, IF THEY'RE GOING TO USE A CHEMICAL WEAPON LIKE THEY DID IN THAT TOWN--
I'M NOT GOING TO LET THAT HAPPEN.
HEY? ARE YOU GOING TO EAT THAT? I'M STARVING. I THOUGHT WE WERE MEETING IN THE DINER, AND THEY'VE GOT THE PUPPY PILE THAT--
IT'S NOT FOR ME.
WAIT-- YOU BRING A *GIRL* BACK TO YOUR PLACE?
NO. BUT I NEED YOU TO LOOK AFTER SOMEONE FOR ME.

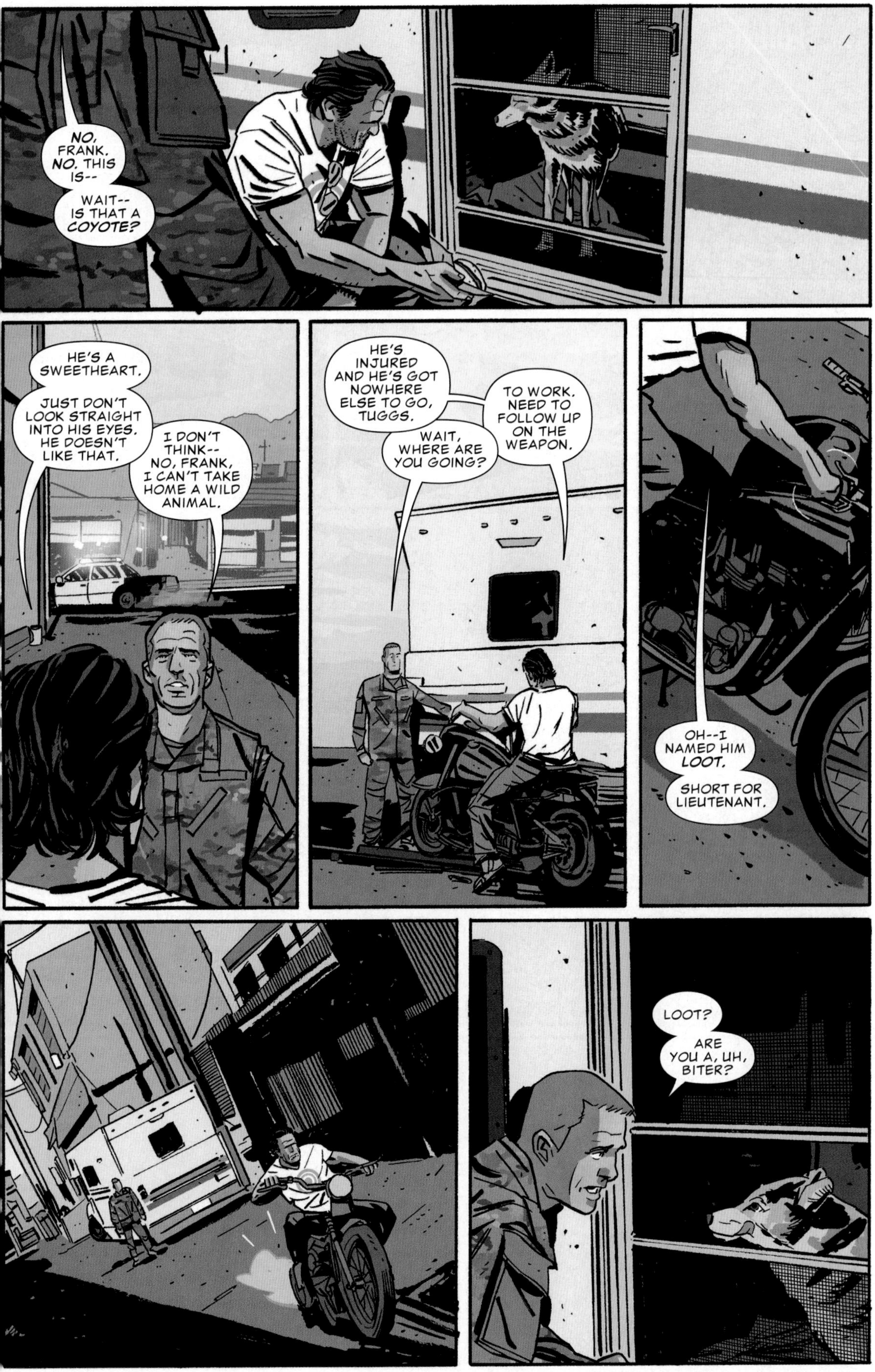
NO, FRANK. NO. THIS IS--
WAIT-- IS THAT A COYOTE?
HE'S A SWEETHEART.
JUST DON'T LOOK STRAIGHT INTO HIS EYES. HE DOESN'T LIKE THAT.
I DON'T THINK-- NO, FRANK, I CAN'T TAKE HOME A WILD ANIMAL.
HE'S INJURED AND HE'S GOT NOWHERE ELSE TO GO, TUGGS.
WAIT, WHERE ARE YOU GOING?
TO WORK. NEED TO FOLLOW UP ON THE WEAPON.
OH--I NAMED HIM LOOT.
SHORT FOR LIEUTENANT.
LOOT?
ARE YOU A, UH, BITER?

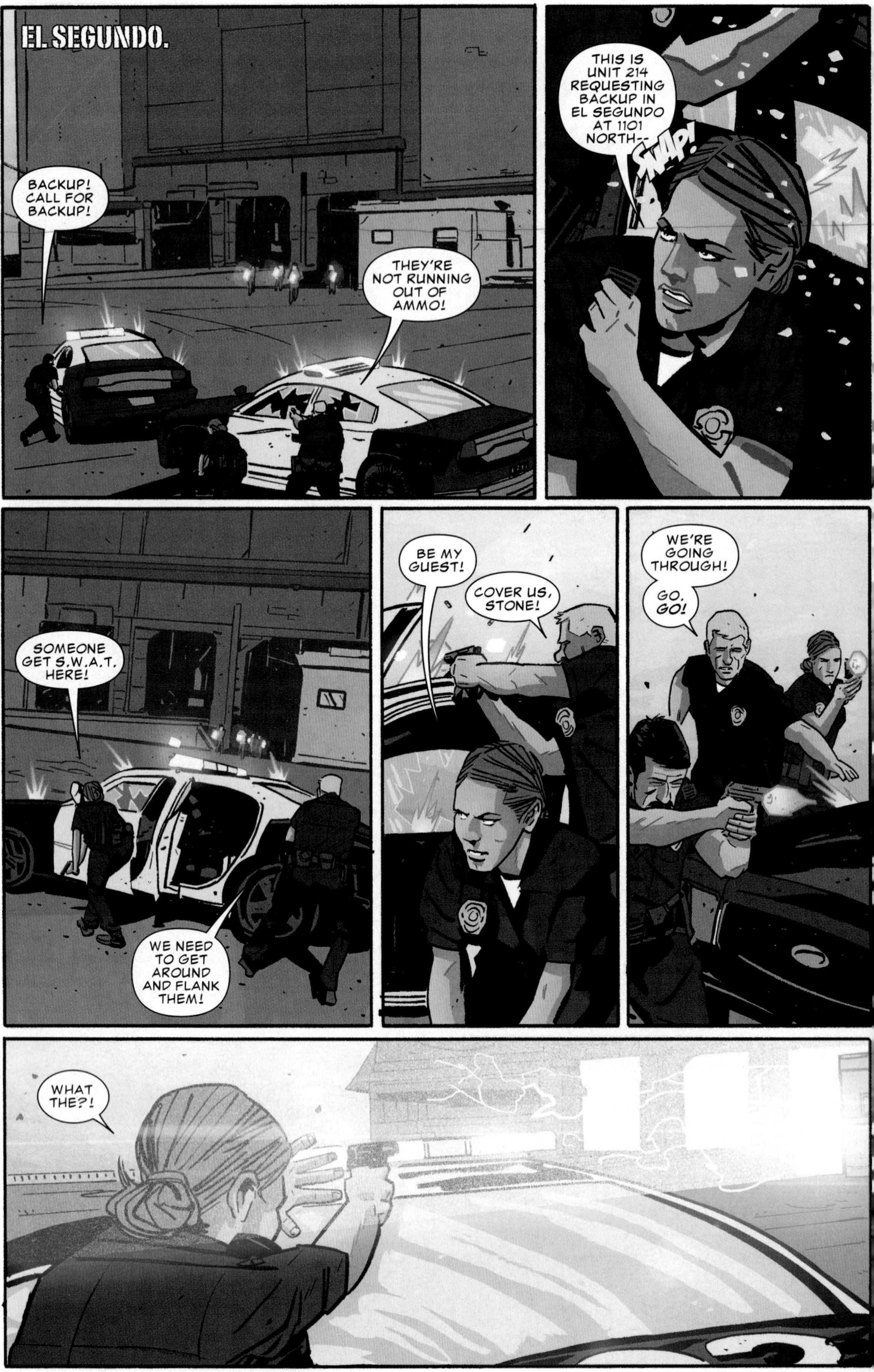
EL SEGUNDO.
BACKUP! CALL FOR BACKUP!
THEY'RE NOT RUNNING OUT OF AMMO!
THIS IS UNIT 214 REQUESTING BACKUP IN EL SEGUNDO AT 1101 NORTH--
SNAP!
SOMEONE GET S.W.A.T. HERE!
WE NEED TO GET AROUND AND FLANK THEM!
COVER US, STONE!
BE MY GUEST!
WE'RE GOING THROUGH!
GO, GO!
WHAT THE?!

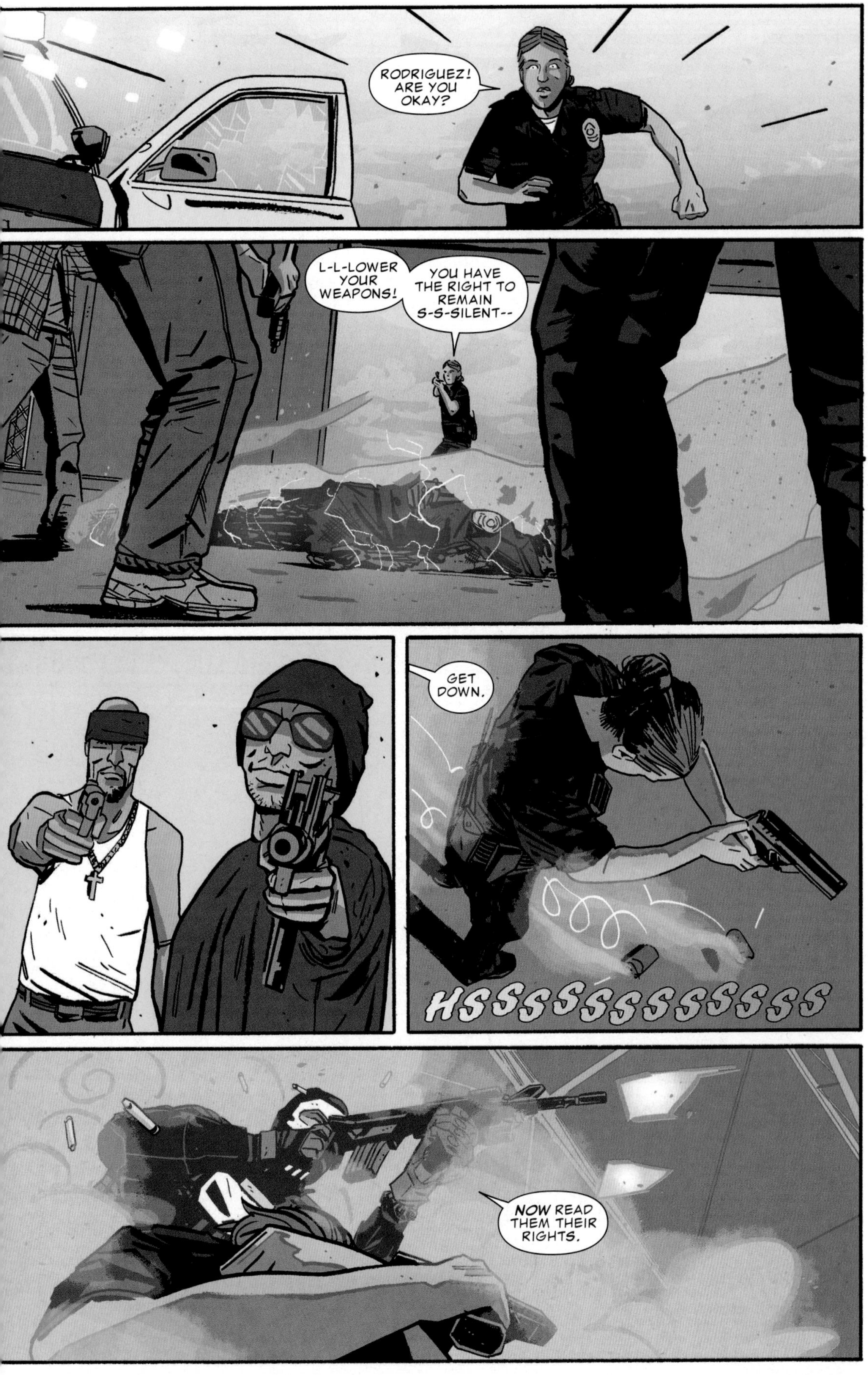
RODRIGUEZ! ARE YOU OKAY?
L-L-LOWER YOUR WEAPONS!
YOU HAVE THE RIGHT TO REMAIN S-S-SILENT--
GET DOWN.
HSSSSSSSSSSSS
NOW READ THEM THEIR RIGHTS.

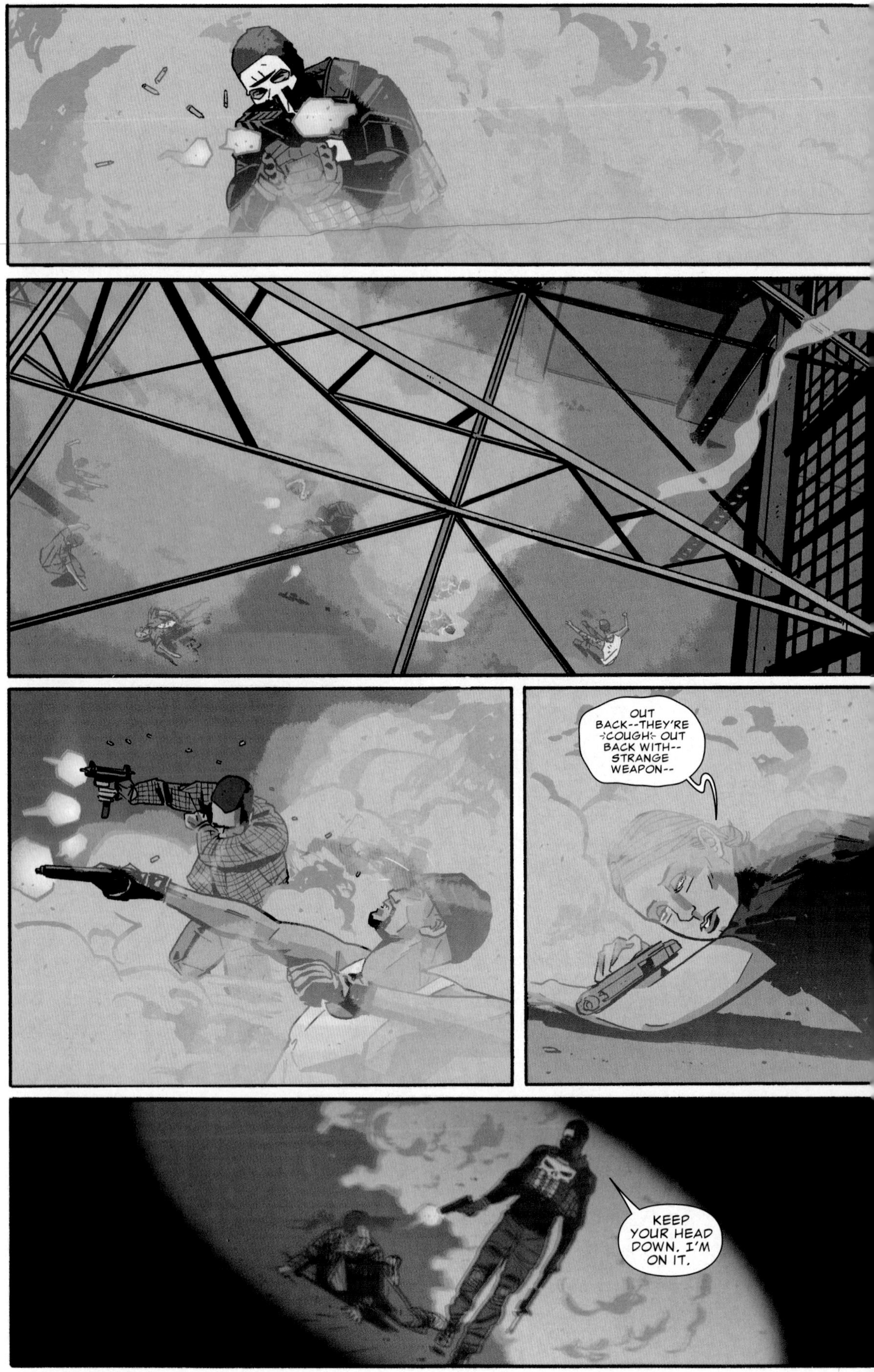
OUT BACK--THEY'RE ⊰COUGH⊱ OUT BACK WITH-- STRANGE WEAPON--
KEEP YOUR HEAD DOWN. I'M ON IT.

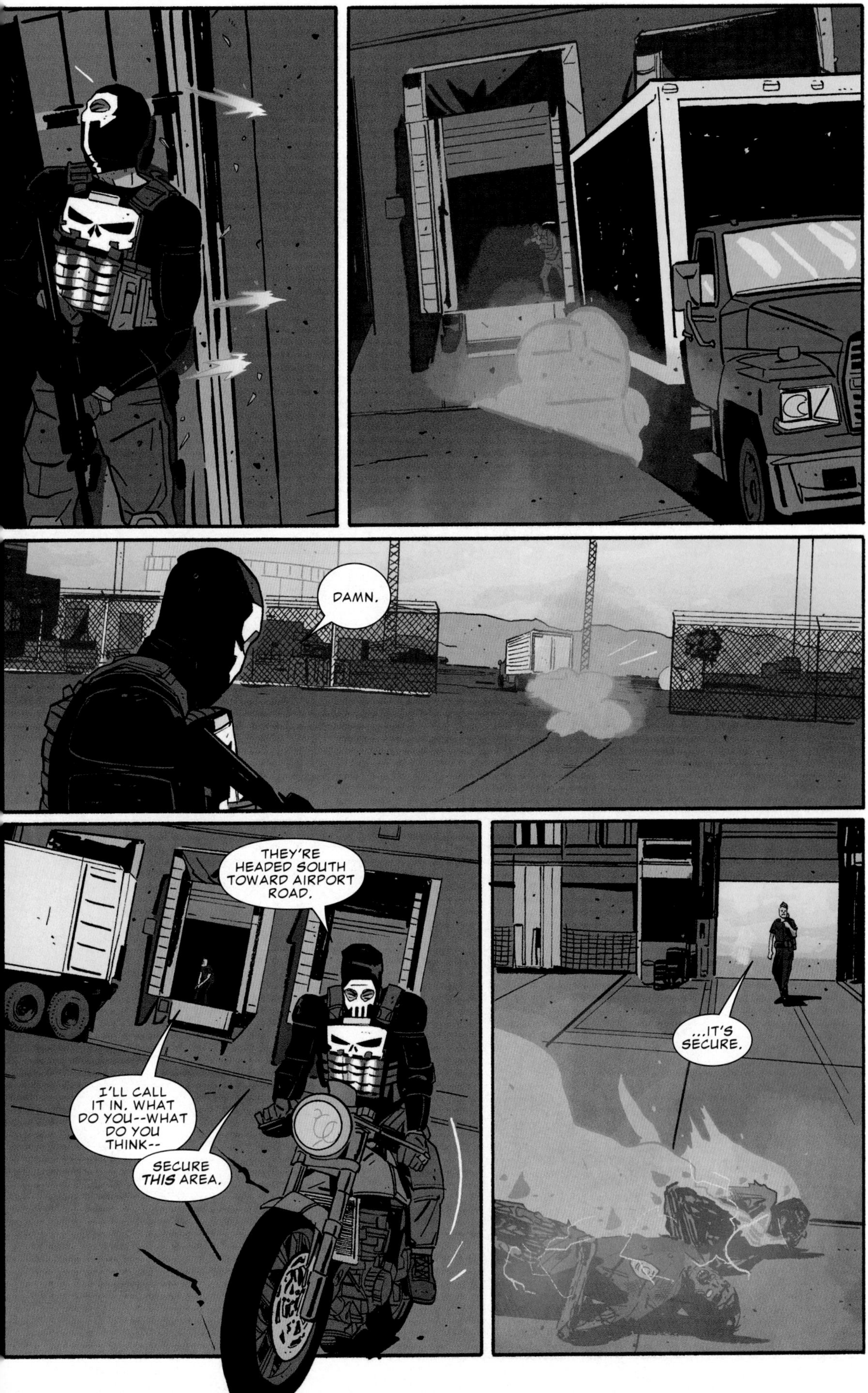
DAMN.
THEY'RE HEADED SOUTH TOWARD AIRPORT ROAD.
I'LL CALL IT IN. WHAT DO YOU--WHAT DO YOU THINK--
SECURE THIS AREA.
...IT'S SECURE.

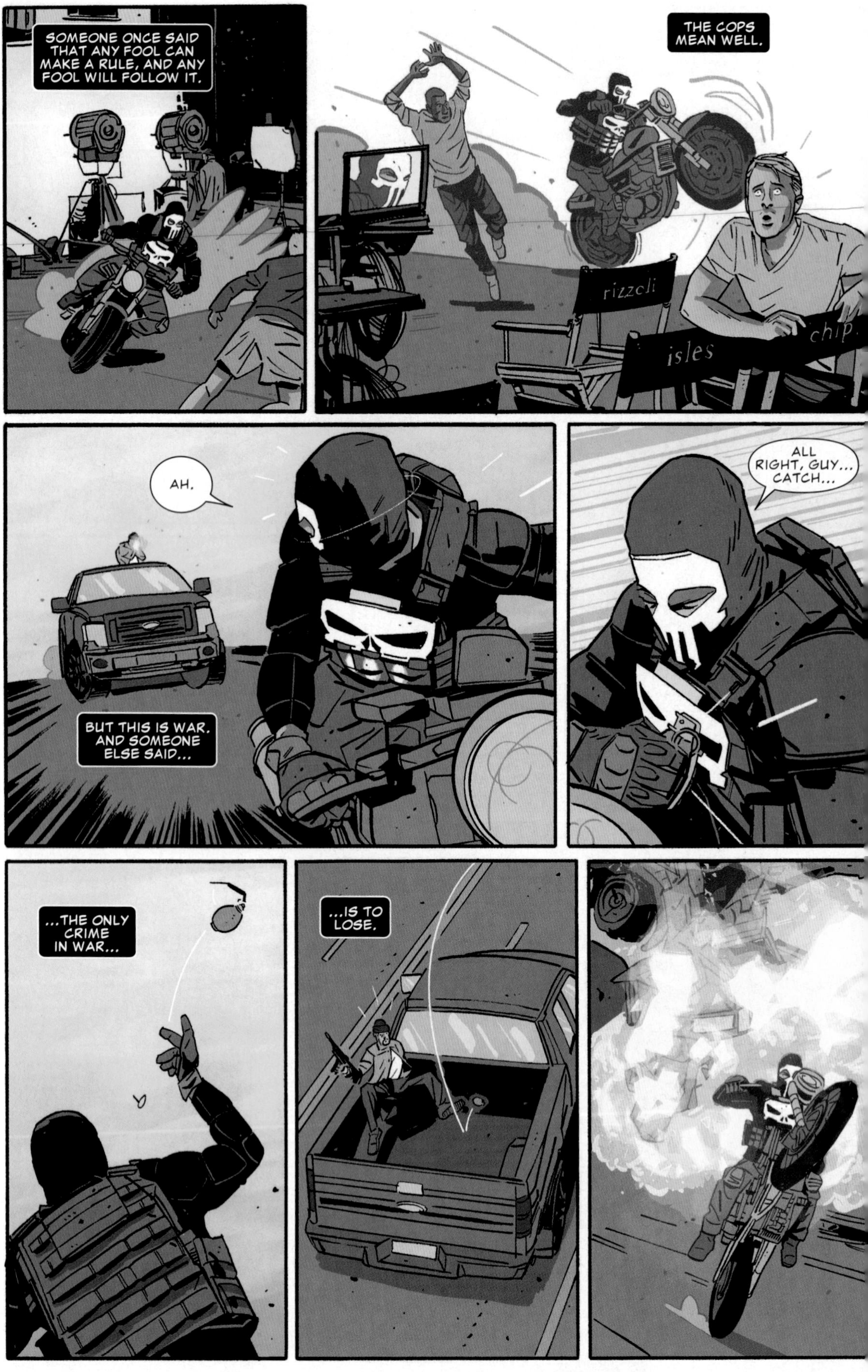
SOMEONE ONCE SAID THAT ANY FOOL CAN MAKE A RULE, AND ANY FOOL WILL FOLLOW IT.
THE COPS MEAN WELL.
rizzoli
isles
chip
AH.
BUT THIS IS WAR. AND SOMEONE ELSE SAID...
ALL RIGHT, GUY... CATCH...
...THE ONLY CRIME IN WAR...
...IS TO LOSE.

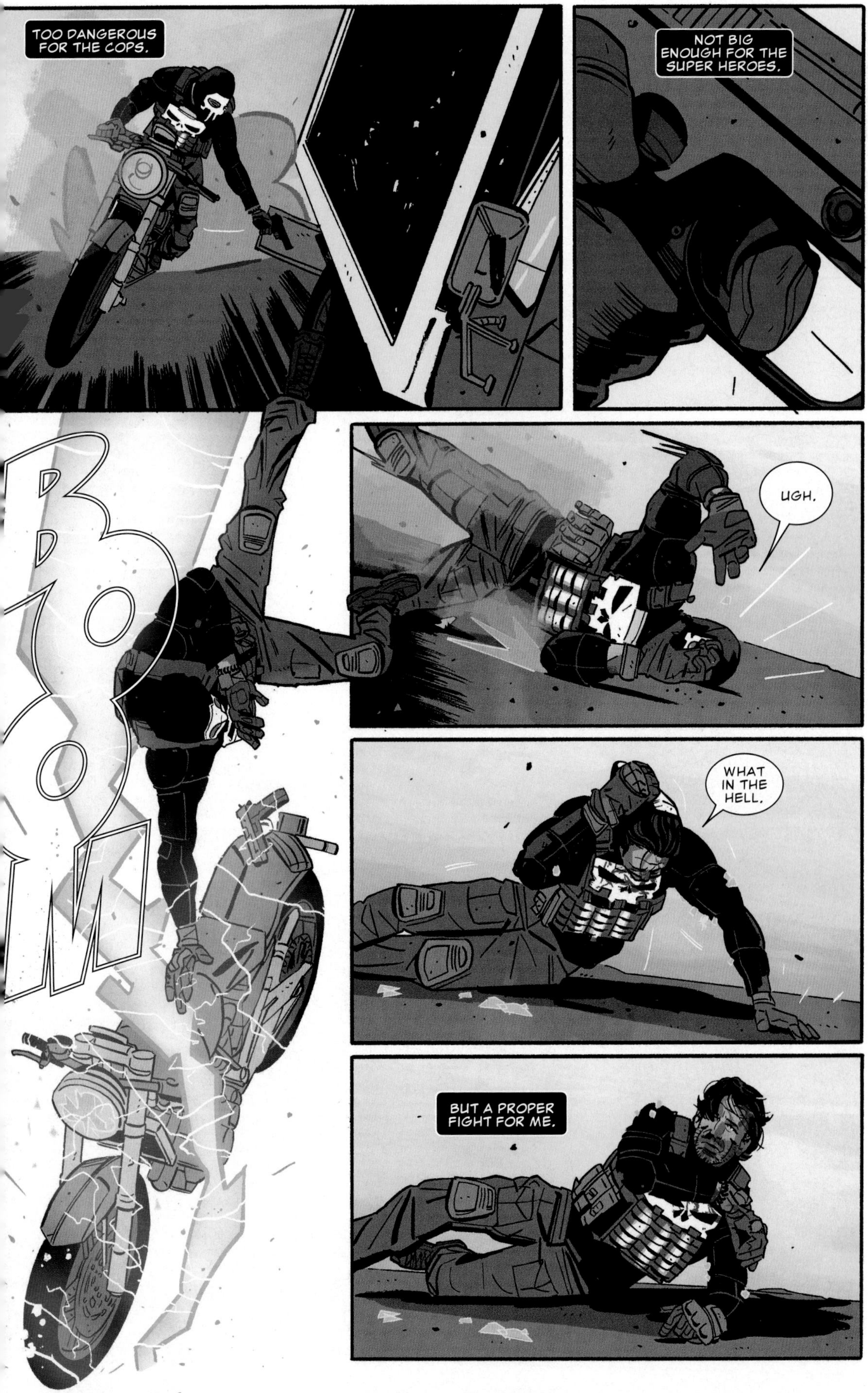
TOO DANGEROUS FOR THE COPS.
NOT BIG ENOUGH FOR THE SUPER HEROES.
BOOM
UGH.
WHAT IN THE HELL.
BUT A PROPER FIGHT FOR ME.

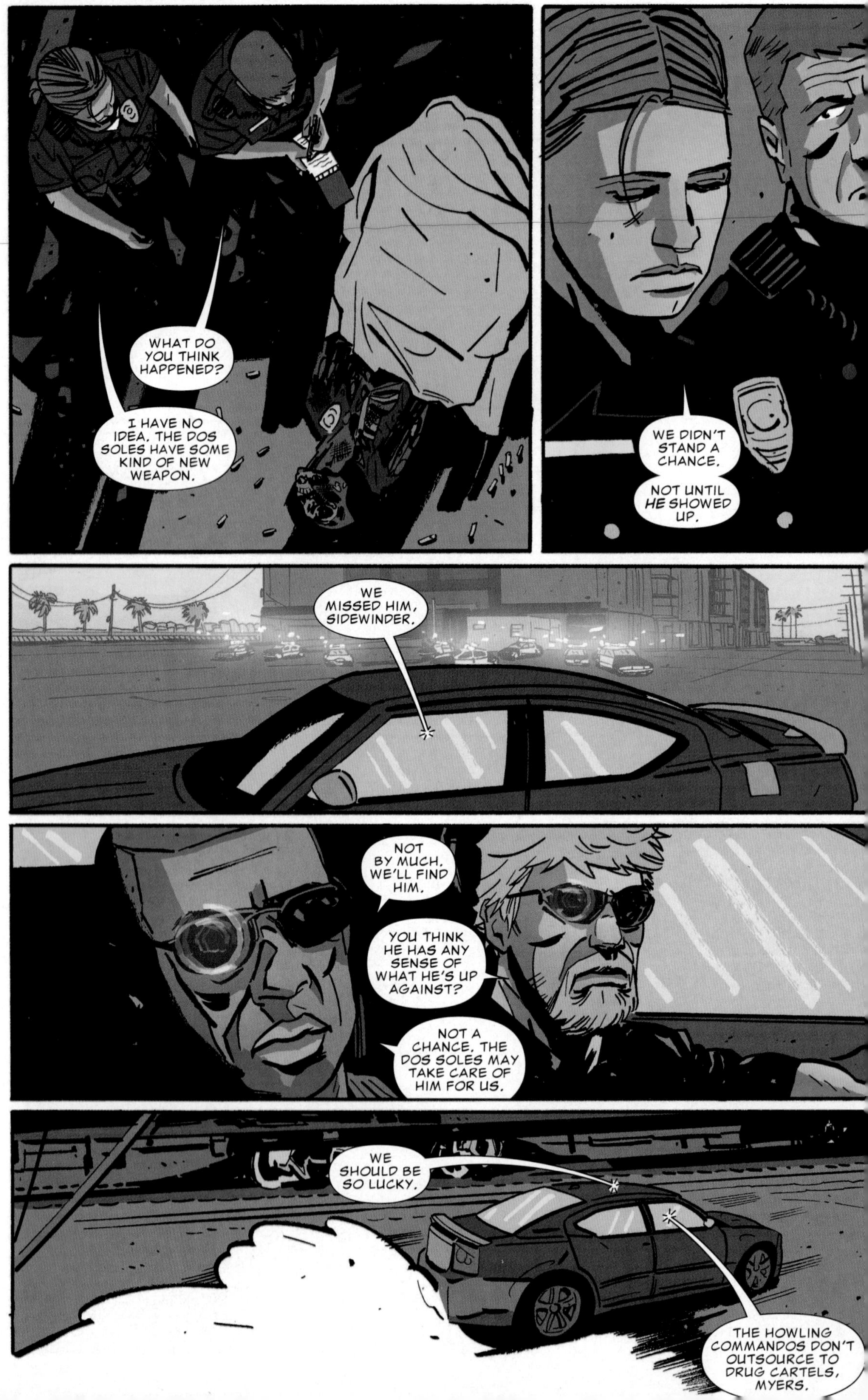
WHAT DO YOU THINK HAPPENED?
I HAVE NO IDEA. THE DOS SOLES HAVE SOME KIND OF NEW WEAPON.
WE DIDN'T STAND A CHANCE.
NOT UNTIL HE SHOWED UP.
WE MISSED HIM, SIDEWINDER.
NOT BY MUCH. WE'LL FIND HIM.
YOU THINK HE HAS ANY SENSE OF WHAT HE'S UP AGAINST?
NOT A CHANCE. THE DOS SOLES MAY TAKE CARE OF HIM FOR US.
WE SHOULD BE SO LUCKY.
THE HOWLING COMMANDOS DON'T OUTSOURCE TO DRUG CARTELS, MYERS.

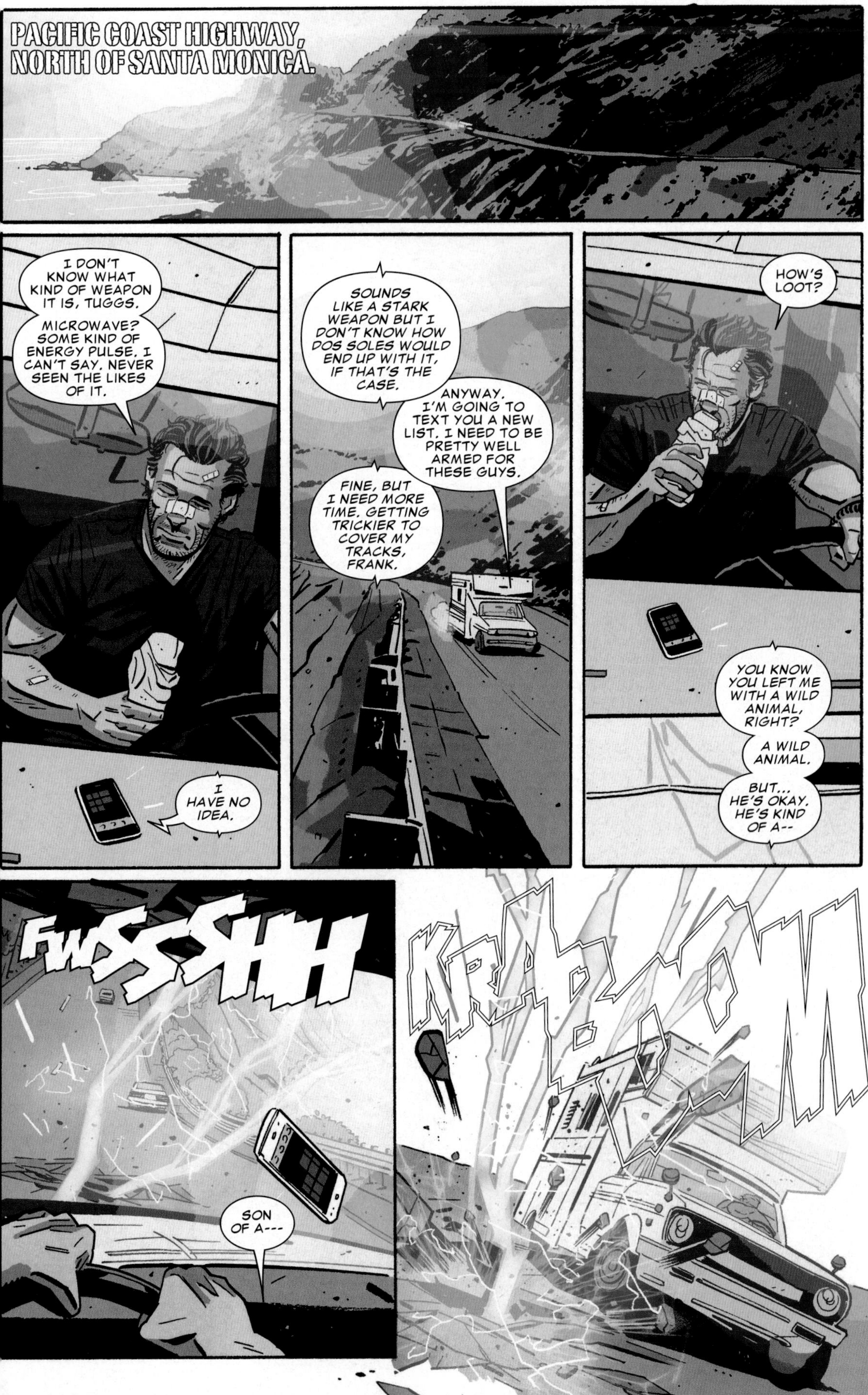
PACIFIC COAST HIGHWAY, NORTH OF SANTA MONICA.
I DON'T KNOW WHAT KIND OF WEAPON IT IS, TUGGS.
MICROWAVE? SOME KIND OF ENERGY PULSE. I CAN'T SAY. NEVER SEEN THE LIKES OF IT.
...
I HAVE NO IDEA.
SOUNDS LIKE A STARK WEAPON BUT I DON'T KNOW HOW DOS SOLES WOULD END UP WITH IT, IF THAT'S THE CASE.
ANYWAY. I'M GOING TO TEXT YOU A NEW LIST. I NEED TO BE PRETTY WELL ARMED FOR THESE GUYS.
FINE, BUT I NEED MORE TIME. GETTING TRICKIER TO COVER MY TRACKS, FRANK.
HOW'S LOOT?
YOU KNOW YOU LEFT ME WITH A WILD ANIMAL, RIGHT?
A WILD ANIMAL.
BUT... HE'S OKAY. HE'S KIND OF A--
FWSSSHH
SON OF A---
KRA-BOOM

SANTA ANA.

FRANK? FRANK? YOU THERE?

DAMN L.A. CELL TOWERS.

"THE SIGNAL IS GONE, BUT I GOT A TRACE."

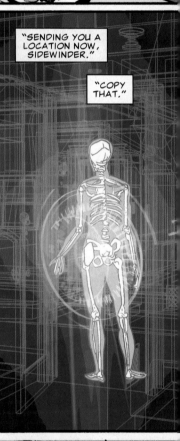

"SENDING YOU A LOCATION NOW, SIDEWINDER."

"COPY THAT."

WHAT DO I DO WITH THIS TARGET?

HE'S AN ASSET, RUBY RED. STAY ON HIM. HE'LL LEAD US TO CASTLE.

SIR, IT'S MYERS, I'M LISTENING TO A POLICE REPORT-- IT'S--YOU NEED TO HEAR THIS. SOMETHING'S GOING DOWN ON THE PCH.

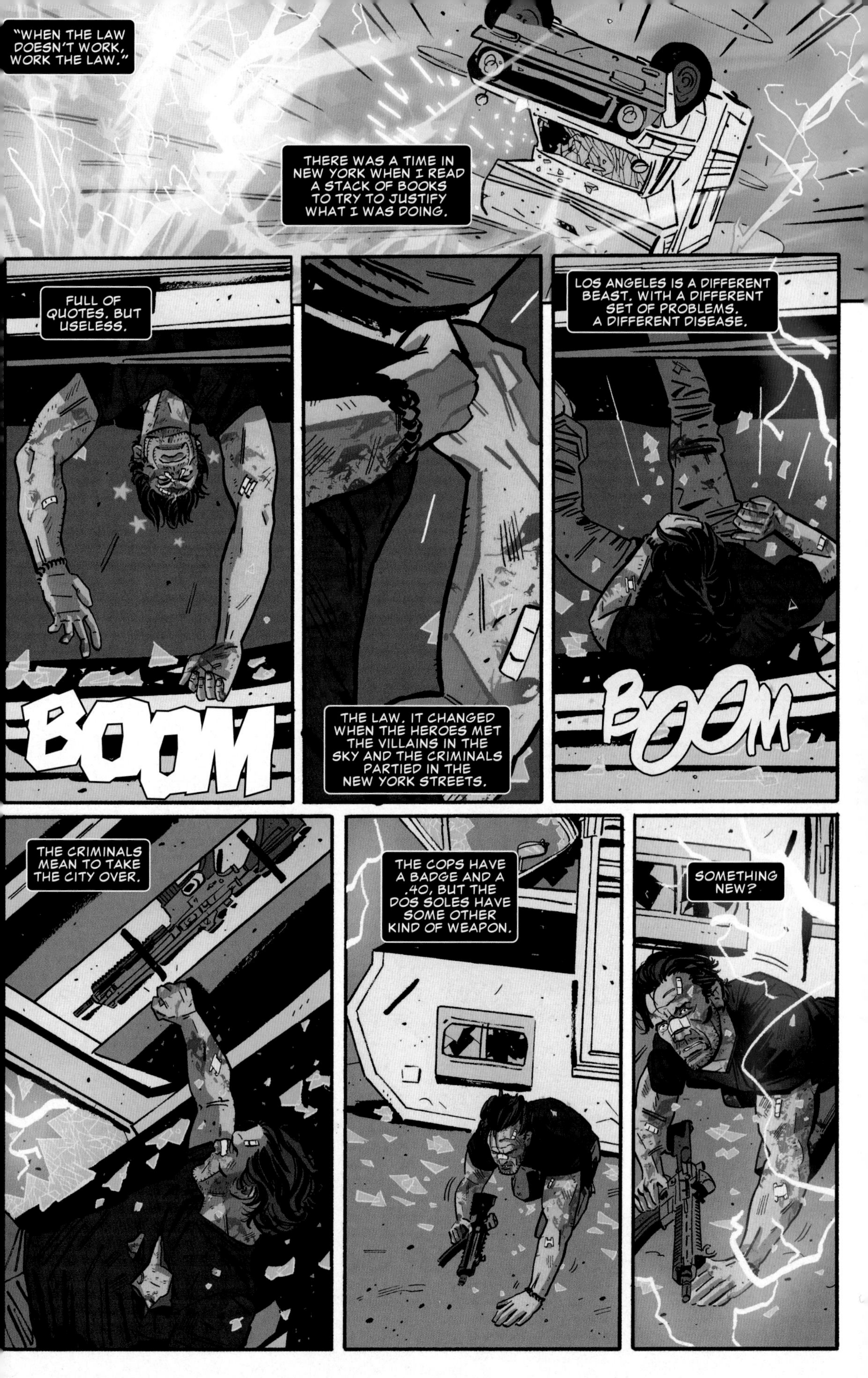
"WHEN THE LAW DOESN'T WORK, WORK THE LAW."
THERE WAS A TIME IN NEW YORK WHEN I READ A STACK OF BOOKS TO TRY TO JUSTIFY WHAT I WAS DOING.
FULL OF QUOTES. BUT USELESS.
BOOM
THE LAW. IT CHANGED WHEN THE HEROES MET THE VILLAINS IN THE SKY AND THE CRIMINALS PARTIED IN THE NEW YORK STREETS.
LOS ANGELES IS A DIFFERENT BEAST. WITH A DIFFERENT SET OF PROBLEMS. A DIFFERENT DISEASE.
BOOM
THE CRIMINALS MEAN TO TAKE THE CITY OVER.
THE COPS HAVE A BADGE AND A .40, BUT THE DOS SOLES HAVE SOME OTHER KIND OF WEAPON.
SOMETHING NEW?

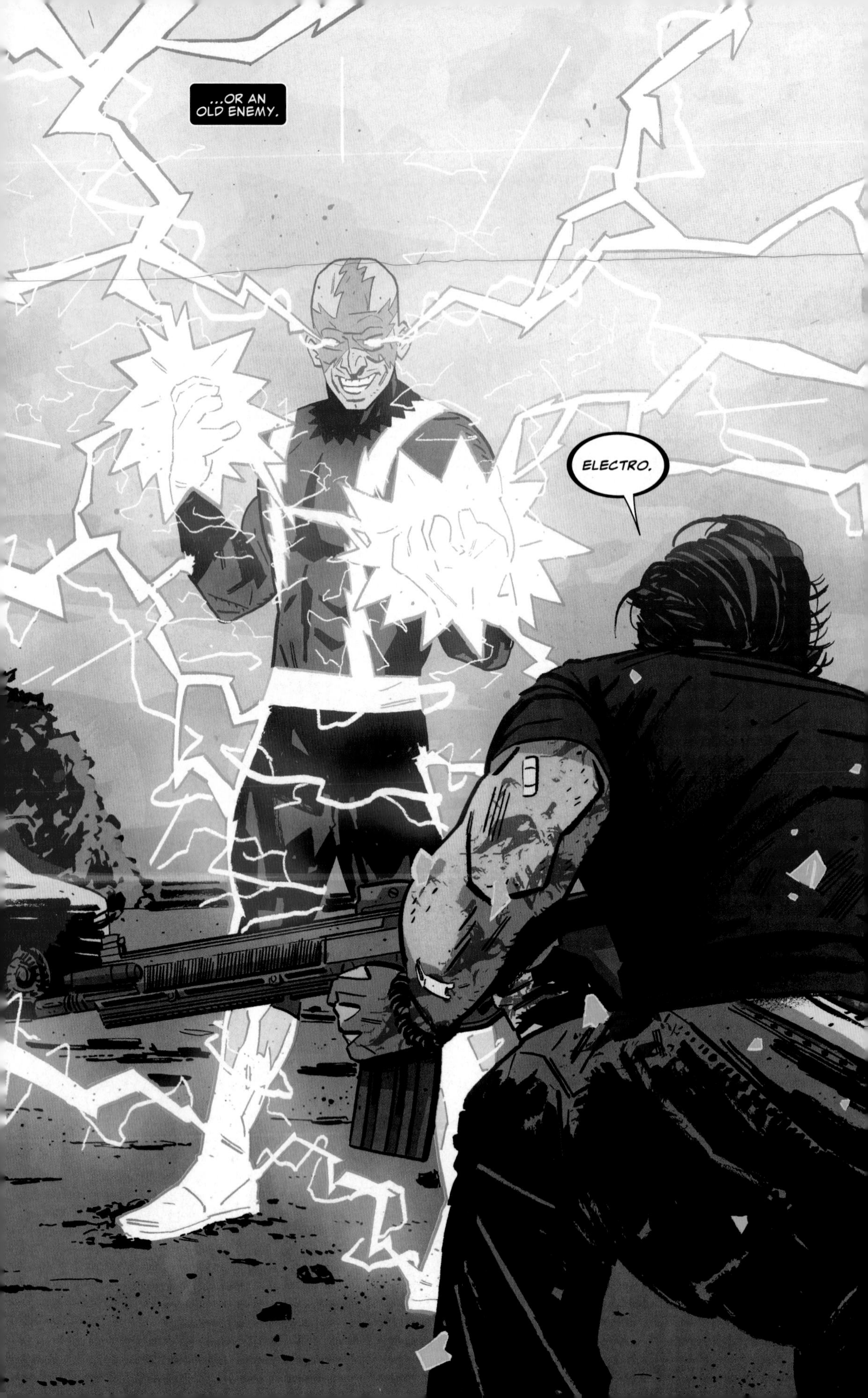
...OR AN OLD ENEMY.
ELECTRO.

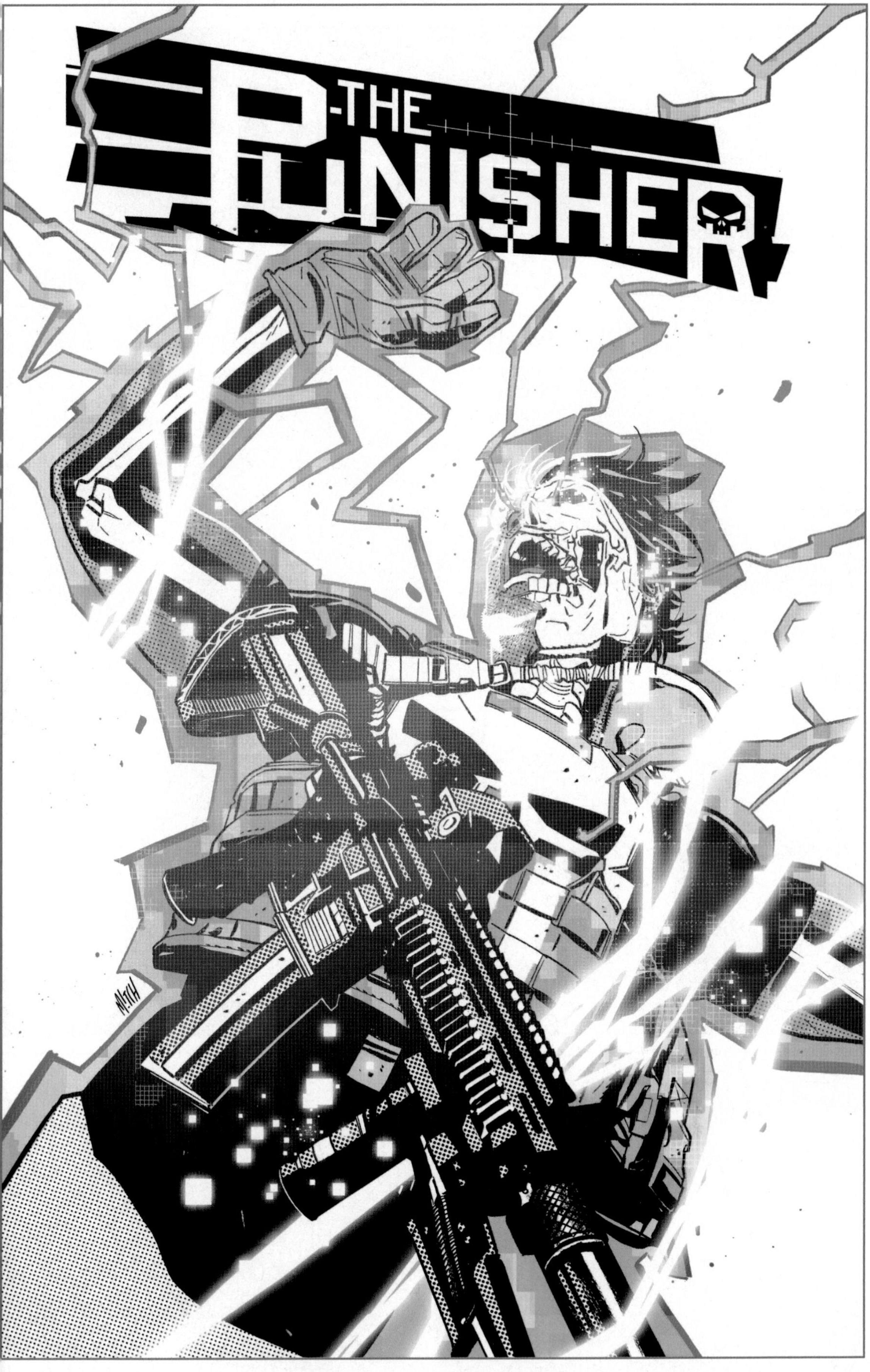
THE PUNISHER

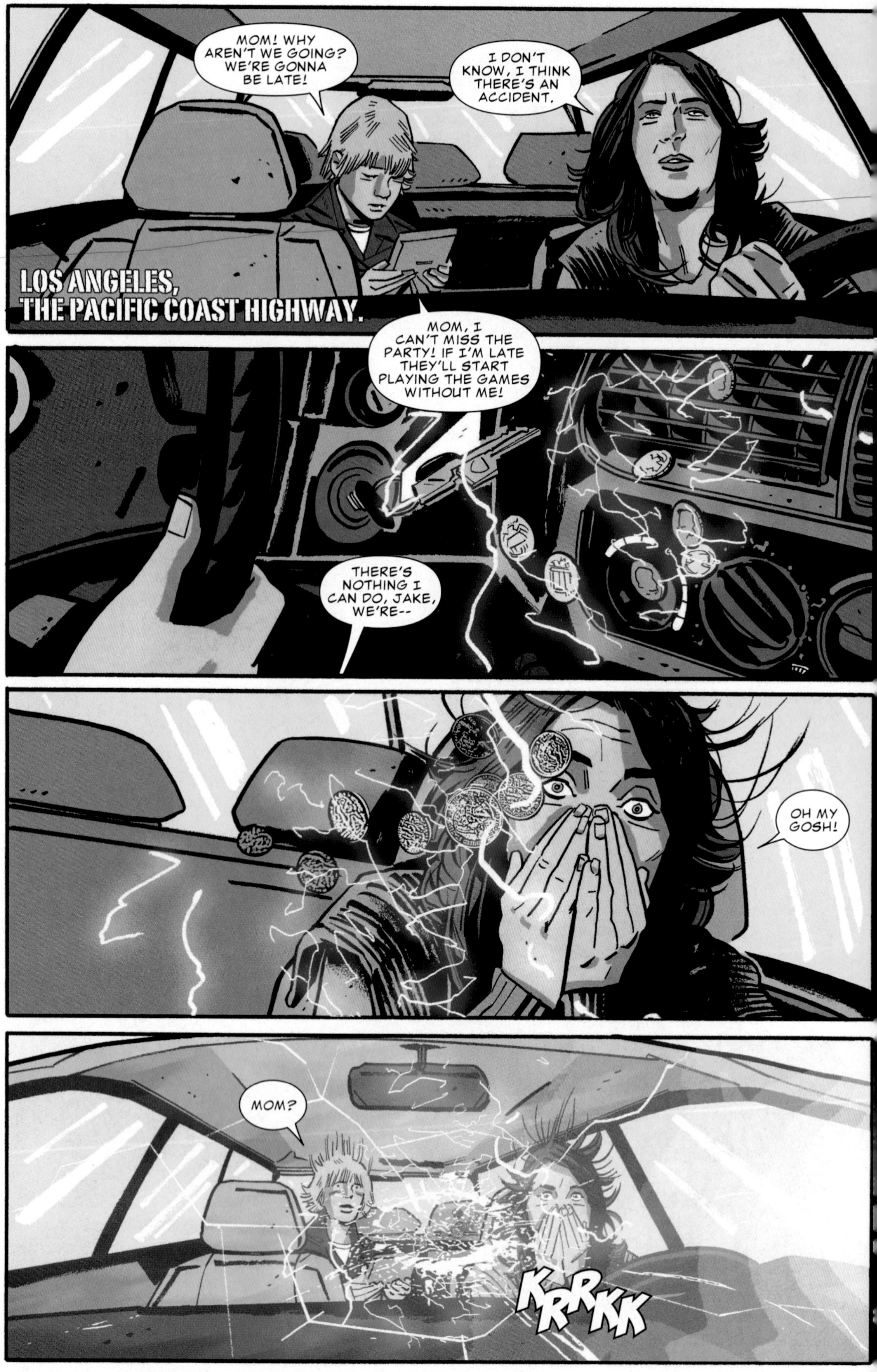

MOM! WHY AREN'T WE GOING? WE'RE GONNA BE LATE!
I DON'T KNOW, I THINK THERE'S AN ACCIDENT.
LOS ANGELES, THE PACIFIC COAST HIGHWAY.
MOM, I CAN'T MISS THE PARTY! IF I'M LATE THEY'LL START PLAYING THE GAMES WITHOUT ME!
THERE'S NOTHING I CAN DO, JAKE, WE'RE--
OH MY GOSH!
MOM?
KRRKK

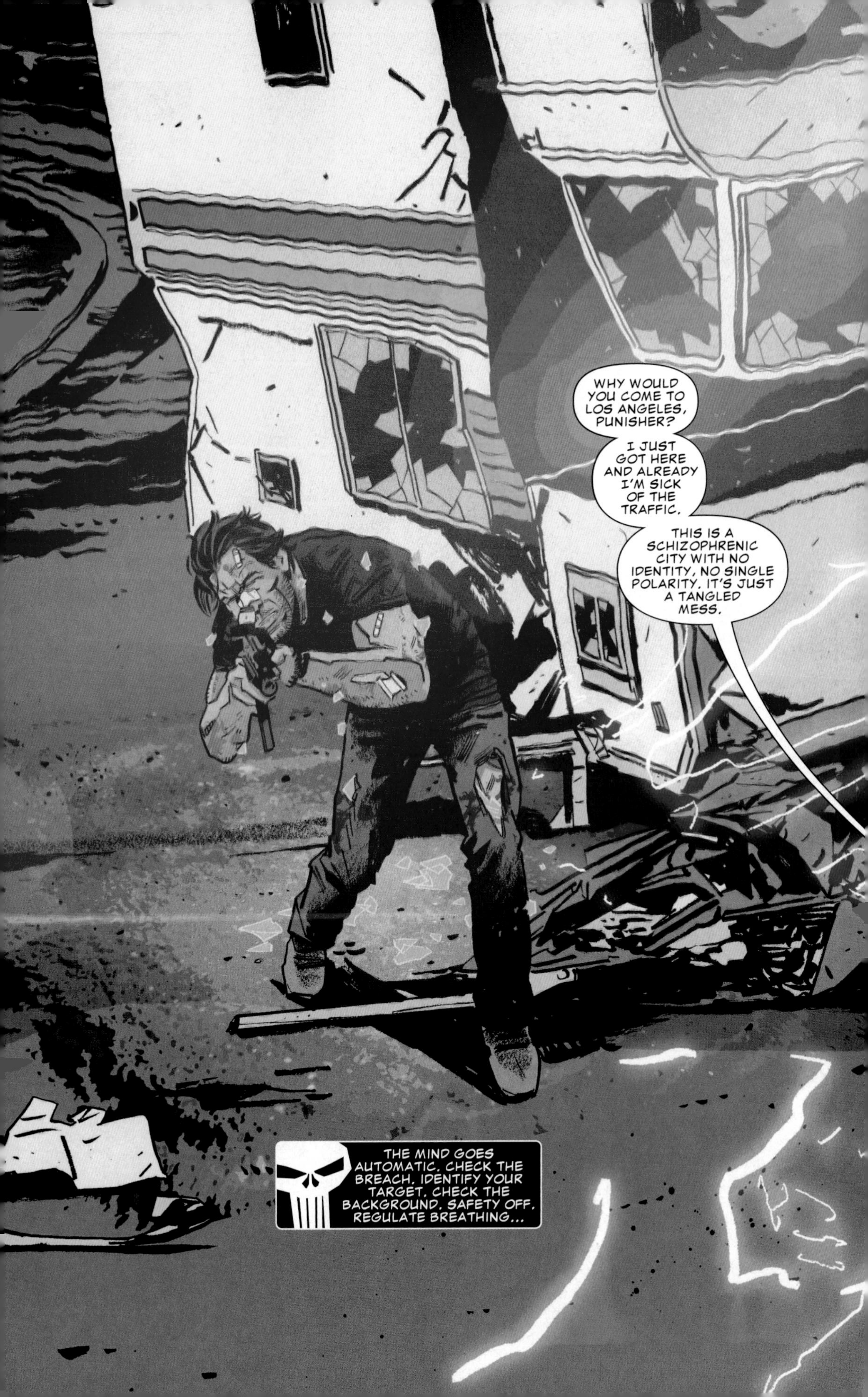
WHY WOULD YOU COME TO LOS ANGELES, PUNISHER?
I JUST GOT HERE AND ALREADY I'M SICK OF THE TRAFFIC.
THIS IS A SCHIZOPHRENIC CITY WITH NO IDENTITY, NO SINGLE POLARITY. IT'S JUST A TANGLED MESS.
THE MIND GOES AUTOMATIC. CHECK THE BREACH. IDENTIFY YOUR TARGET. CHECK THE BACKGROUND. SAFETY OFF. REGULATE BREATHING...

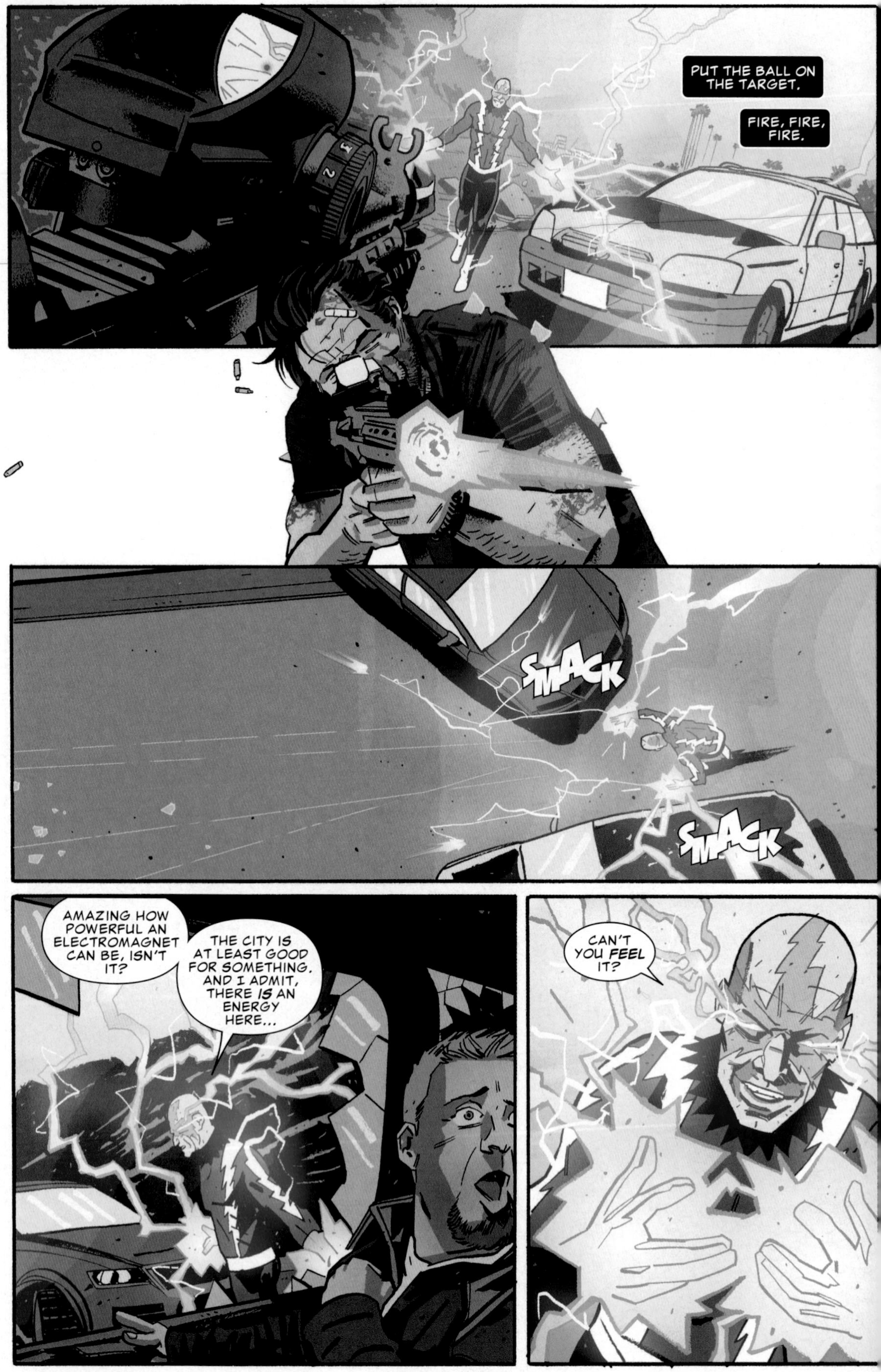
PUT THE BALL ON THE TARGET.
FIRE, FIRE, FIRE.
SMACK
SMACK
AMAZING HOW POWERFUL AN ELECTROMAGNET CAN BE, ISN'T IT?
THE CITY IS AT LEAST GOOD FOR SOMETHING. AND I ADMIT, THERE IS AN ENERGY HERE...
CAN'T YOU FEEL IT?

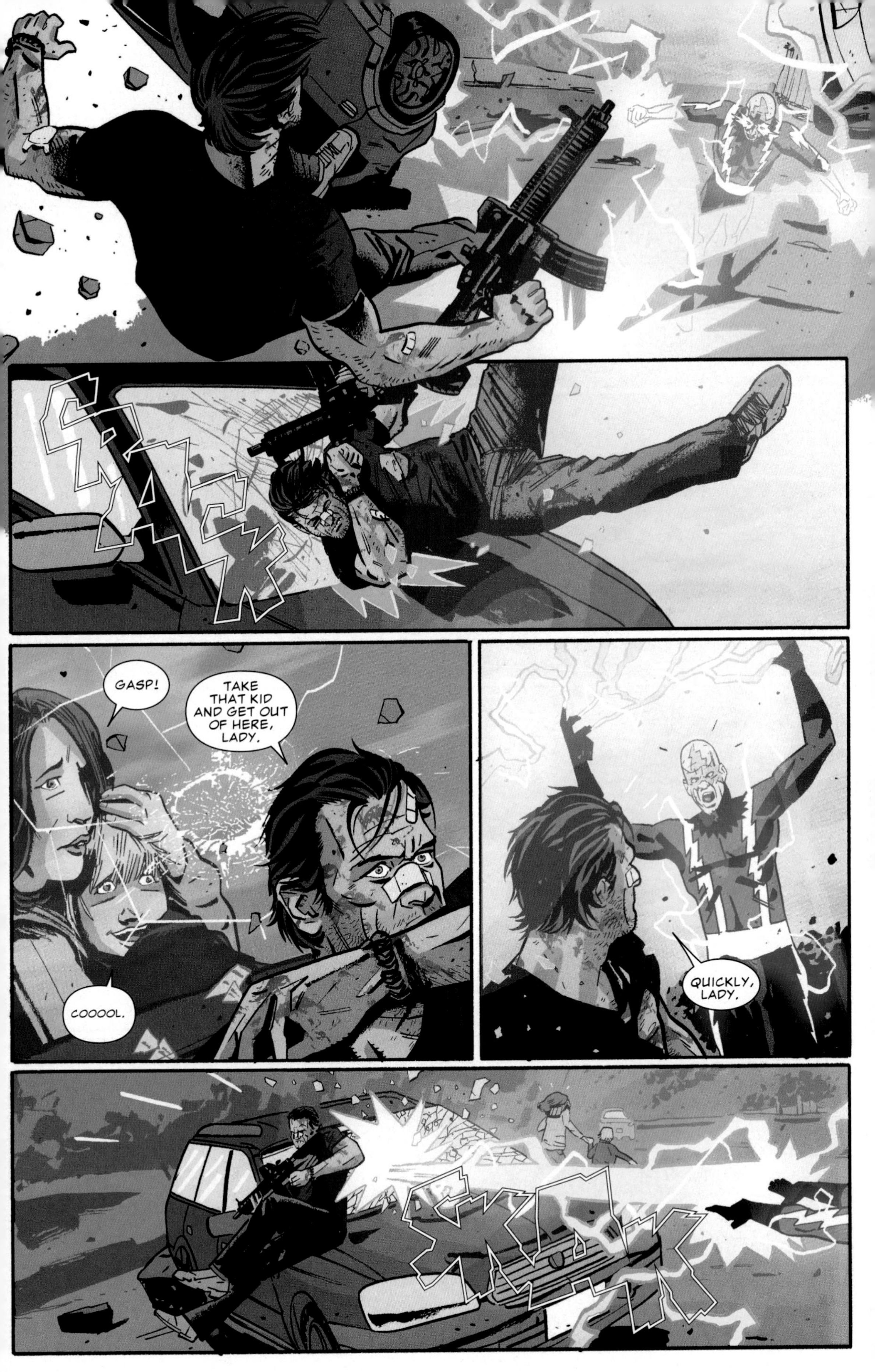
GASP!
TAKE THAT KID AND GET OUT OF HERE, LADY.
COOOOL.
QUICKLY, LADY.

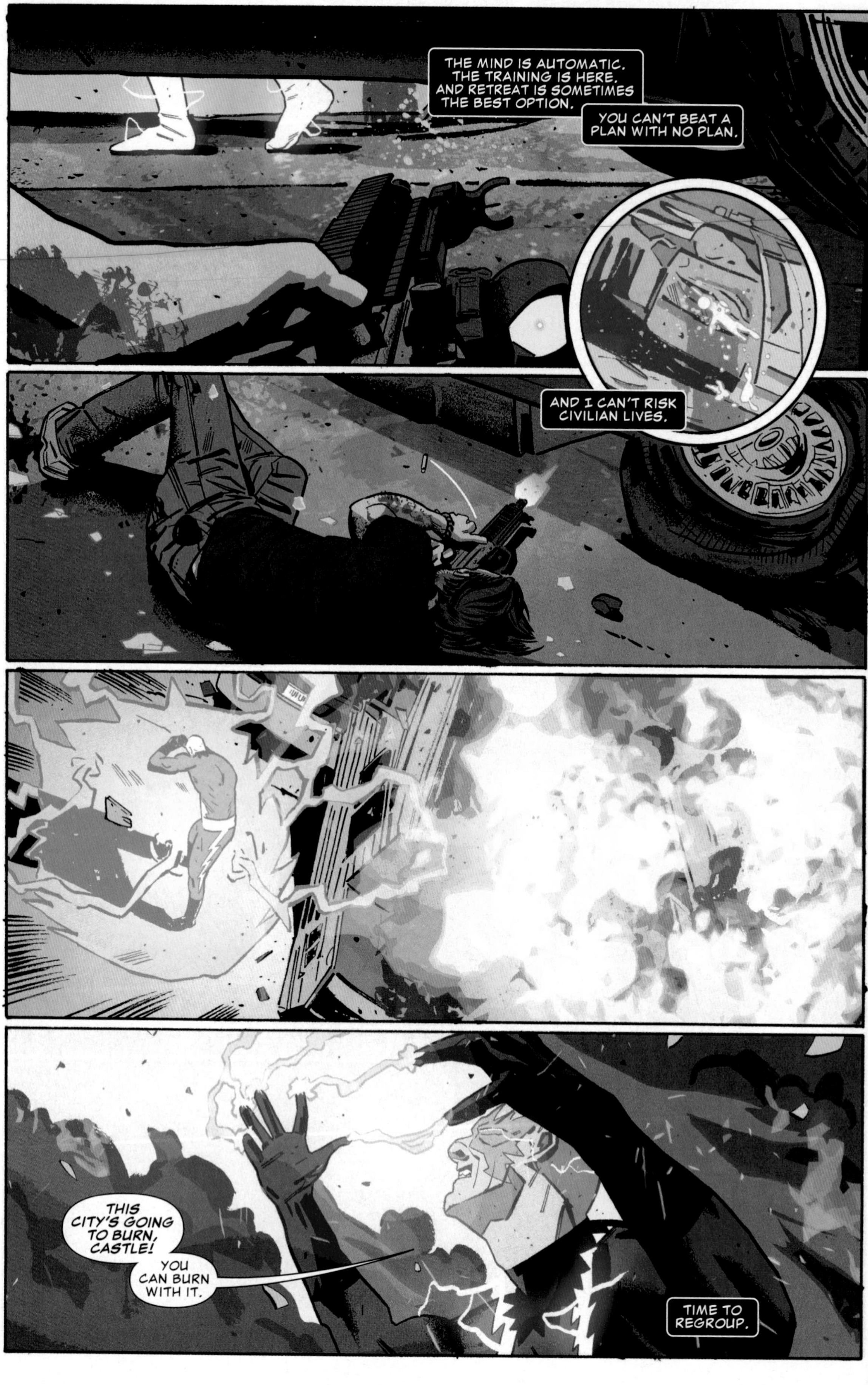
THE MIND IS AUTOMATIC. THE TRAINING IS HERE. AND RETREAT IS SOMETIMES THE BEST OPTION.
YOU CAN'T BEAT A PLAN WITH NO PLAN.
AND I CAN'T RISK CIVILIAN LIVES.
THIS CITY'S GOING TO BURN, CASTLE!
YOU CAN BURN WITH IT.
TIME TO REGROUP.

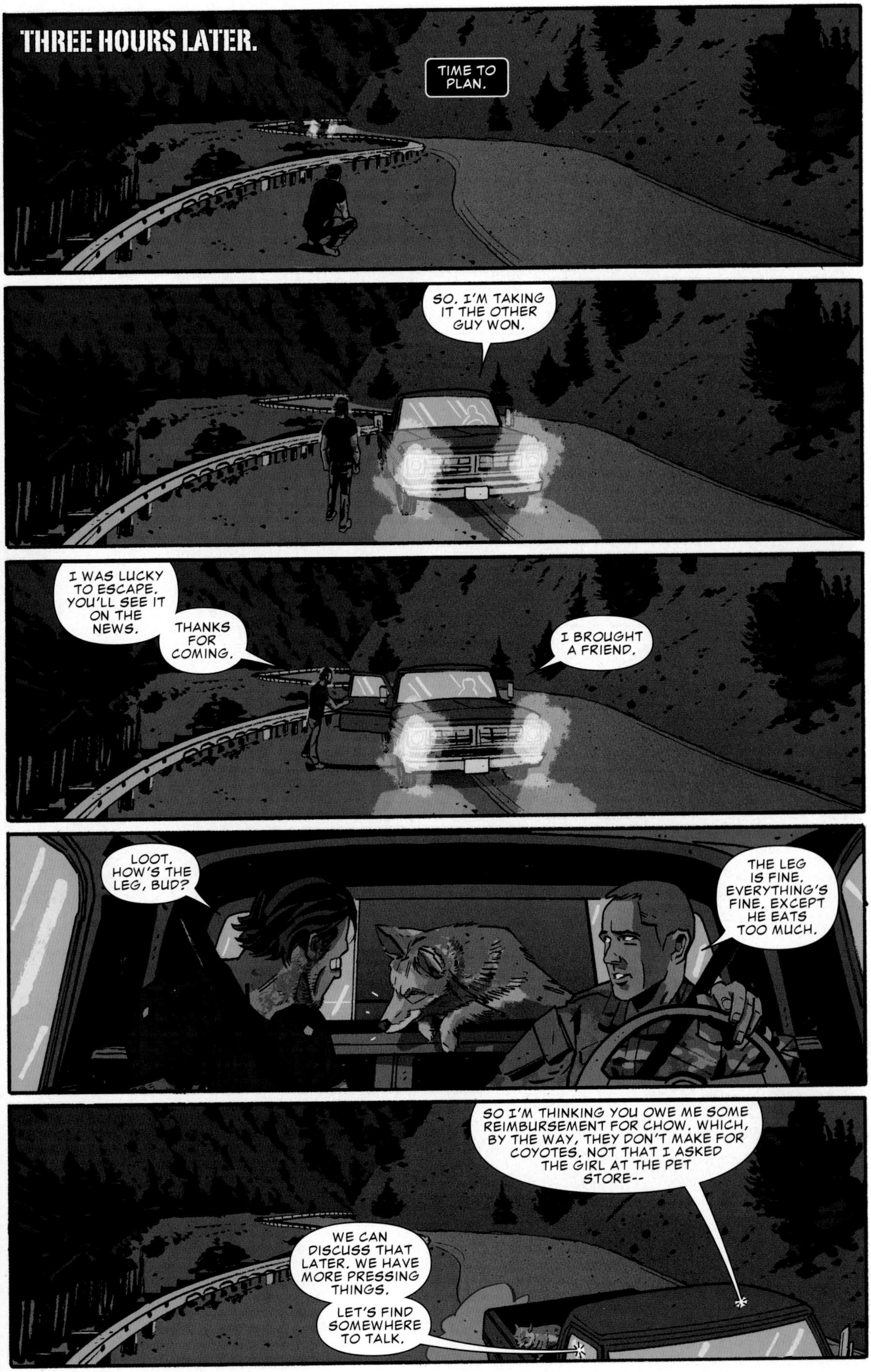
THREE HOURS LATER.
TIME TO PLAN.
SO. I'M TAKING IT THE OTHER GUY WON.
I WAS LUCKY TO ESCAPE. YOU'LL SEE IT ON THE NEWS.
THANKS FOR COMING.
I BROUGHT A FRIEND.
LOOT. HOW'S THE LEG, BUD?
THE LEG IS FINE. EVERYTHING'S FINE. EXCEPT HE EATS TOO MUCH.
SO I'M THINKING YOU OWE ME SOME REIMBURSEMENT FOR CHOW. WHICH, BY THE WAY, THEY DON'T MAKE FOR COYOTES. NOT THAT I ASKED THE GIRL AT THE PET STORE--
WE CAN DISCUSS THAT LATER. WE HAVE MORE PRESSING THINGS.
LET'S FIND SOMEWHERE TO TALK.

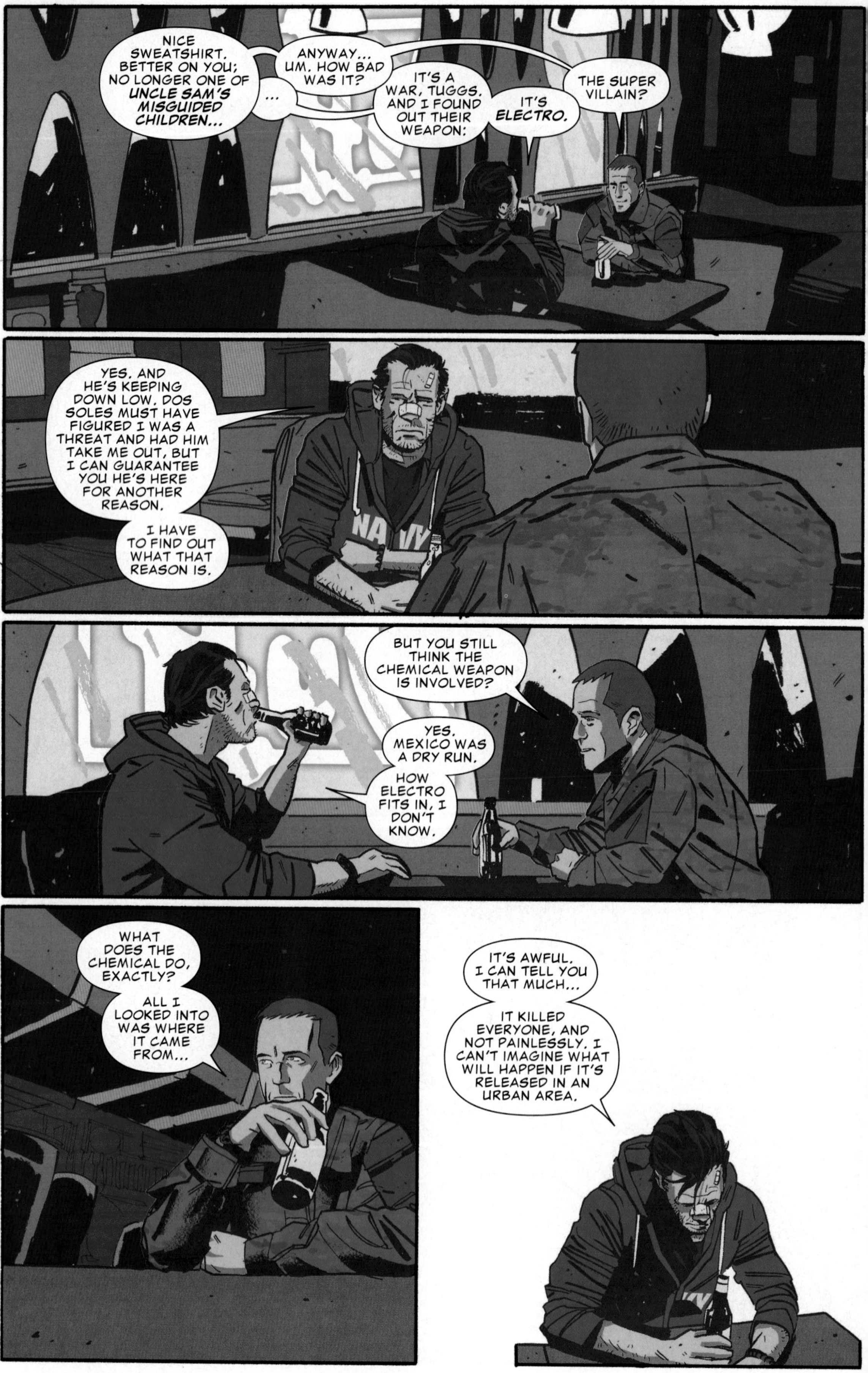
NICE SWEATSHIRT. BETTER ON YOU; NO LONGER ONE OF UNCLE SAM'S MISGUIDED CHILDREN...
...
ANYWAY... UM. HOW BAD WAS IT?
IT'S A WAR, TUGGS. AND I FOUND OUT THEIR WEAPON:
IT'S ELECTRO.
THE SUPER VILLAIN?
YES. AND HE'S KEEPING DOWN LOW. DOS SOLES MUST HAVE FIGURED I WAS A THREAT AND HAD HIM TAKE ME OUT, BUT I CAN GUARANTEE YOU HE'S HERE FOR ANOTHER REASON.
I HAVE TO FIND OUT WHAT THAT REASON IS.
NAVY
BUT YOU STILL THINK THE CHEMICAL WEAPON IS INVOLVED?
YES. MEXICO WAS A DRY RUN.
HOW ELECTRO FITS IN, I DON'T KNOW.
WHAT DOES THE CHEMICAL DO, EXACTLY?
ALL I LOOKED INTO WAS WHERE IT CAME FROM...
IT'S AWFUL. I CAN TELL YOU THAT MUCH...
IT KILLED EVERYONE, AND NOT PAINLESSLY. I CAN'T IMAGINE WHAT WILL HAPPEN IF IT'S RELEASED IN AN URBAN AREA.

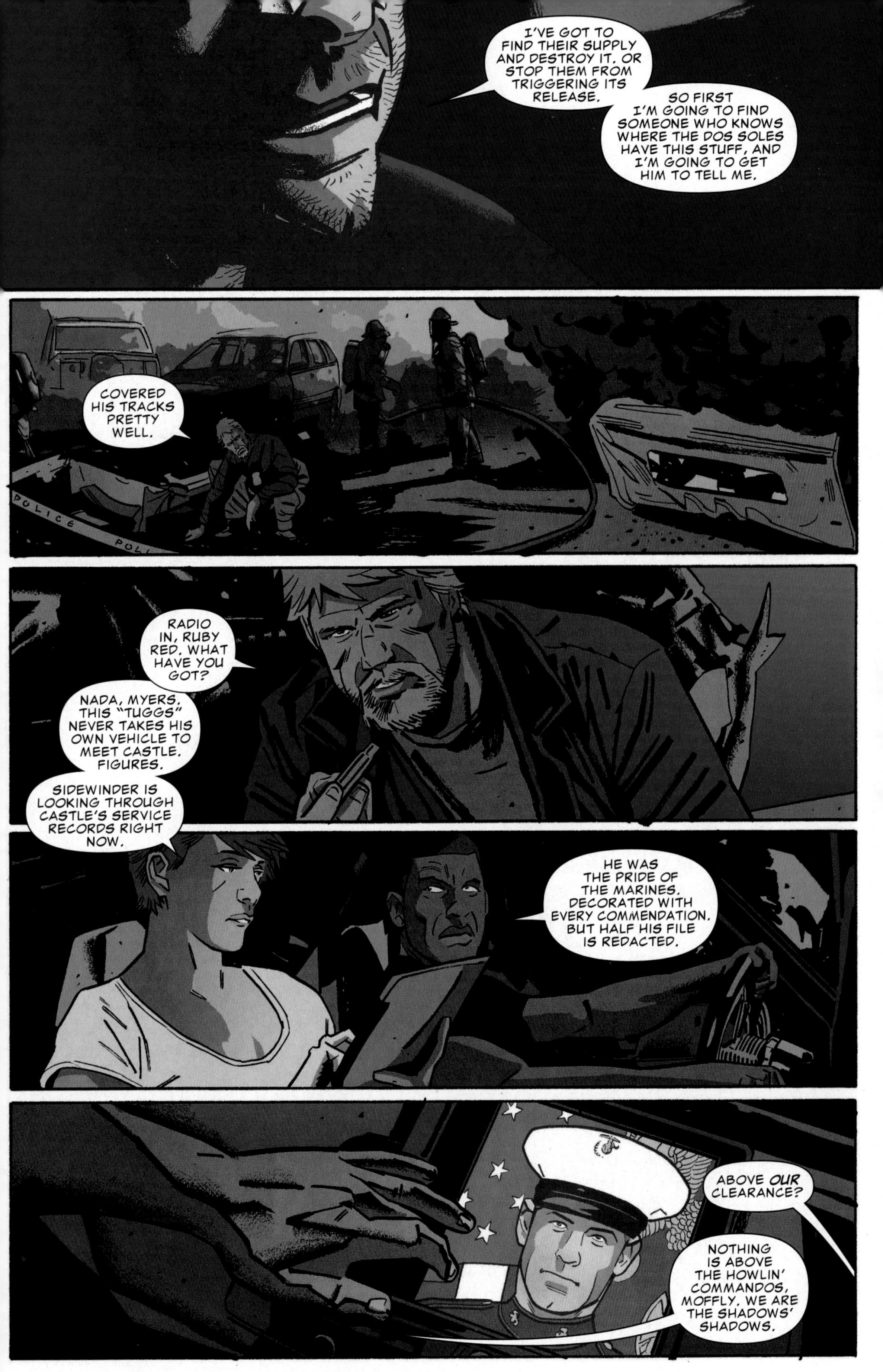
I'VE GOT TO FIND THEIR SUPPLY AND DESTROY IT. OR STOP THEM FROM TRIGGERING ITS RELEASE.
SO FIRST I'M GOING TO FIND SOMEONE WHO KNOWS WHERE THE DOS SOLES HAVE THIS STUFF, AND I'M GOING TO GET HIM TO TELL ME.
COVERED HIS TRACKS PRETTY WELL.
POLICE
RADIO IN, RUBY RED. WHAT HAVE YOU GOT?
NADA, MYERS. THIS "TUGGS" NEVER TAKES HIS OWN VEHICLE TO MEET CASTLE. FIGURES.
SIDEWINDER IS LOOKING THROUGH CASTLE'S SERVICE RECORDS RIGHT NOW.
HE WAS THE PRIDE OF THE MARINES. DECORATED WITH EVERY COMMENDATION. BUT HALF HIS FILE IS REDACTED.
ABOVE *OUR* CLEARANCE?
NOTHING IS ABOVE THE HOWLIN' COMMANDOS, MOFFLY. WE ARE THE SHADOWS' SHADOWS.

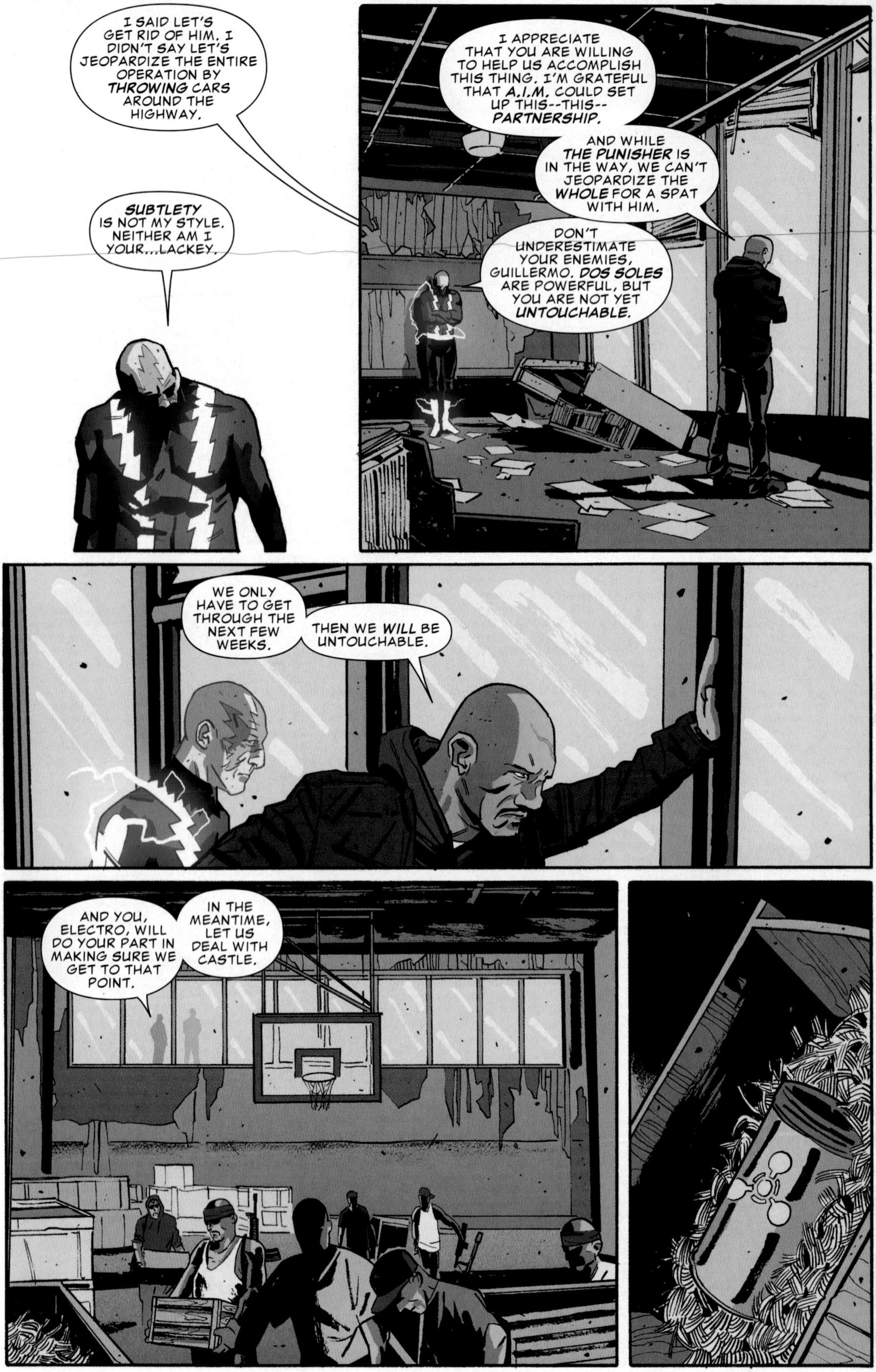
I SAID LET'S GET RID OF HIM. I DIDN'T SAY LET'S JEOPARDIZE THE ENTIRE OPERATION BY THROWING CARS AROUND THE HIGHWAY.
SUBTLETY IS NOT MY STYLE. NEITHER AM I YOUR...LACKEY.
I APPRECIATE THAT YOU ARE WILLING TO HELP US ACCOMPLISH THIS THING. I'M GRATEFUL THAT A.I.M. COULD SET UP THIS--THIS-- PARTNERSHIP.
AND WHILE THE PUNISHER IS IN THE WAY, WE CAN'T JEOPARDIZE THE WHOLE FOR A SPAT WITH HIM.
DON'T UNDERESTIMATE YOUR ENEMIES, GUILLERMO. DOS SOLES ARE POWERFUL, BUT YOU ARE NOT YET UNTOUCHABLE.
WE ONLY HAVE TO GET THROUGH THE NEXT FEW WEEKS.
THEN WE WILL BE UNTOUCHABLE.
AND YOU, ELECTRO, WILL DO YOUR PART IN MAKING SURE WE GET TO THAT POINT.
IN THE MEANTIME, LET US DEAL WITH CASTLE.

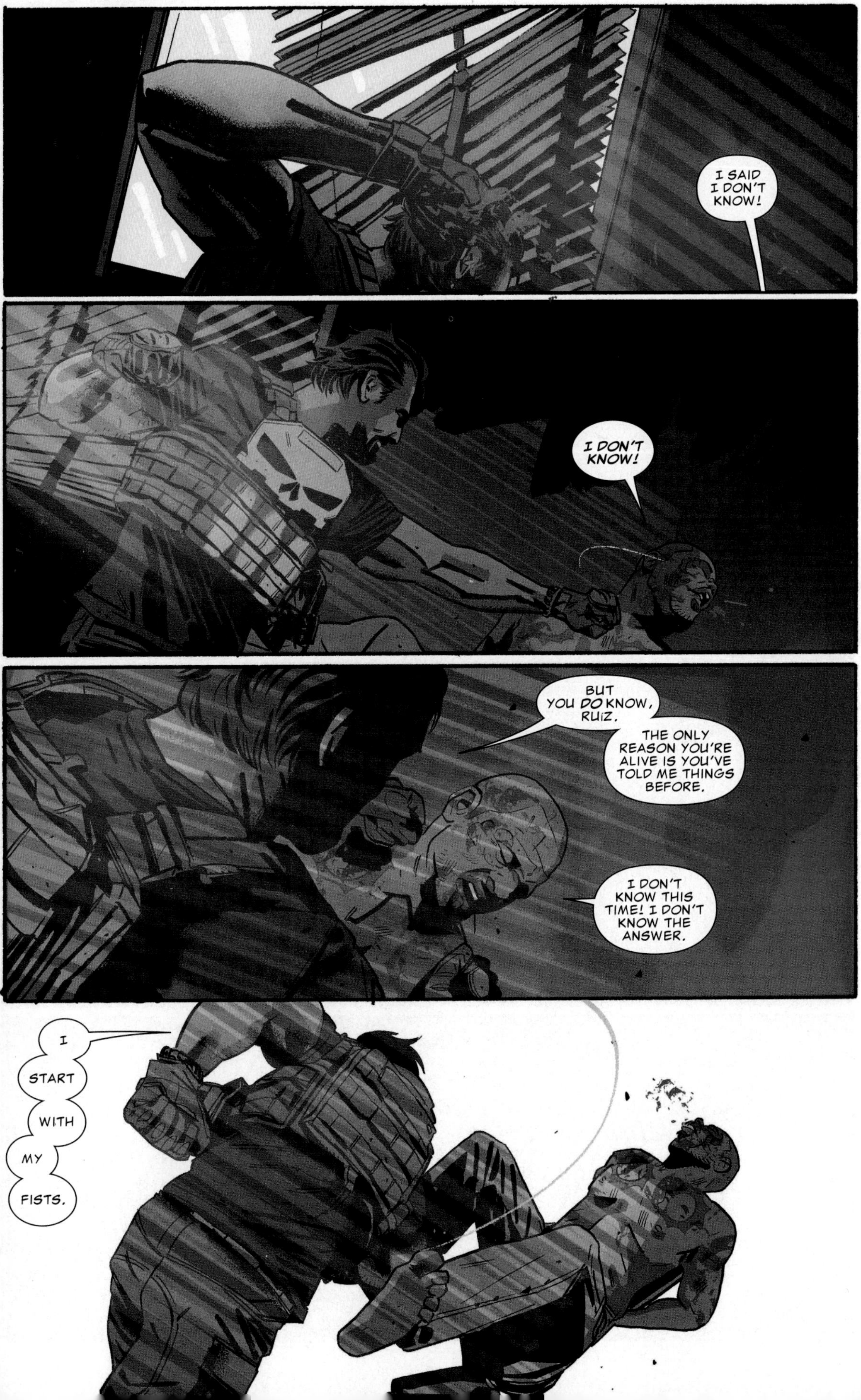
I SAID I DON'T KNOW!
I DON'T KNOW!
BUT YOU DO KNOW, RUIZ.
THE ONLY REASON YOU'RE ALIVE IS YOU'VE TOLD ME THINGS BEFORE.
I DON'T KNOW THIS TIME! I DON'T KNOW THE ANSWER.
I
START
WITH
MY
FISTS.

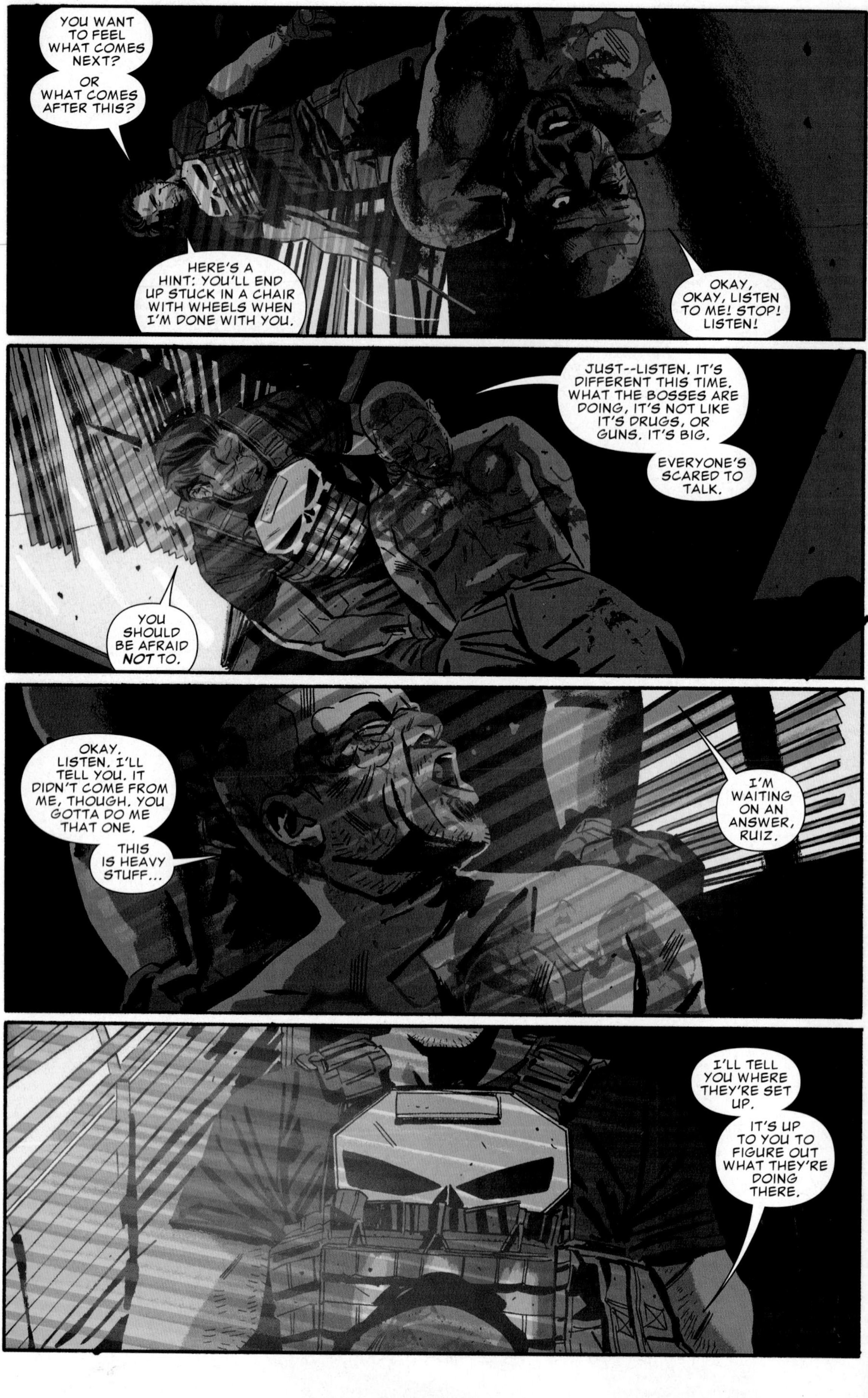

YOU WANT TO FEEL WHAT COMES NEXT?
OR WHAT COMES AFTER THIS?
HERE'S A HINT: YOU'LL END UP STUCK IN A CHAIR WITH WHEELS WHEN I'M DONE WITH YOU.
OKAY, OKAY, LISTEN TO ME! STOP! LISTEN!
JUST--LISTEN. IT'S DIFFERENT THIS TIME. WHAT THE BOSSES ARE DOING, IT'S NOT LIKE IT'S DRUGS, OR GUNS. IT'S BIG.
EVERYONE'S SCARED TO TALK.
YOU SHOULD BE AFRAID **NOT** TO.
OKAY. LISTEN. I'LL TELL YOU. IT DIDN'T COME FROM ME, THOUGH. YOU GOTTA DO ME THAT ONE.
THIS IS HEAVY STUFF...
I'M WAITING ON AN ANSWER, RUIZ.
I'LL TELL YOU WHERE THEY'RE SET UP.
IT'S UP TO YOU TO FIGURE OUT WHAT THEY'RE DOING THERE.

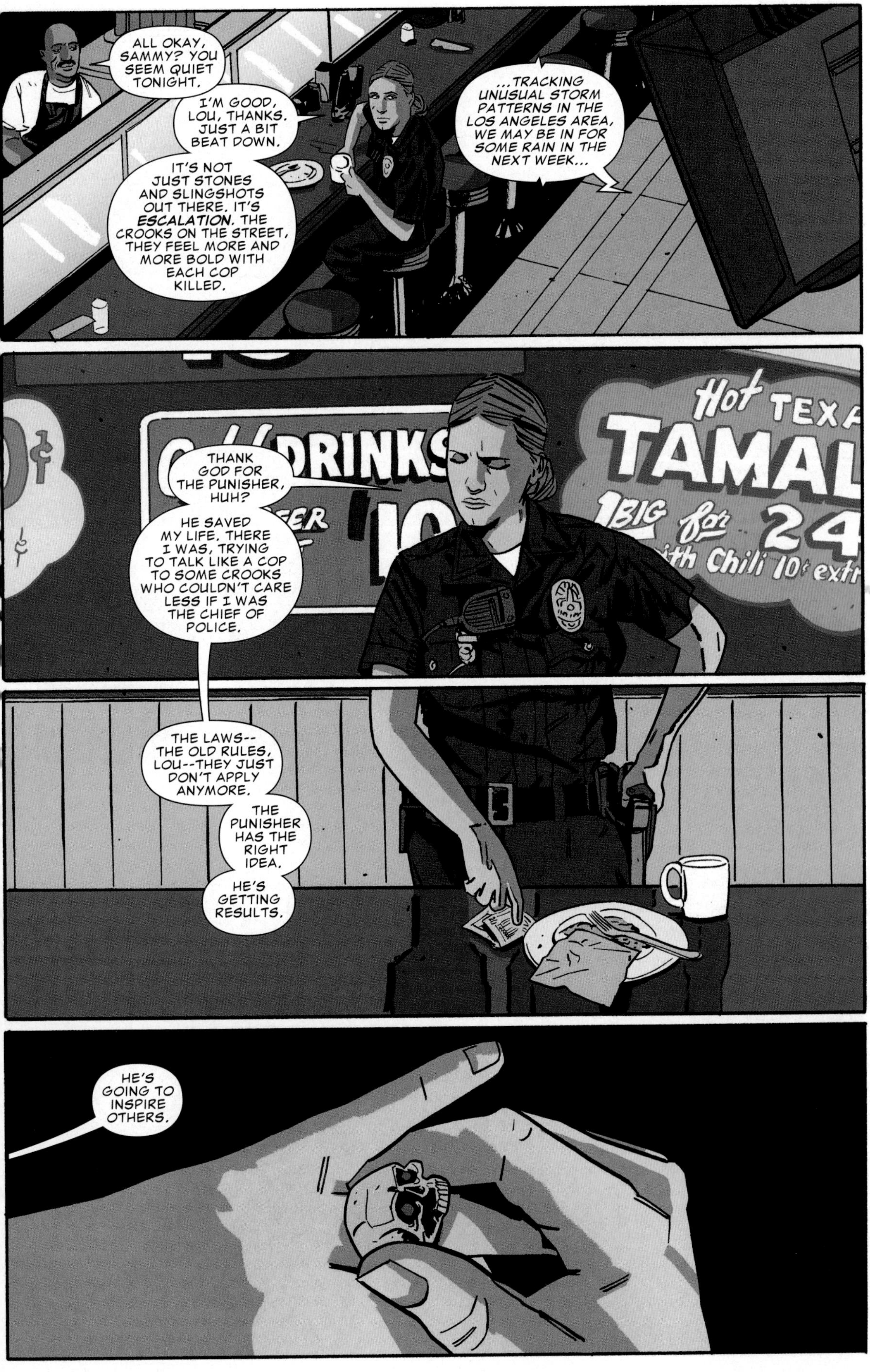
ALL OKAY, SAMMY? YOU SEEM QUIET TONIGHT.
I'M GOOD, LOU, THANKS. JUST A BIT BEAT DOWN.
IT'S NOT JUST STONES AND SLINGSHOTS OUT THERE. IT'S ESCALATION. THE CROOKS ON THE STREET, THEY FEEL MORE AND MORE BOLD WITH EACH COP KILLED.
...TRACKING UNUSUAL STORM PATTERNS IN THE LOS ANGELES AREA, WE MAY BE IN FOR SOME RAIN IN THE NEXT WEEK...
DRINKS
Hot TEXA
TAMAL
1 BIG for 24
ith Chili 10¢ extr
THANK GOD FOR THE PUNISHER, HUH?
HE SAVED MY LIFE. THERE I WAS, TRYING TO TALK LIKE A COP TO SOME CROOKS WHO COULDN'T CARE LESS IF I WAS THE CHIEF OF POLICE.
THE LAWS-- THE OLD RULES, LOU--THEY JUST DON'T APPLY ANYMORE.
THE PUNISHER HAS THE RIGHT IDEA.
HE'S GETTING RESULTS.
HE'S GOING TO INSPIRE OTHERS.

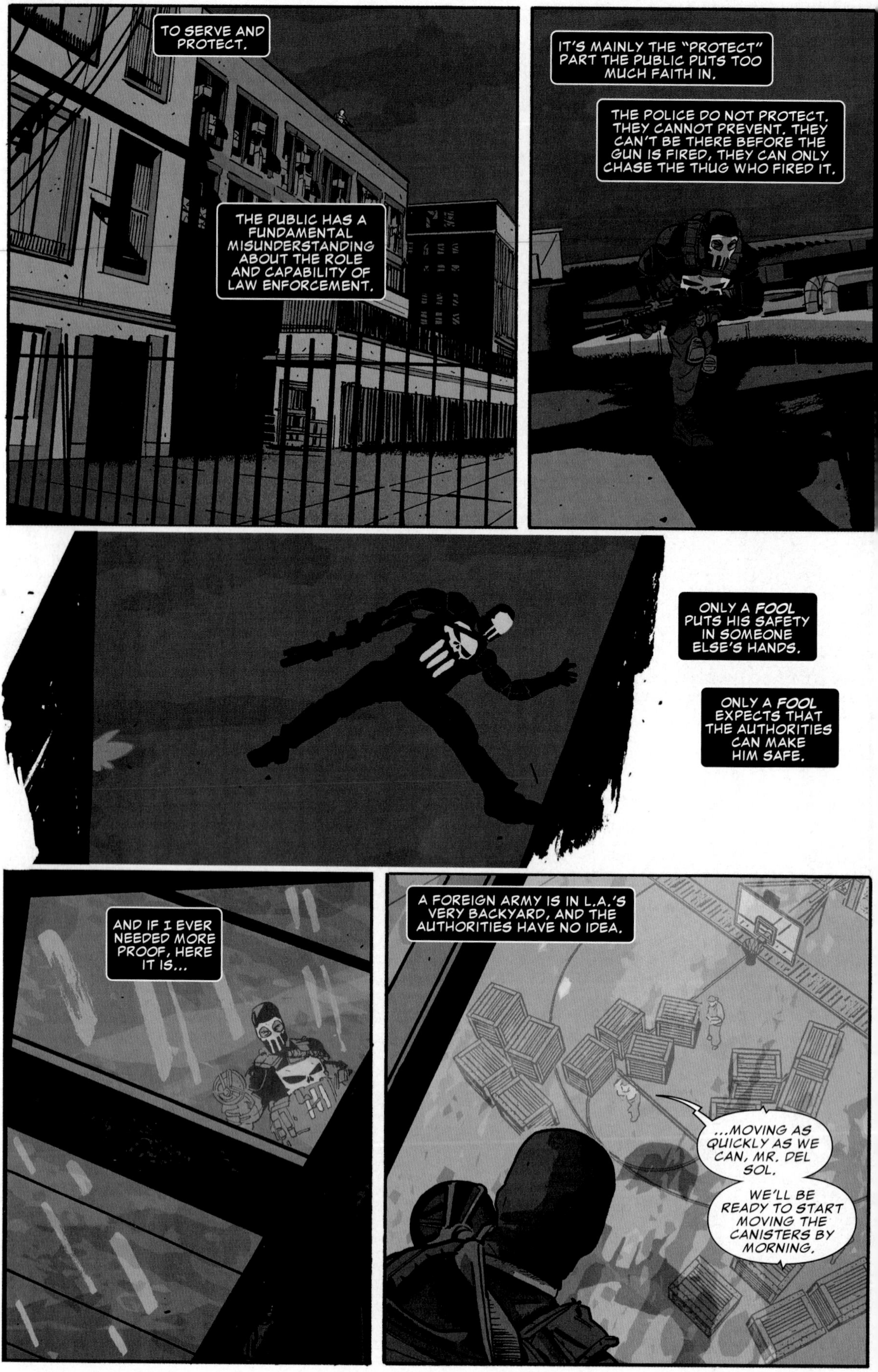
TO SERVE AND PROTECT.
THE PUBLIC HAS A FUNDAMENTAL MISUNDERSTANDING ABOUT THE ROLE AND CAPABILITY OF LAW ENFORCEMENT.
IT'S MAINLY THE "PROTECT" PART THE PUBLIC PUTS TOO MUCH FAITH IN.
THE POLICE DO NOT PROTECT. THEY CANNOT PREVENT. THEY CAN'T BE THERE BEFORE THE GUN IS FIRED, THEY CAN ONLY CHASE THE THUG WHO FIRED IT.
ONLY A *FOOL* PUTS HIS SAFETY IN SOMEONE ELSE'S HANDS.
ONLY A *FOOL* EXPECTS THAT THE AUTHORITIES CAN MAKE HIM SAFE.
AND IF I EVER NEEDED MORE PROOF, HERE IT IS...
A FOREIGN ARMY IS IN L.A.'S VERY BACKYARD, AND THE AUTHORITIES HAVE NO IDEA.
...MOVING AS QUICKLY AS WE CAN, MR. DEL SOL.
WE'LL BE READY TO START MOVING THE CANISTERS BY MORNING.

WE HAVE TO BE READY BY TOMORROW NIGHT.

ELECTRO WILL BLACK OUT THE CITY AND THEN WE BEGIN.

WHEN THE FUSE IS LIT, THERE IS NO STOPPING IT.

I UNDERSTAND, MR. DEL SOL. WE WON'T LET YOU DOWN.

SEÑOR! ESTA AQUI.

PERIMETER IS BREACHED.

AWAITING OUR ORDER.

ARE THE MEN IN PLACE?

THEY DON'T *NEED* MY ORDER. GO! GO!

THE WORST FEELING ON THE BATTLEFIELD IS THIS ONE:

THE FEELING THAT YOU HAVE UNDERESTIMATED YOUR ENEMY.

IT IS A COLD WASH ACROSS YOUR SKIN, LIKE BLOOD LOSS.

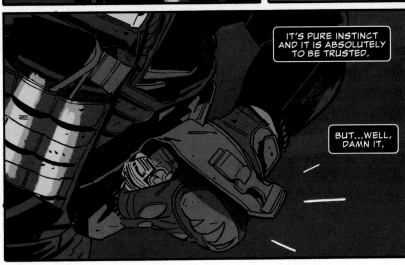

IT'S PURE INSTINCT AND IT IS ABSOLUTELY TO BE TRUSTED.

BUT...WELL, DAMN IT.

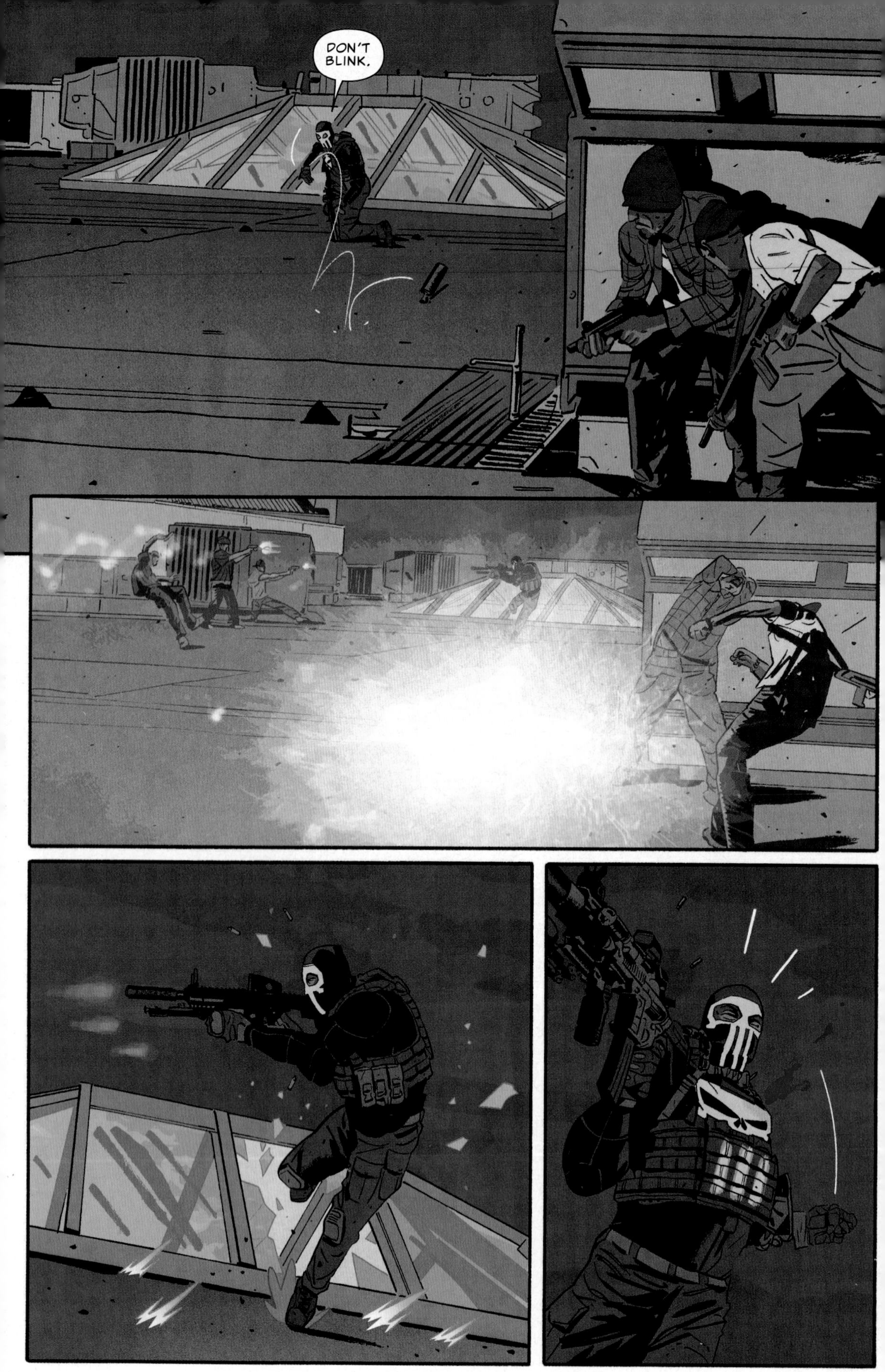
DON'T BLINK.

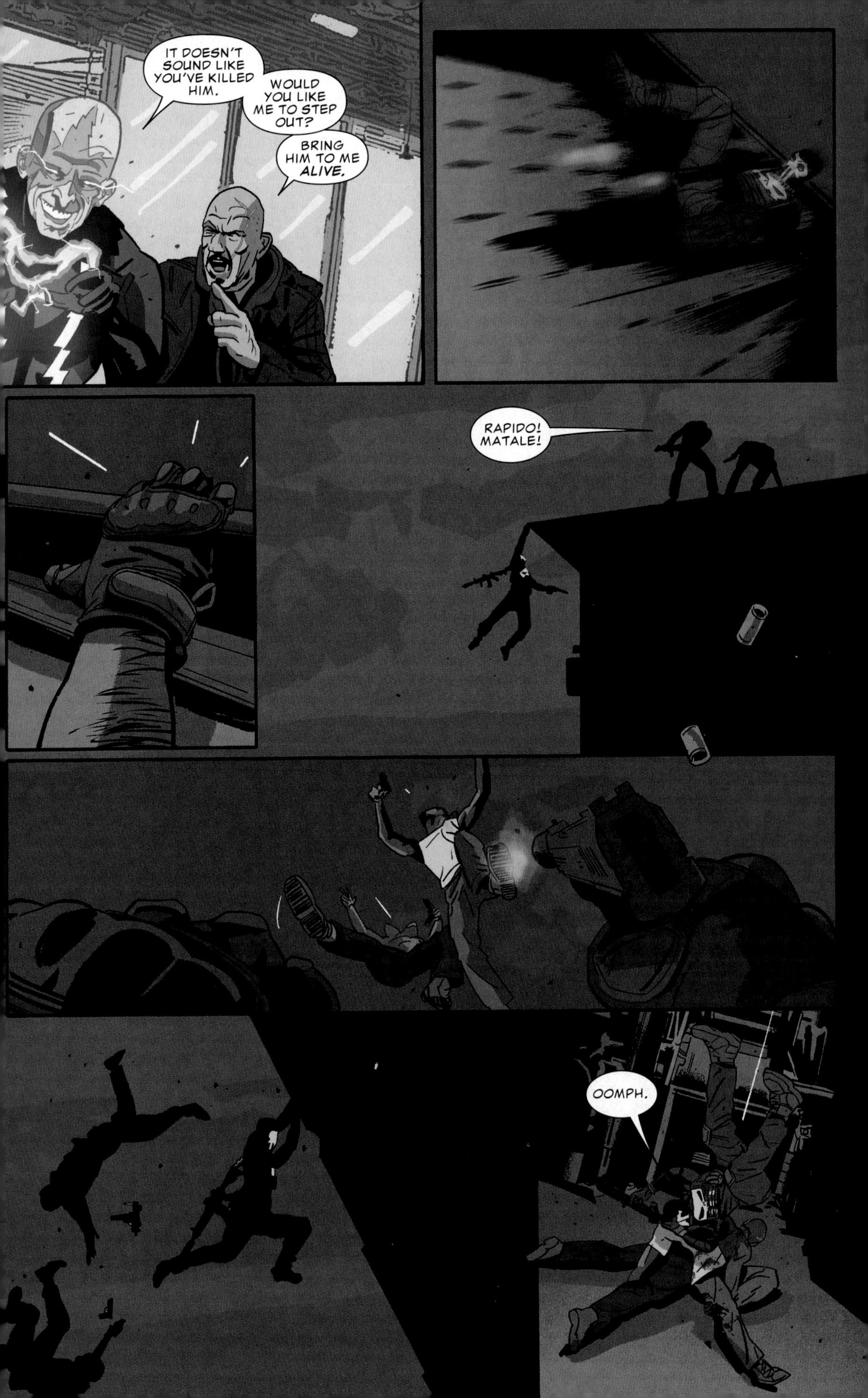
IT DOESN'T SOUND LIKE YOU'VE KILLED HIM.
WOULD YOU LIKE ME TO STEP OUT?
BRING HIM TO ME ALIVE.
RAPIDO! MATALE!
OOMPH.

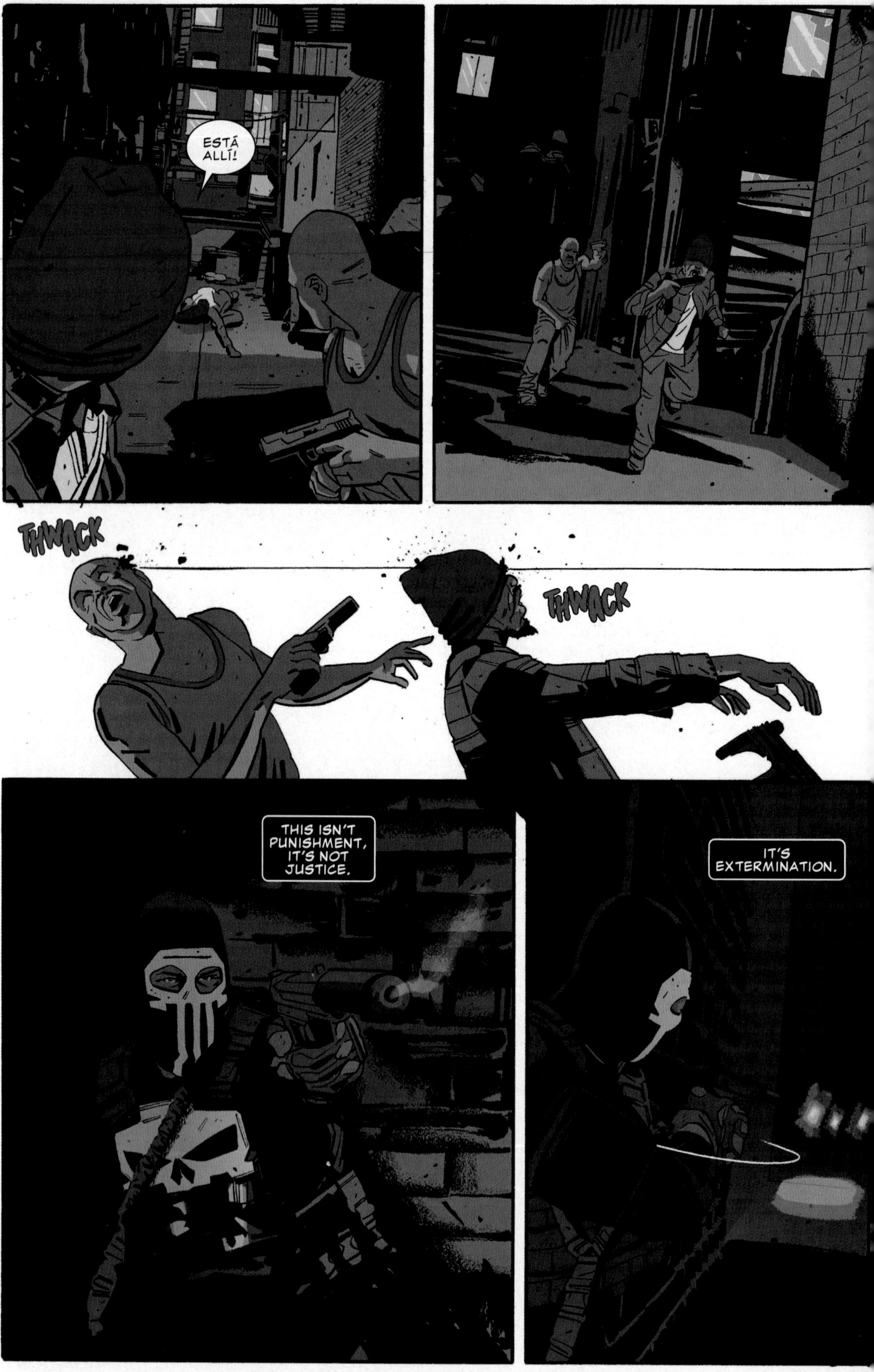
ESTÁ ALLÍ!
THWACK
THWACK
THIS ISN'T PUNISHMENT, IT'S NOT JUSTICE.
IT'S EXTERMINATION.

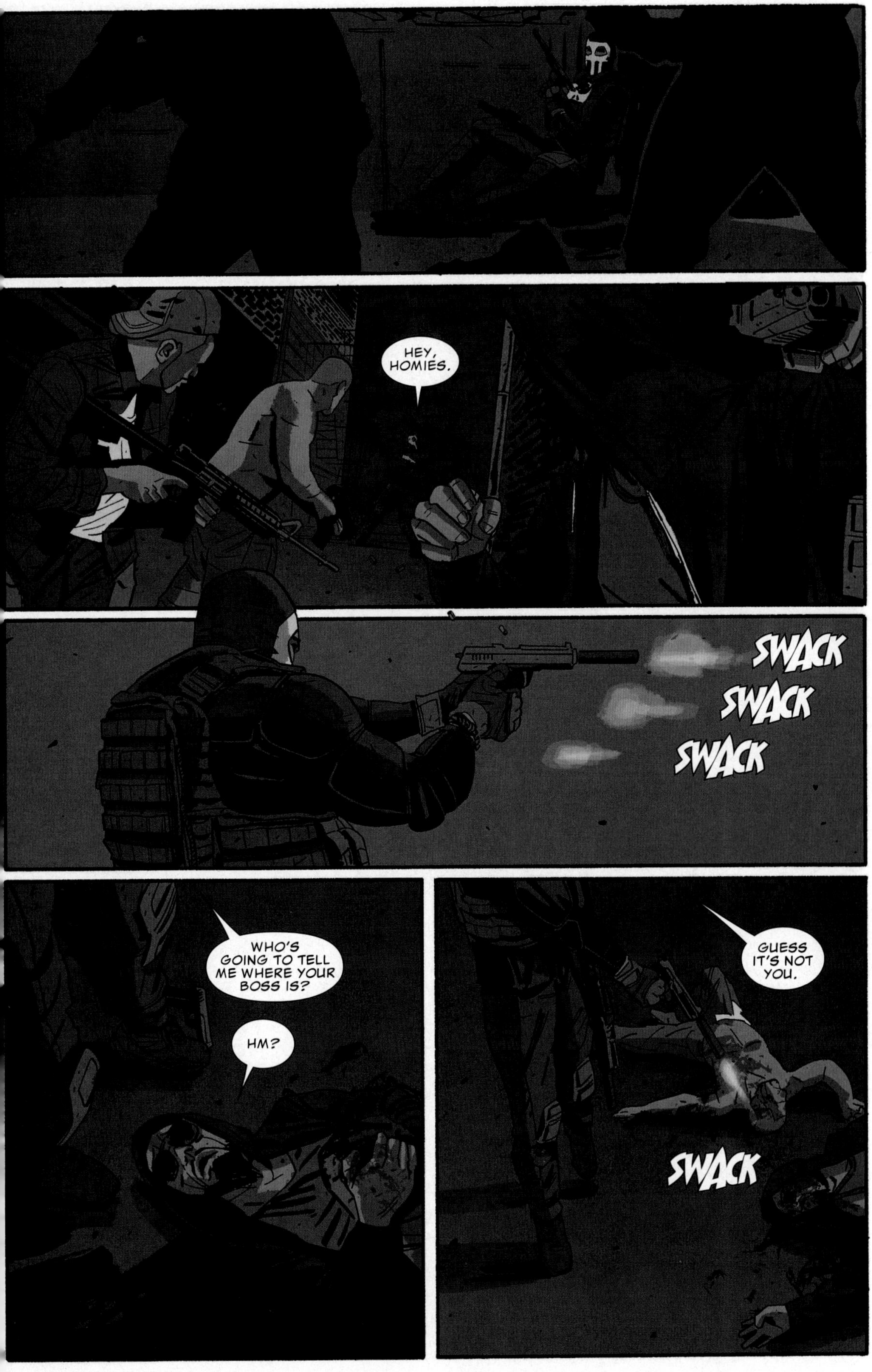
HEY, HOMIES.
SWACK
SWACK
SWACK
WHO'S GOING TO TELL ME WHERE YOUR BOSS IS?
HM?
GUESS IT'S NOT YOU.
SWACK

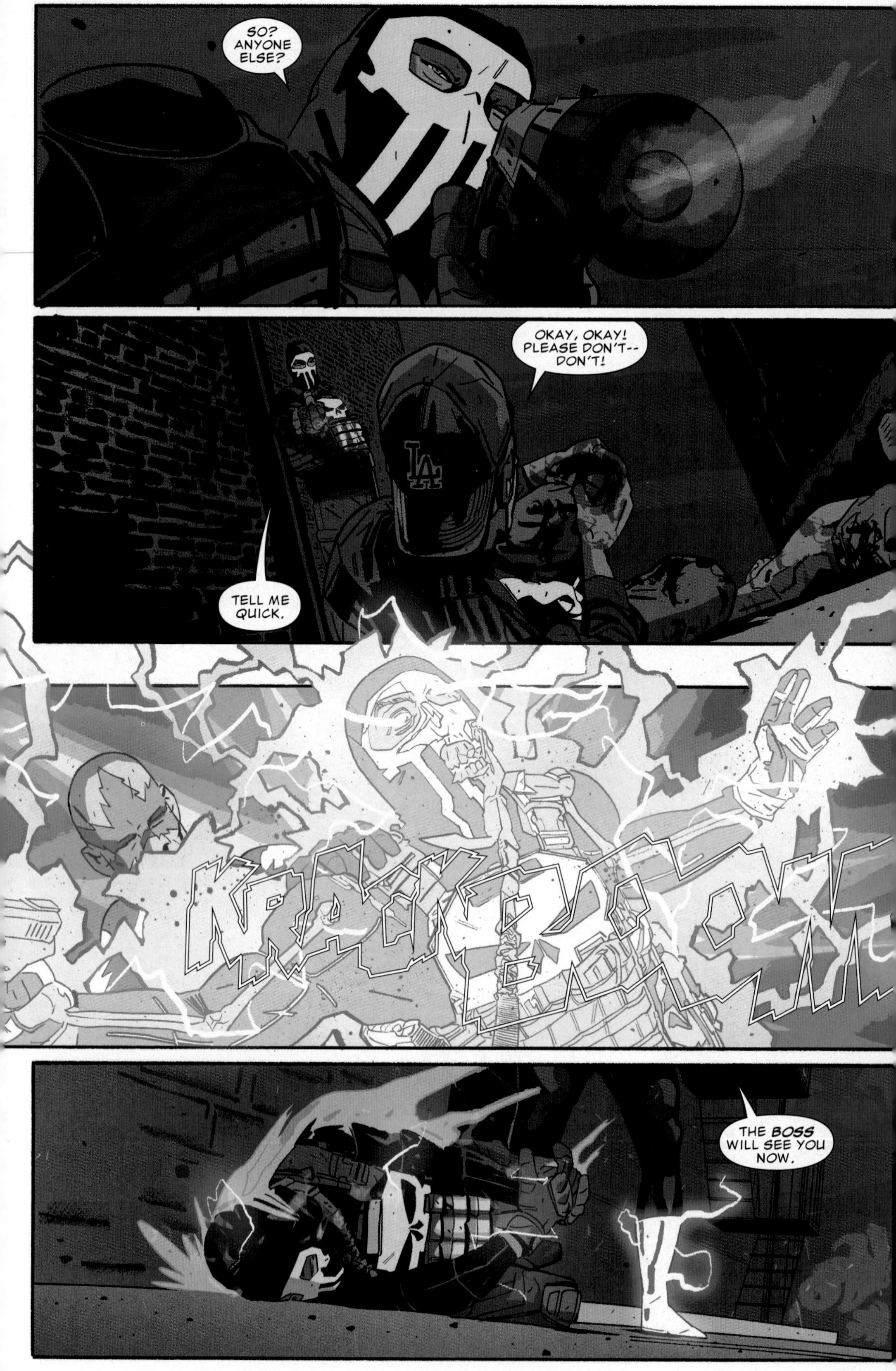
SO? ANYONE ELSE?
OKAY, OKAY! PLEASE DON'T-- DON'T!
TELL ME QUICK.
THE BOSS WILL SEE YOU NOW.

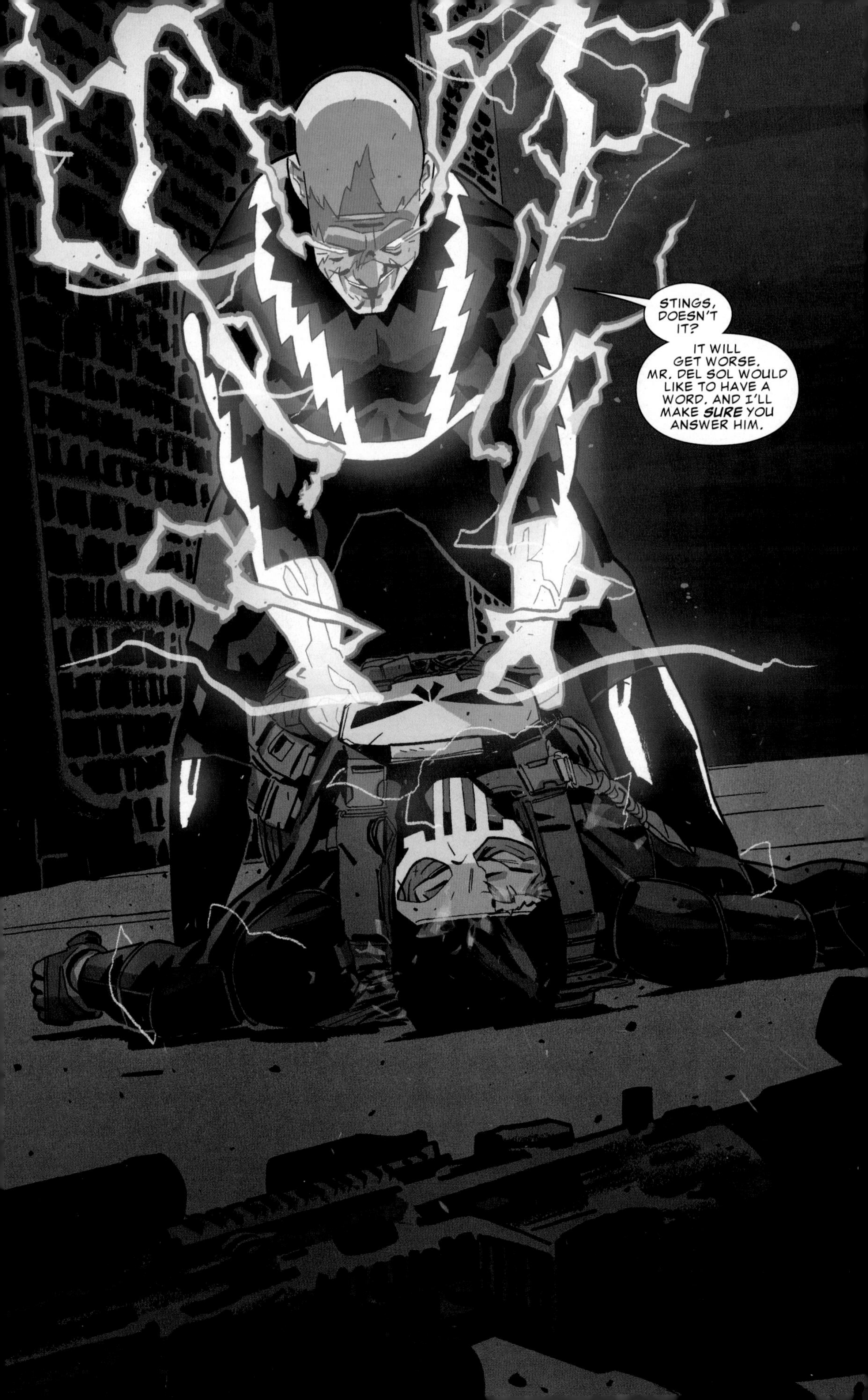
STINGS, DOESN'T IT?
IT WILL GET WORSE. MR. DEL SOL WOULD LIKE TO HAVE A WORD. AND I'LL MAKE *SURE* YOU ANSWER HIM.

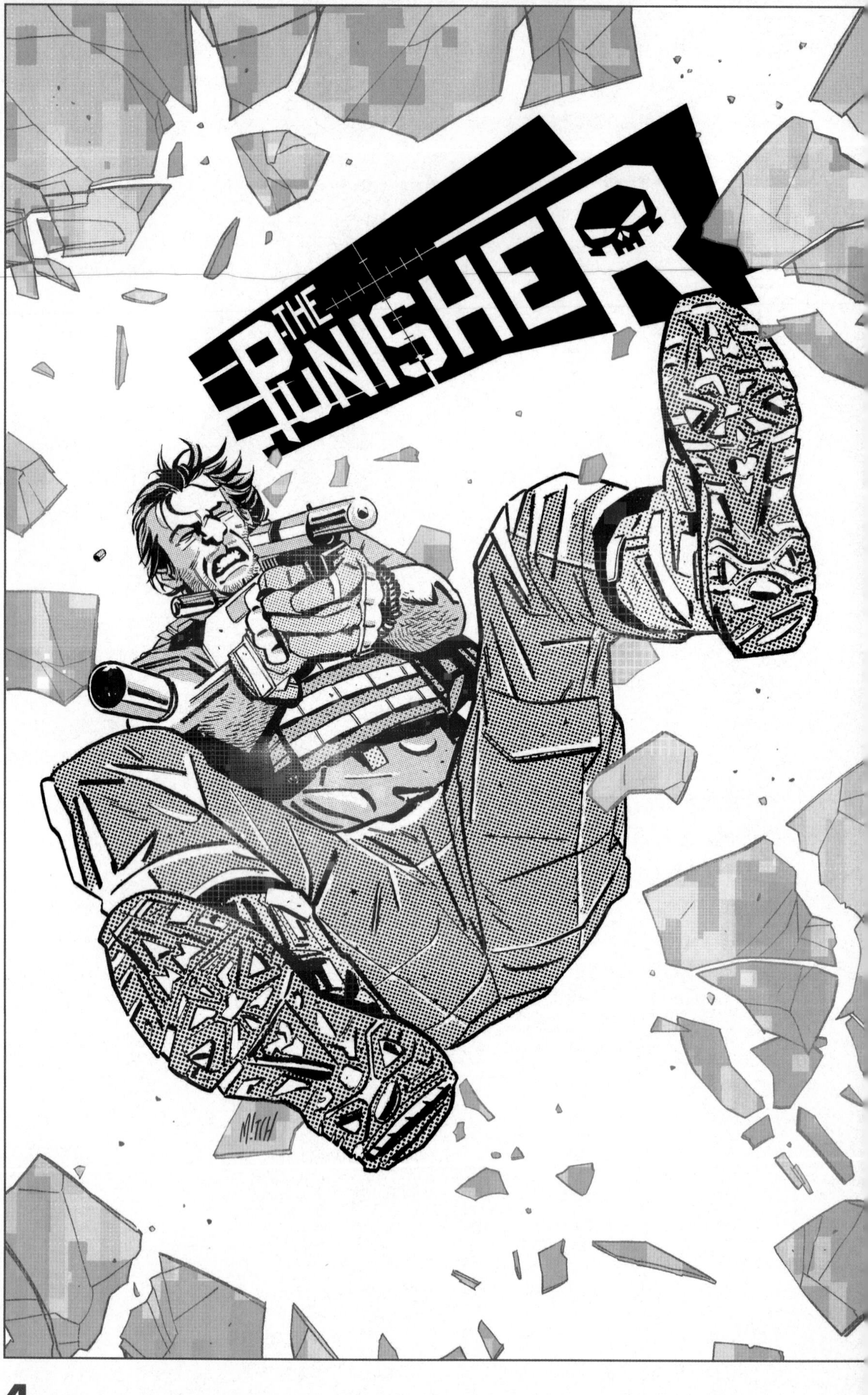
THE PUNISHER
MITCH

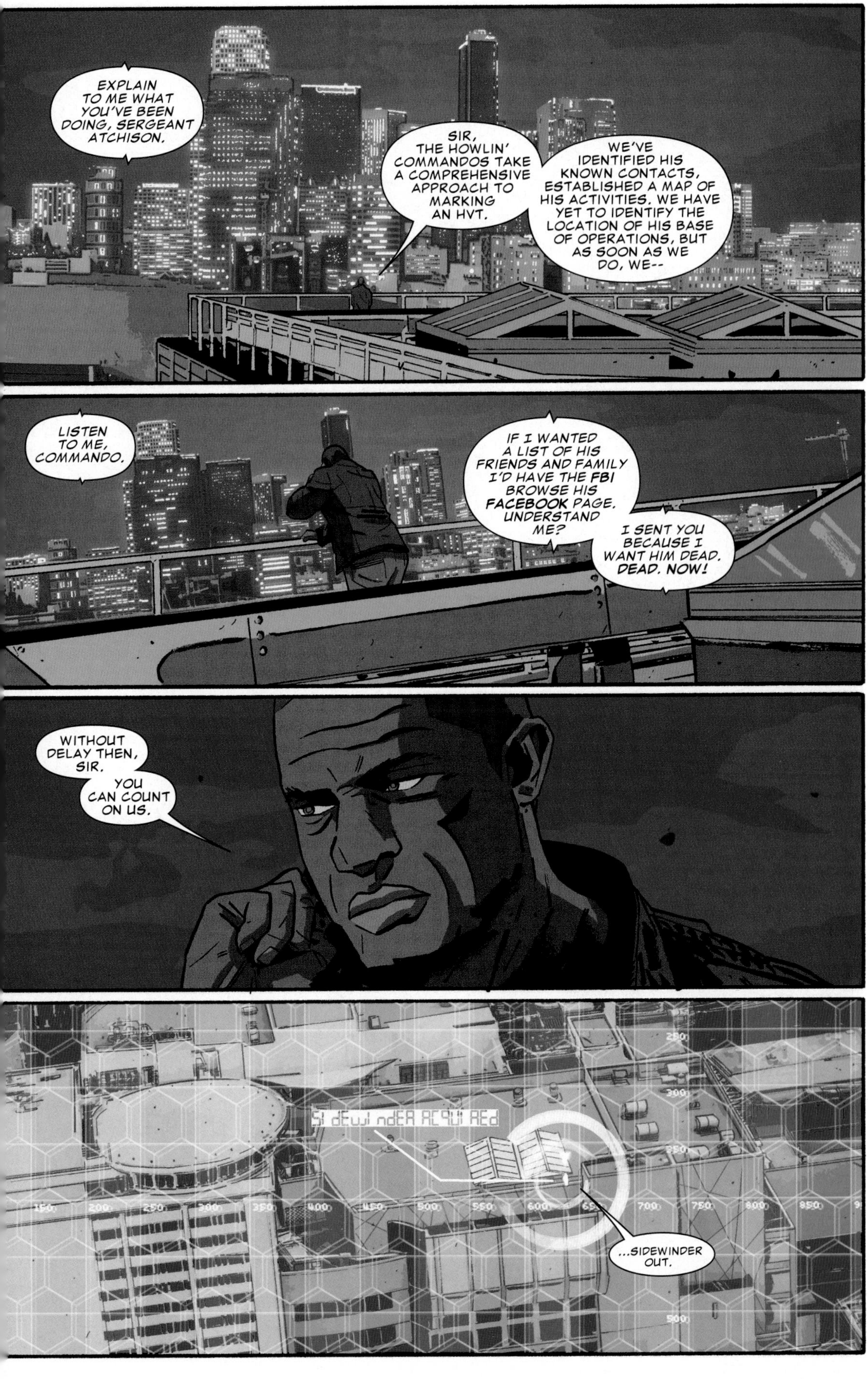
EXPLAIN TO ME WHAT YOU'VE BEEN DOING, SERGEANT ATCHISON.
SIR, THE HOWLIN' COMMANDOS TAKE A COMPREHENSIVE APPROACH TO MARKING AN HVT.
WE'VE IDENTIFIED HIS KNOWN CONTACTS, ESTABLISHED A MAP OF HIS ACTIVITIES. WE HAVE YET TO IDENTIFY THE LOCATION OF HIS BASE OF OPERATIONS, BUT AS SOON AS WE DO, WE--
LISTEN TO ME, COMMANDO.
IF I WANTED A LIST OF HIS FRIENDS AND FAMILY I'D HAVE THE **FBI** BROWSE HIS **FACEBOOK** PAGE. UNDERSTAND ME?
I SENT YOU BECAUSE I WANT HIM DEAD. **DEAD. NOW!**
WITHOUT DELAY THEN, SIR.
YOU CAN COUNT ON US.
SIDEWINDER ACQUIRED
...SIDEWINDER OUT.

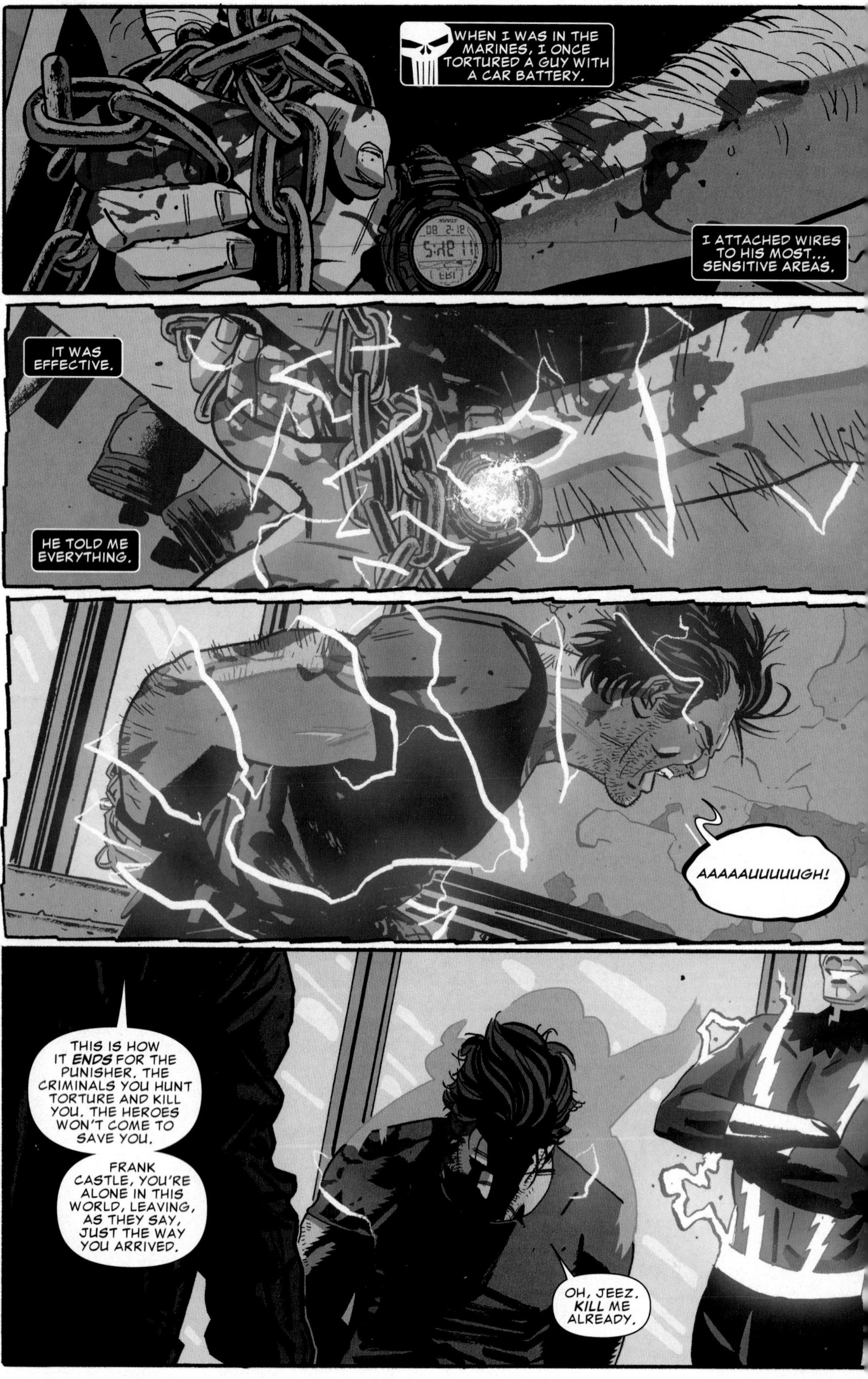

WHEN I WAS IN THE MARINES, I ONCE TORTURED A GUY WITH A CAR BATTERY.
I ATTACHED WIRES TO HIS MOST... SENSITIVE AREAS.
IT WAS EFFECTIVE.
HE TOLD ME EVERYTHING.
AAAAAUUUUUGH!
THIS IS HOW IT ENDS FOR THE PUNISHER. THE CRIMINALS YOU HUNT TORTURE AND KILL YOU. THE HEROES WON'T COME TO SAVE YOU.
FRANK CASTLE, YOU'RE ALONE IN THIS WORLD, LEAVING, AS THEY SAY, JUST THE WAY YOU ARRIVED.
OH, JEEZ. KILL ME ALREADY.

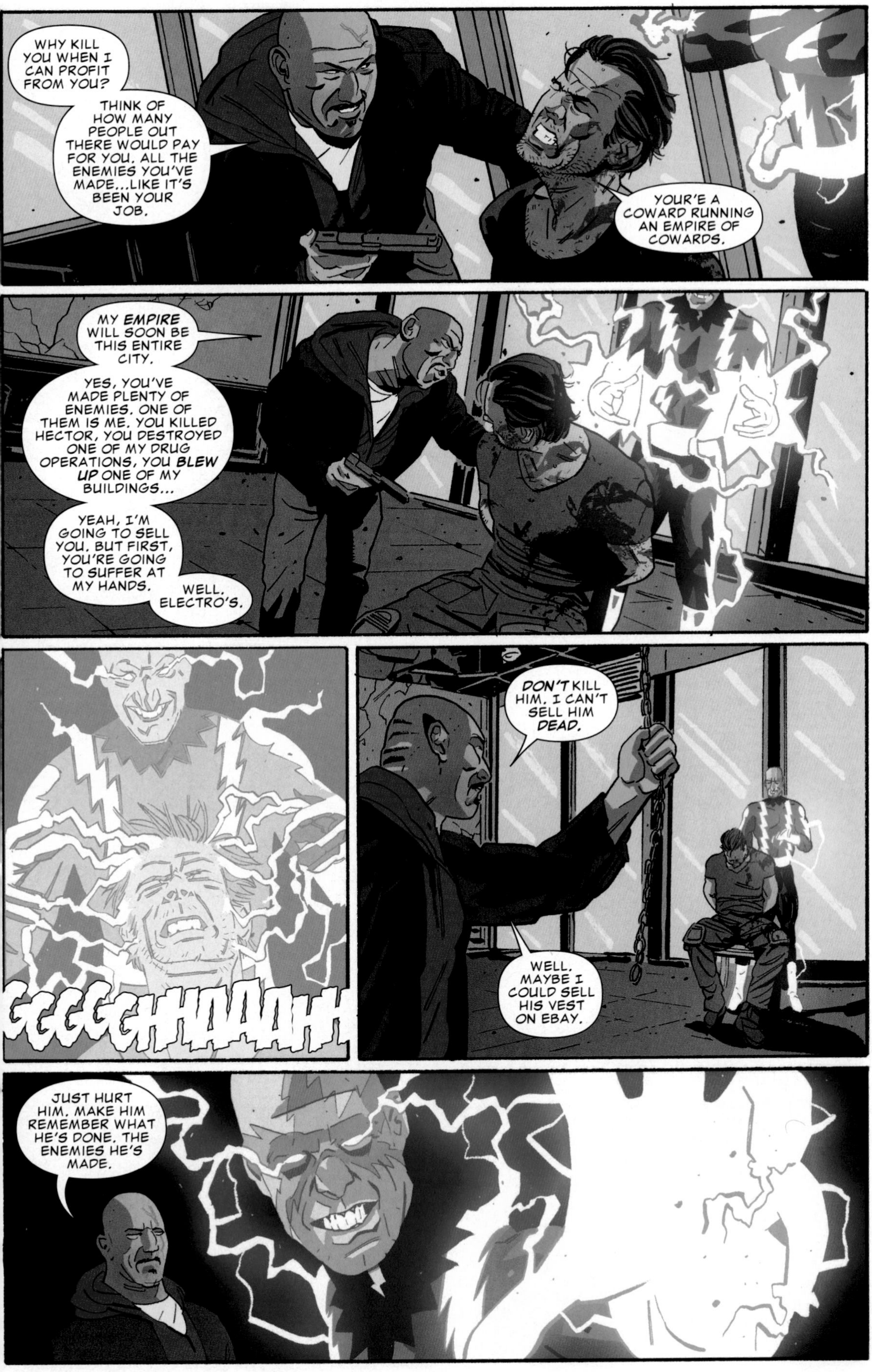
WHY KILL YOU WHEN I CAN PROFIT FROM YOU?
THINK OF HOW MANY PEOPLE OUT THERE WOULD PAY FOR YOU. ALL THE ENEMIES YOU'VE MADE...LIKE IT'S BEEN YOUR JOB.
YOUR'E A COWARD RUNNING AN EMPIRE OF COWARDS.
MY EMPIRE WILL SOON BE THIS ENTIRE CITY.
YES, YOU'VE MADE PLENTY OF ENEMIES. ONE OF THEM IS ME. YOU KILLED HECTOR, YOU DESTROYED ONE OF MY DRUG OPERATIONS, YOU BLEW UP ONE OF MY BUILDINGS...
YEAH, I'M GOING TO SELL YOU. BUT FIRST, YOU'RE GOING TO SUFFER AT MY HANDS.
WELL, ELECTRO'S.
GGGGGHHAAAAHH
DON'T KILL HIM. I CAN'T SELL HIM DEAD.
WELL, MAYBE I COULD SELL HIS VEST ON EBAY.
JUST HURT HIM. MAKE HIM REMEMBER WHAT HE'S DONE. THE ENEMIES HE'S MADE.

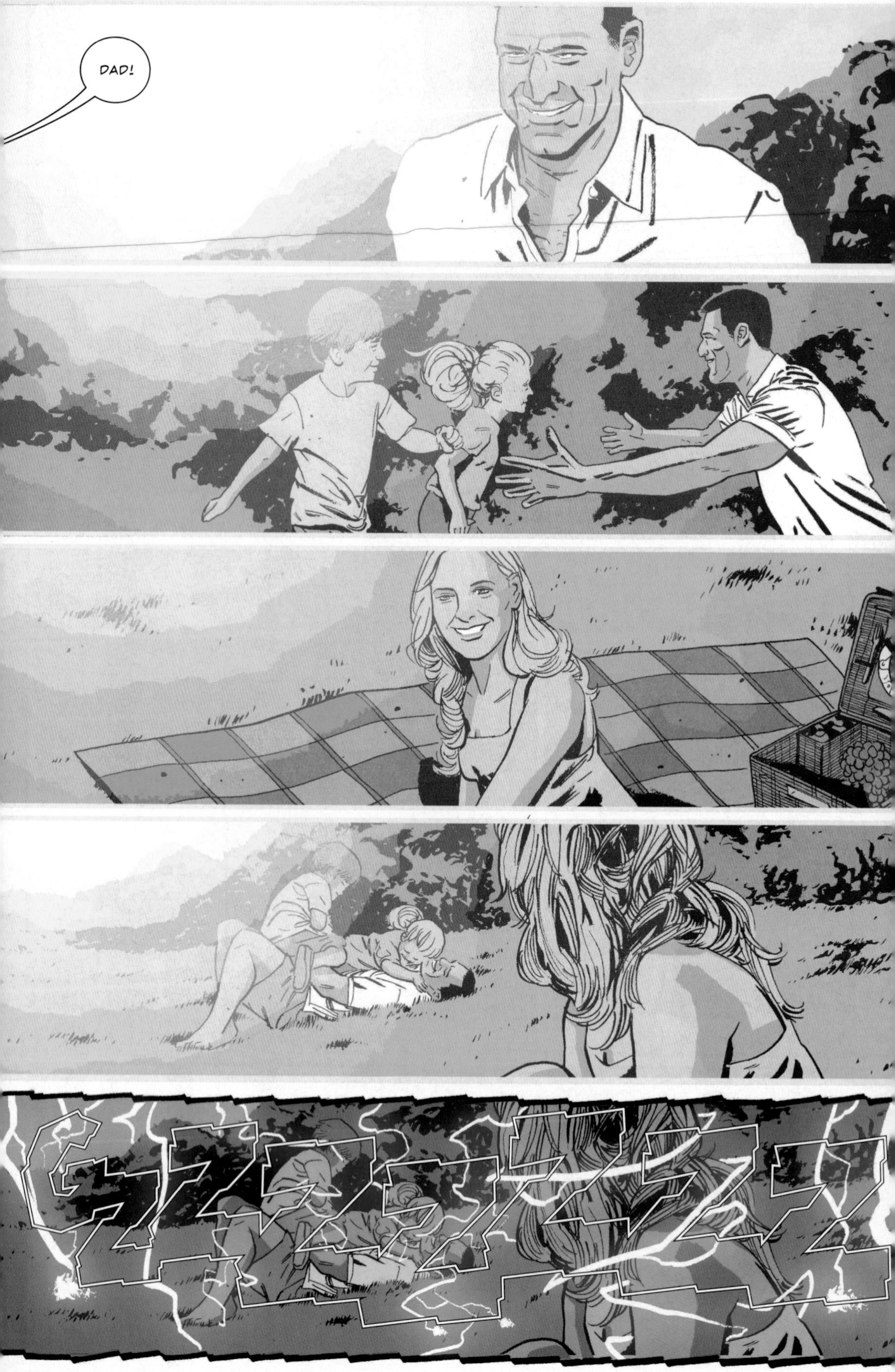
DAD!
GZZZZZZ

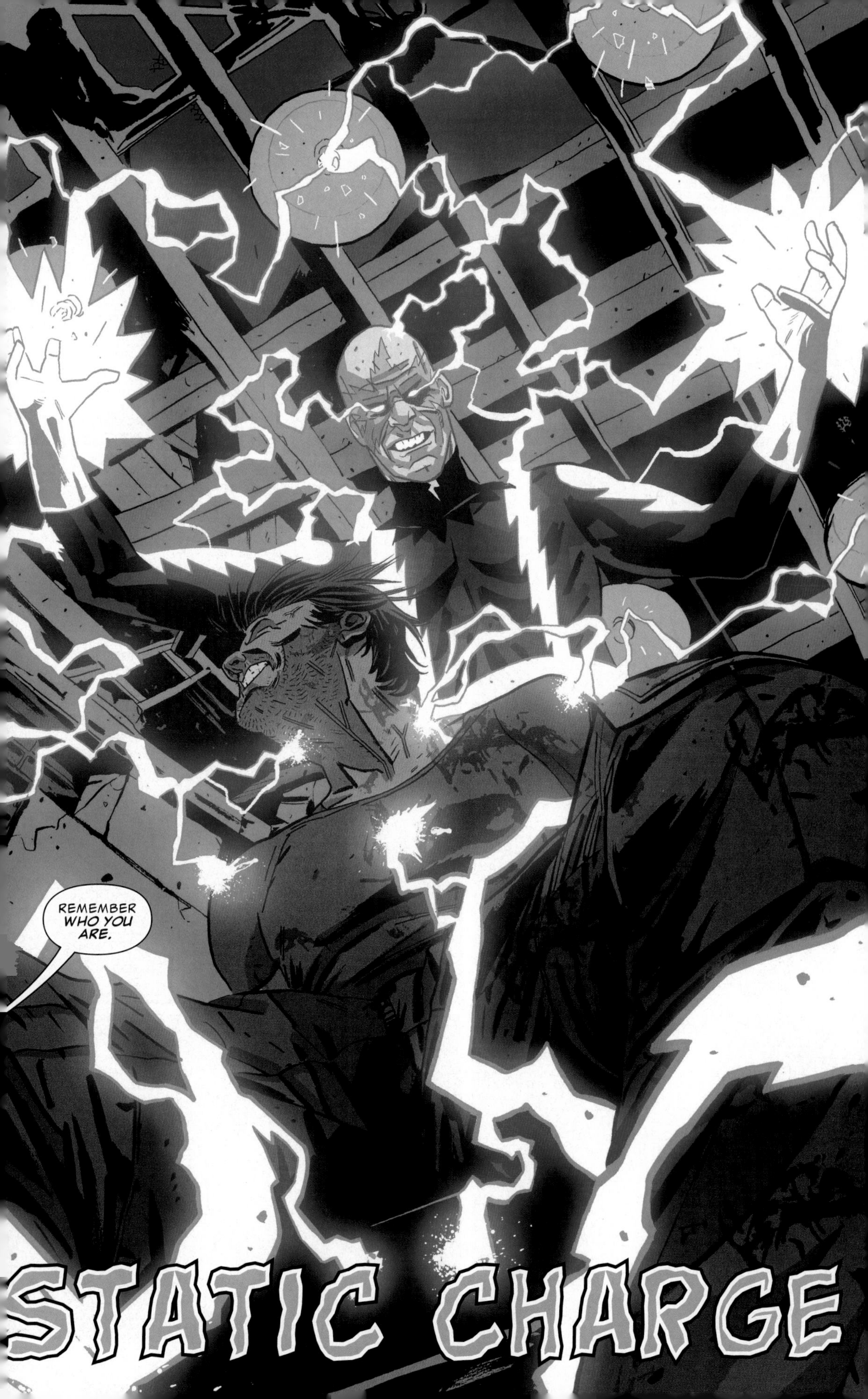
REMEMBER WHO YOU ARE.
STATIC CHARGE

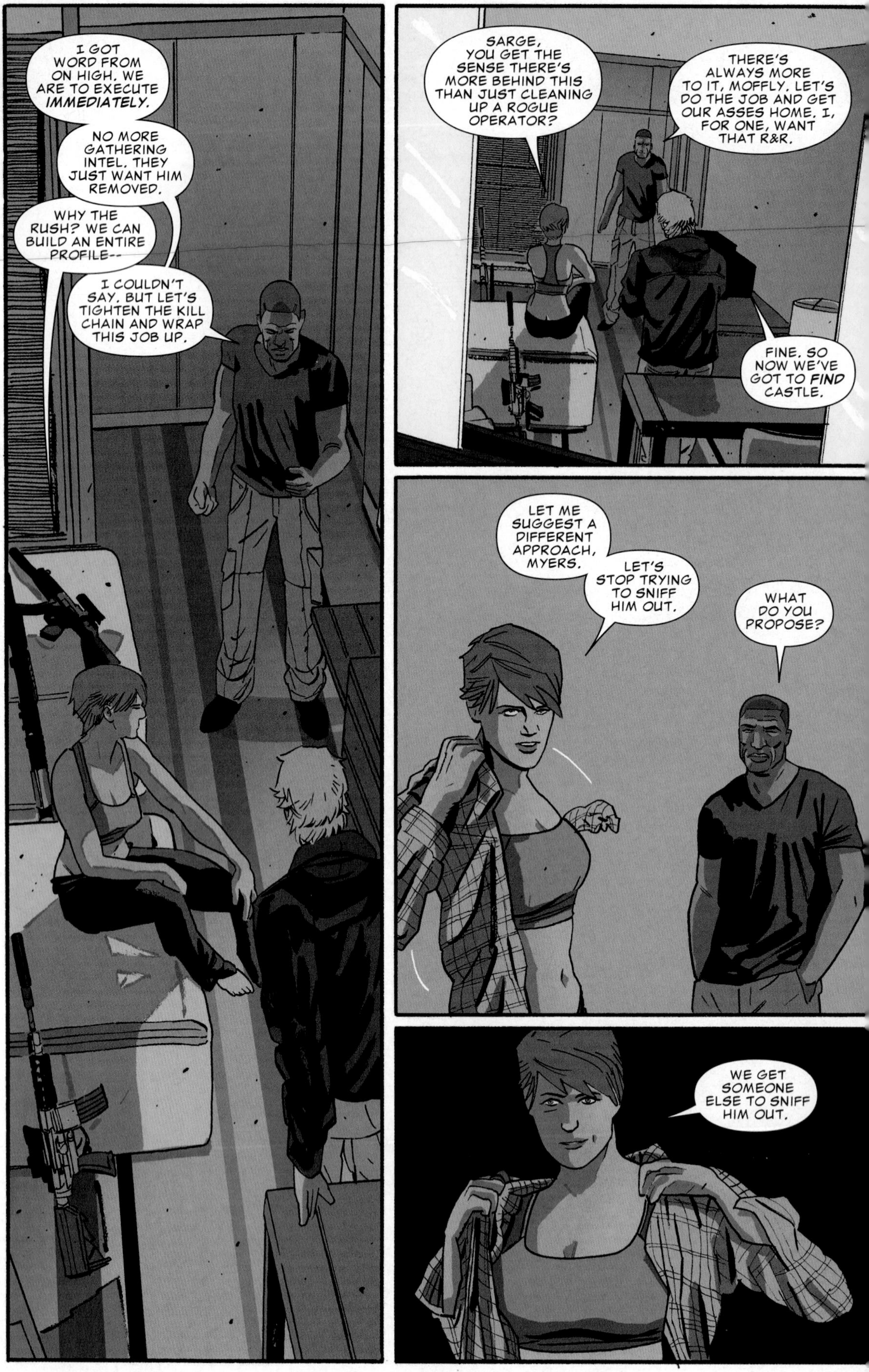

I GOT WORD FROM ON HIGH. WE ARE TO EXECUTE *IMMEDIATELY.*
NO MORE GATHERING INTEL. THEY JUST WANT HIM REMOVED.
WHY THE RUSH? WE CAN BUILD AN ENTIRE PROFILE--
I COULDN'T SAY. BUT LET'S TIGHTEN THE KILL CHAIN AND WRAP THIS JOB UP.
SARGE, YOU GET THE SENSE THERE'S MORE BEHIND THIS THAN JUST CLEANING UP A ROGUE OPERATOR?
THERE'S ALWAYS MORE TO IT, MOFFLY. LET'S DO THE JOB AND GET OUR ASSES HOME. I, FOR ONE, WANT THAT R&R.
FINE. SO NOW WE'VE GOT TO **FIND** CASTLE.
LET ME SUGGEST A DIFFERENT APPROACH, MYERS.
LET'S STOP TRYING TO SNIFF HIM OUT.
WHAT DO YOU PROPOSE?
WE GET SOMEONE ELSE TO SNIFF HIM OUT.

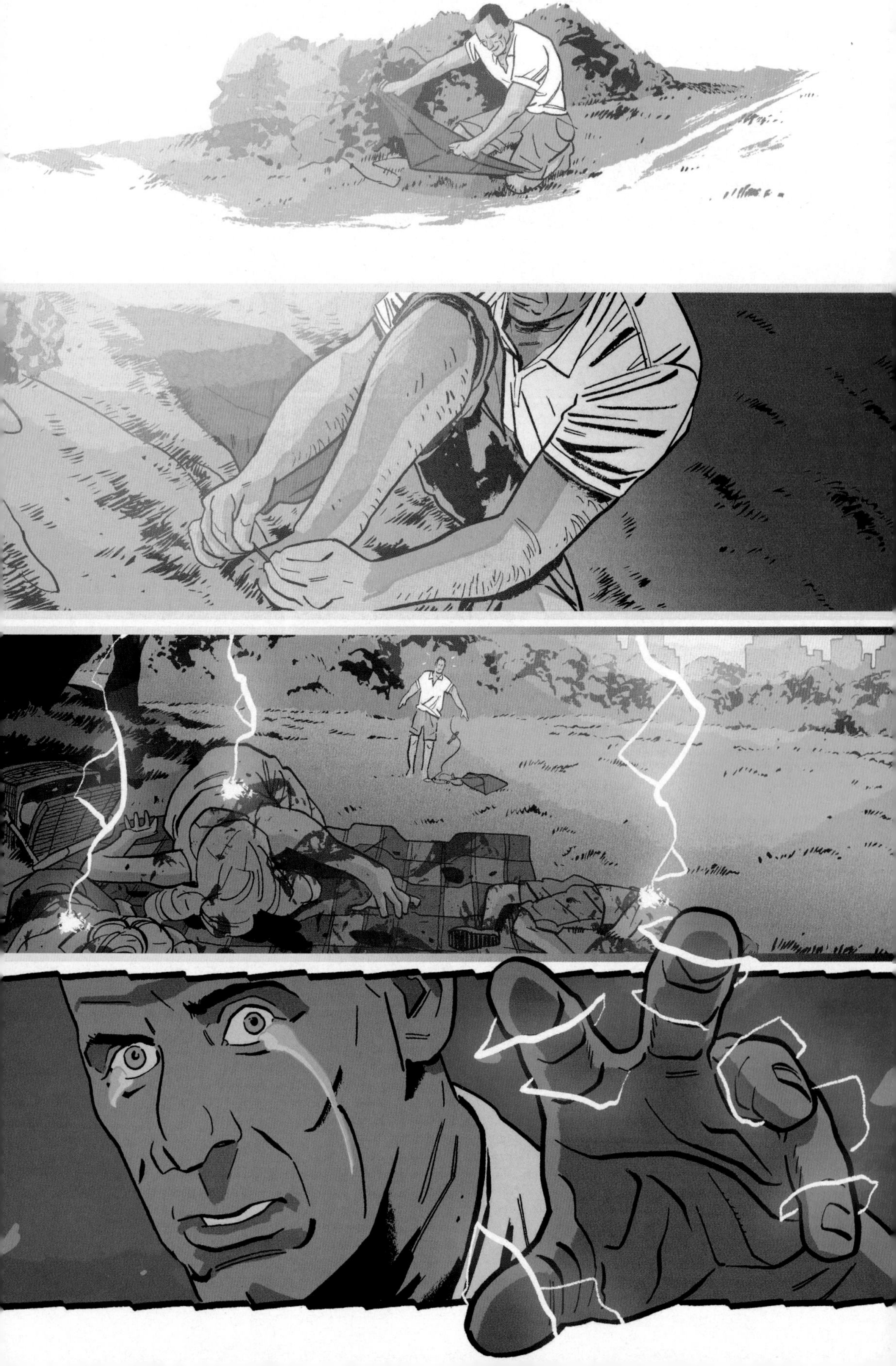

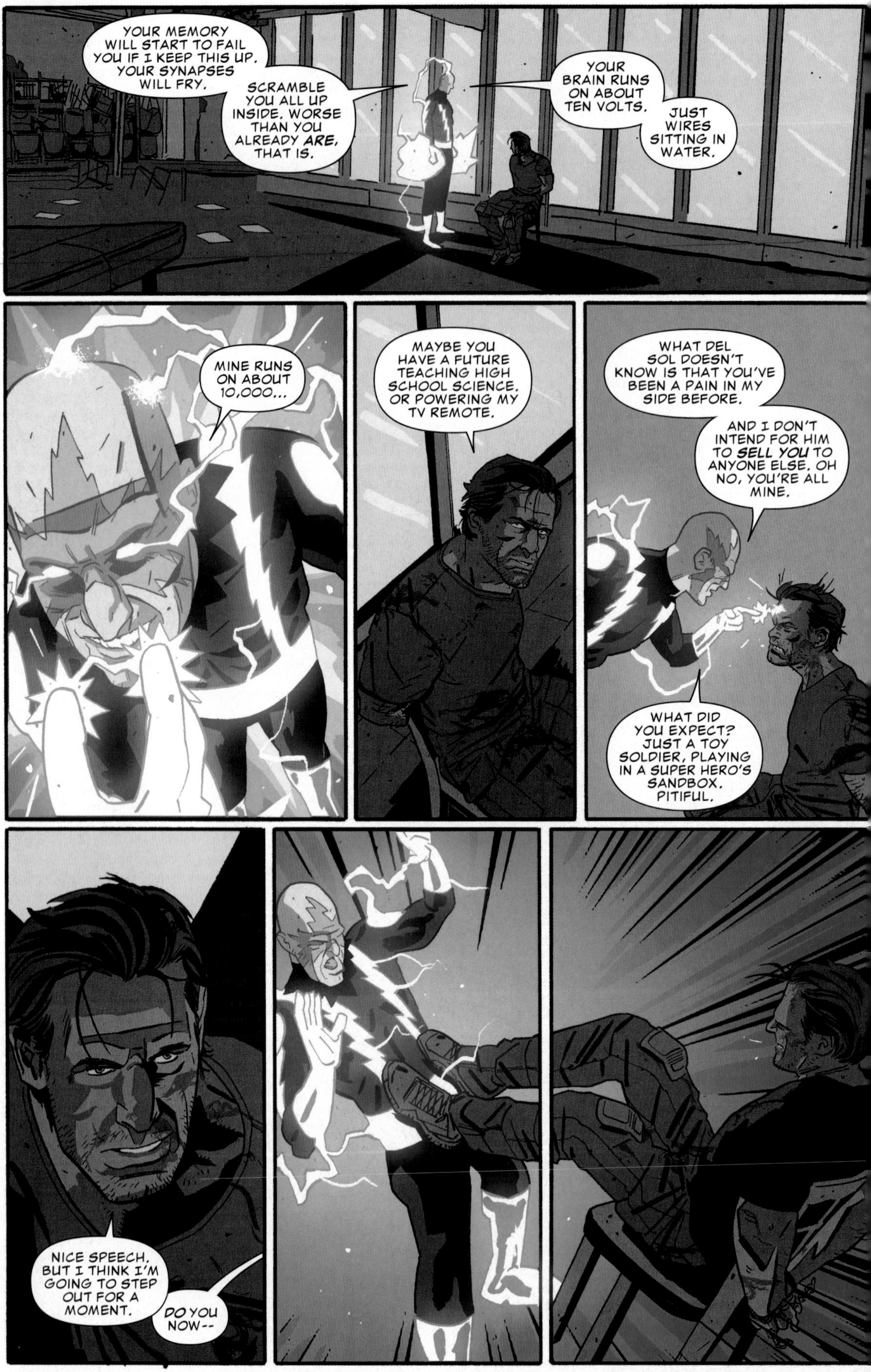

YOUR MEMORY WILL START TO FAIL YOU IF I KEEP THIS UP. YOUR SYNAPSES WILL FRY.
SCRAMBLE YOU ALL UP INSIDE. WORSE THAN YOU ALREADY **ARE**, THAT IS.
YOUR BRAIN RUNS ON ABOUT TEN VOLTS.
JUST WIRES SITTING IN WATER.
MINE RUNS ON ABOUT 10,000...
MAYBE YOU HAVE A FUTURE TEACHING HIGH SCHOOL SCIENCE, OR POWERING MY TV REMOTE.
WHAT DEL SOL DOESN'T KNOW IS THAT YOU'VE BEEN A PAIN IN MY SIDE BEFORE.
AND I DON'T INTEND FOR HIM TO **SELL YOU** TO ANYONE ELSE. OH NO, YOU'RE ALL MINE.
WHAT DID YOU EXPECT? JUST A TOY SOLDIER, PLAYING IN A SUPER HERO'S SANDBOX. PITIFUL.
NICE SPEECH. BUT I THINK I'M GOING TO STEP OUT FOR A MOMENT.
DO YOU NOW--

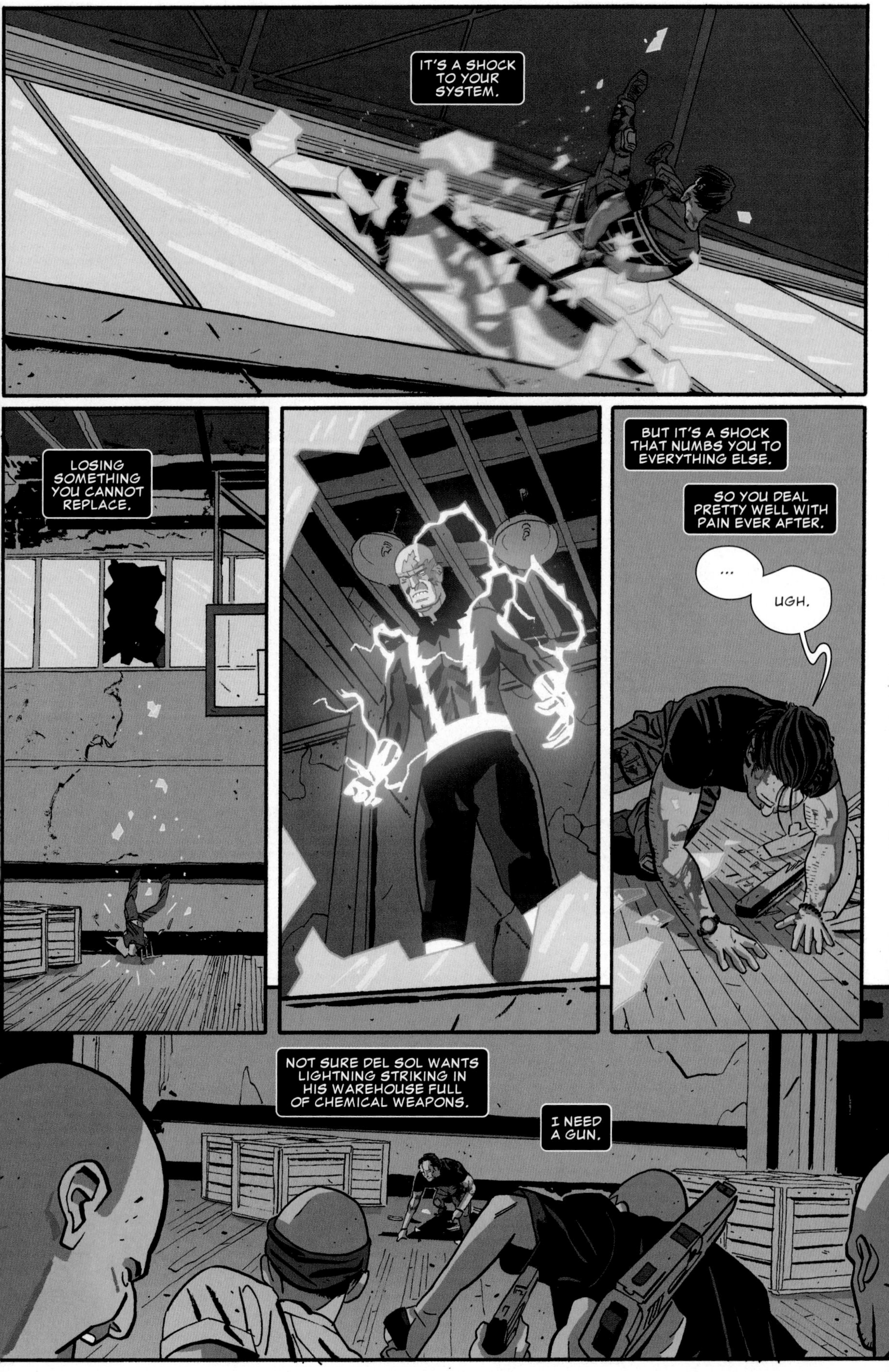
IT'S A SHOCK TO YOUR SYSTEM.
LOSING SOMETHING YOU CANNOT REPLACE.
BUT IT'S A SHOCK THAT NUMBS YOU TO EVERYTHING ELSE.
SO YOU DEAL PRETTY WELL WITH PAIN EVER AFTER.
...
UGH.
NOT SURE DEL SOL WANTS LIGHTNING STRIKING IN HIS WAREHOUSE FULL OF CHEMICAL WEAPONS.
I NEED A GUN.

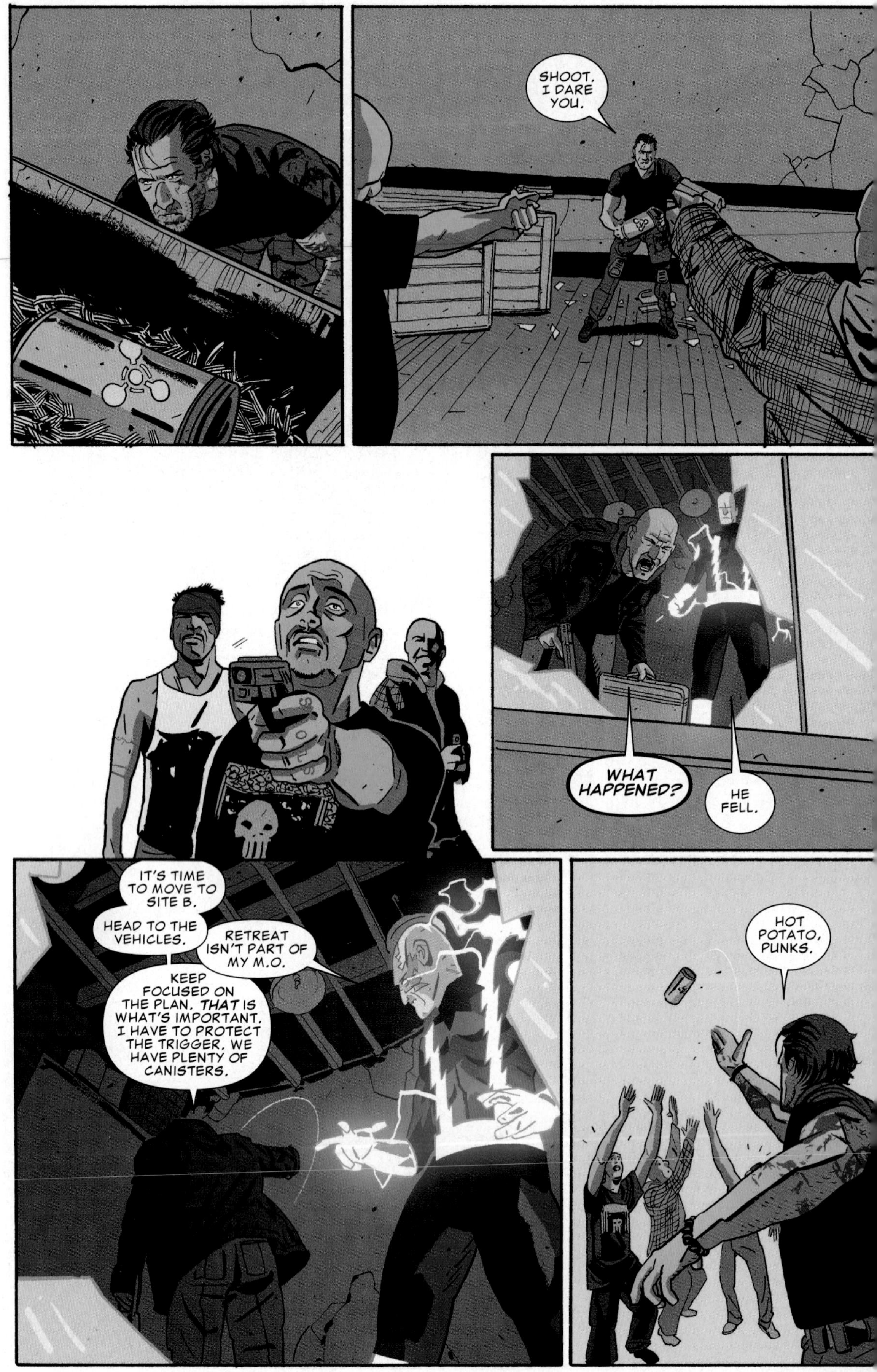
SHOOT. I DARE YOU.
WHAT HAPPENED?
HE FELL.
IT'S TIME TO MOVE TO SITE B.
HEAD TO THE VEHICLES.
RETREAT ISN'T PART OF MY M.O.
KEEP FOCUSED ON THE PLAN. THAT IS WHAT'S IMPORTANT. I HAVE TO PROTECT THE TRIGGER. WE HAVE PLENTY OF CANISTERS.
HOT POTATO, PUNKS.

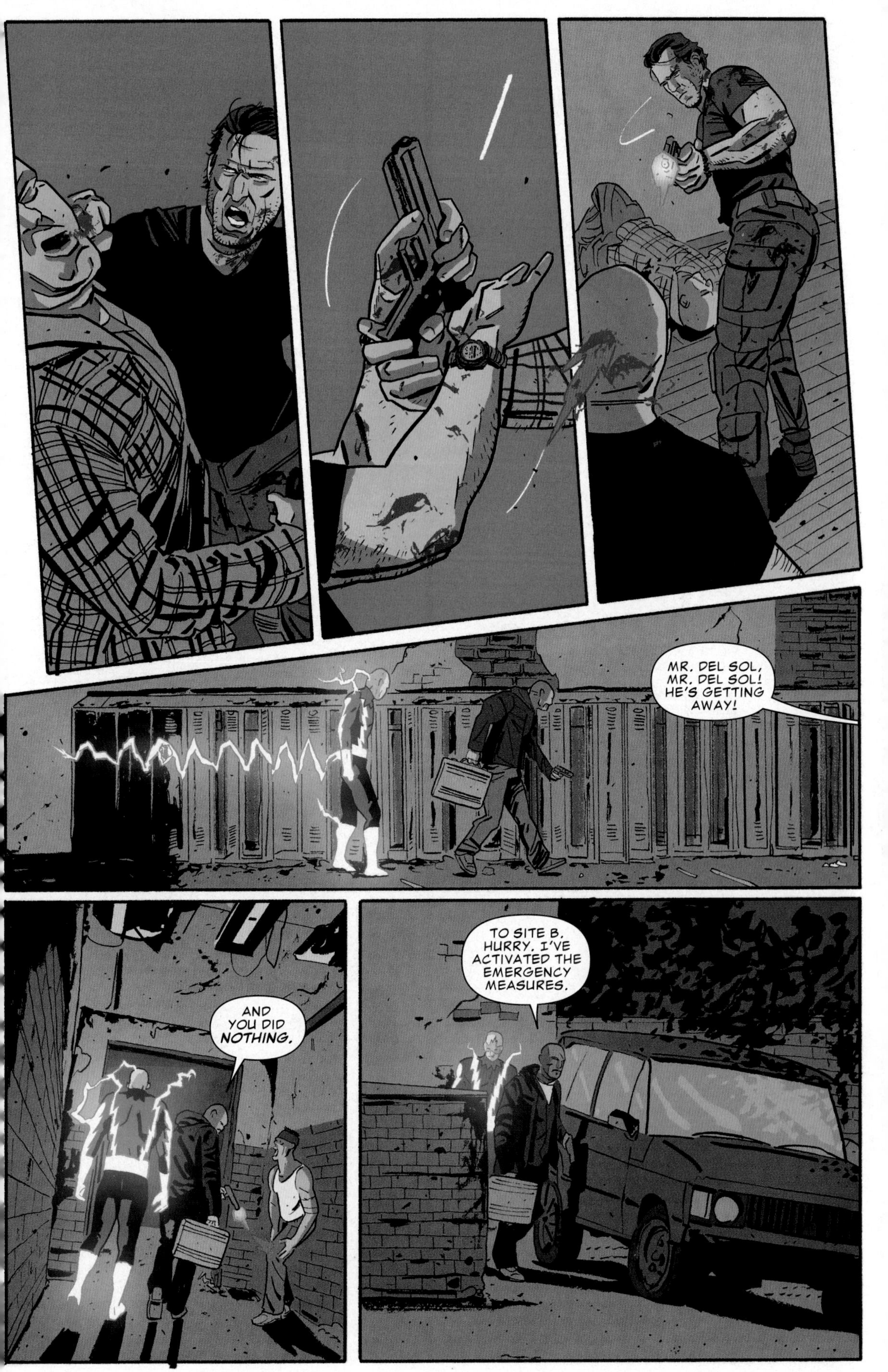
MR. DEL SOL, MR. DEL SOL! HE'S GETTING AWAY!
AND YOU DID NOTHING.
TO SITE B. HURRY. I'VE ACTIVATED THE EMERGENCY MEASURES.

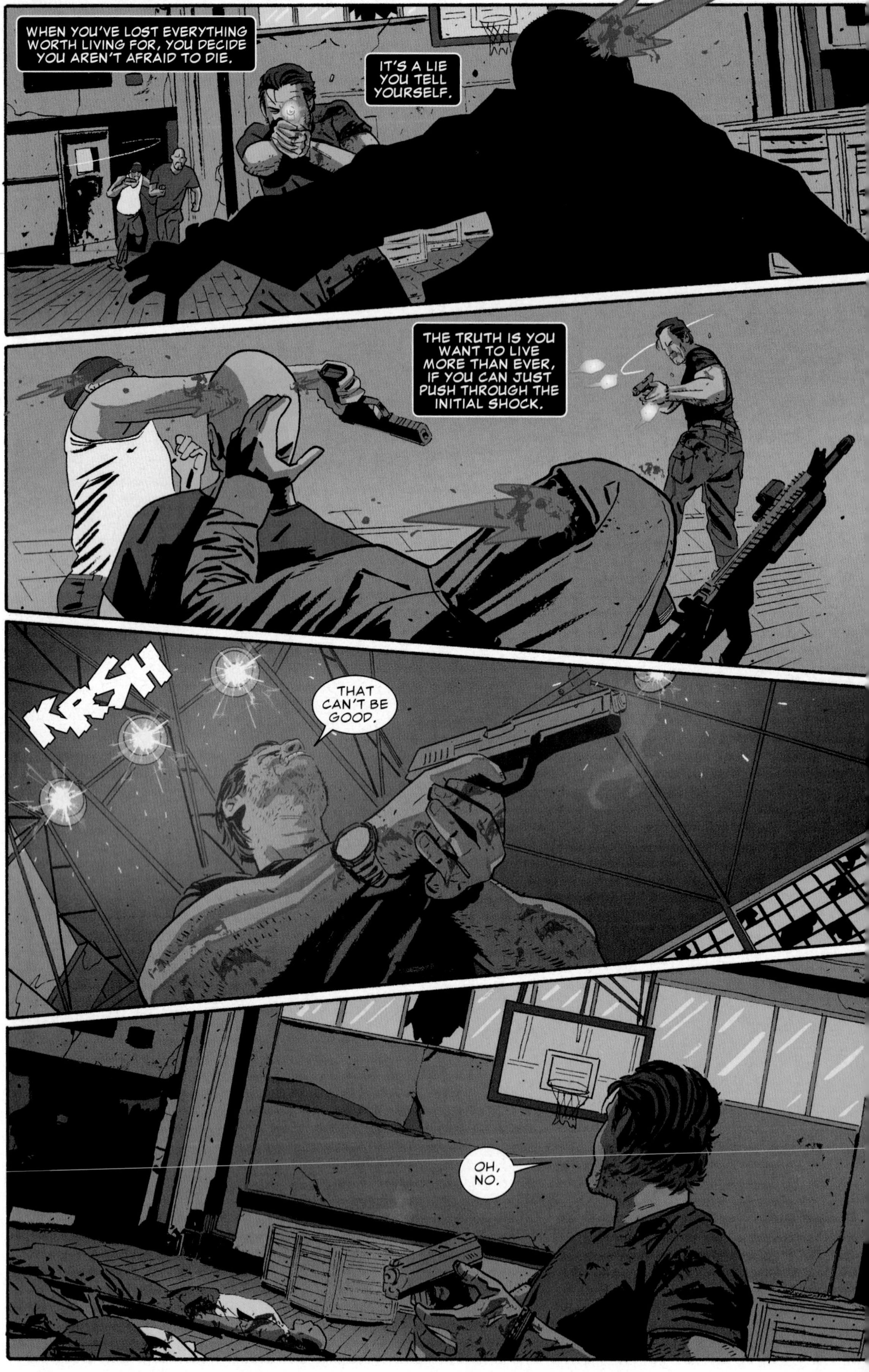
WHEN YOU'VE LOST EVERYTHING WORTH LIVING FOR, YOU DECIDE YOU AREN'T AFRAID TO DIE.
IT'S A LIE YOU TELL YOURSELF.
THE TRUTH IS YOU WANT TO LIVE MORE THAN EVER, IF YOU CAN JUST PUSH THROUGH THE INITIAL SHOCK.
KRSH
THAT CAN'T BE GOOD.
OH, NO.

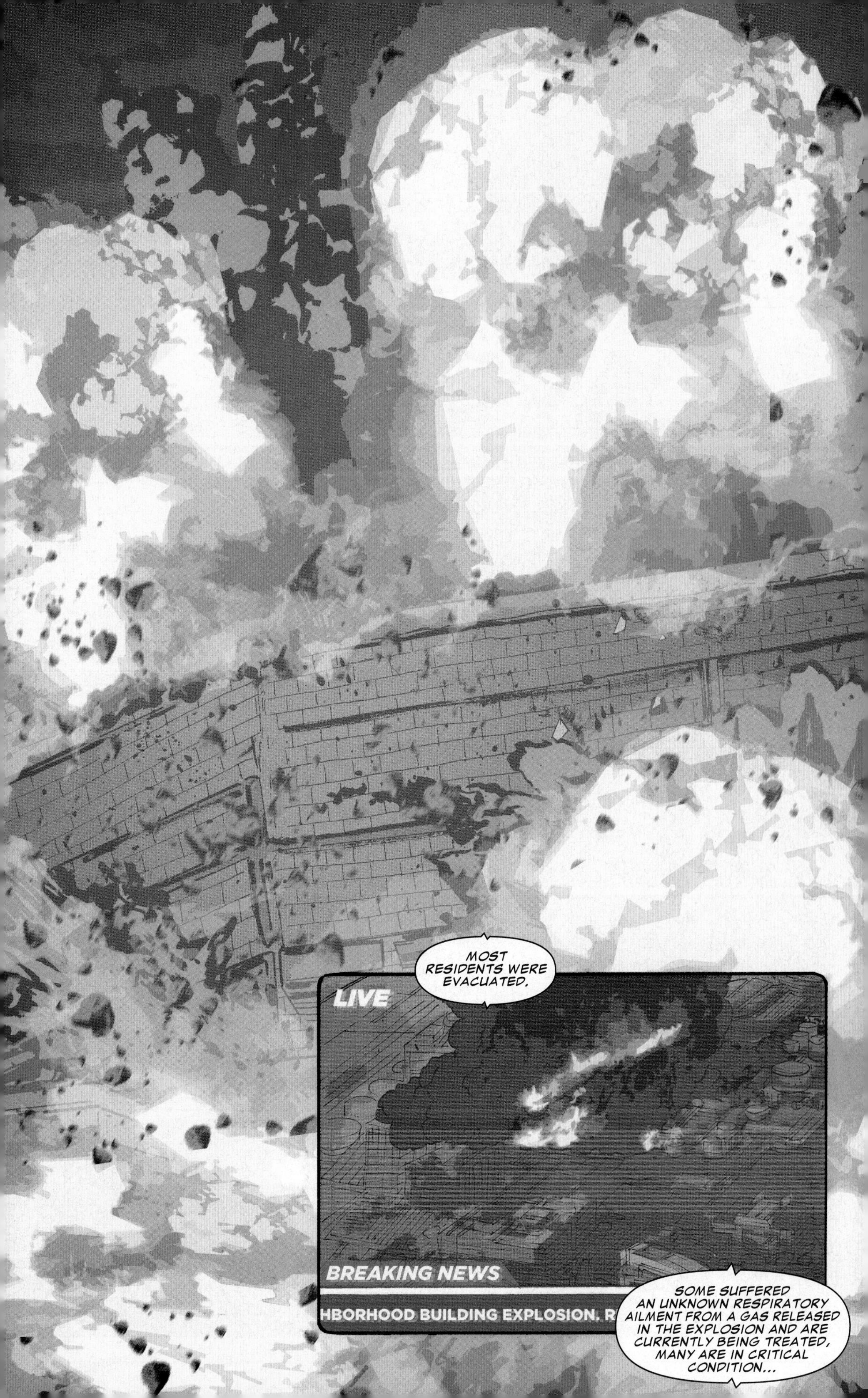

MOST RESIDENTS WERE EVACUATED.
LIVE
BREAKING NEWS
HBORHOOD BUILDING EXPLOSION. R
SOME SUFFERED AN UNKNOWN RESPIRATORY AILMENT FROM A GAS RELEASED IN THE EXPLOSION AND ARE CURRENTLY BEING TREATED, MANY ARE IN CRITICAL CONDITION...

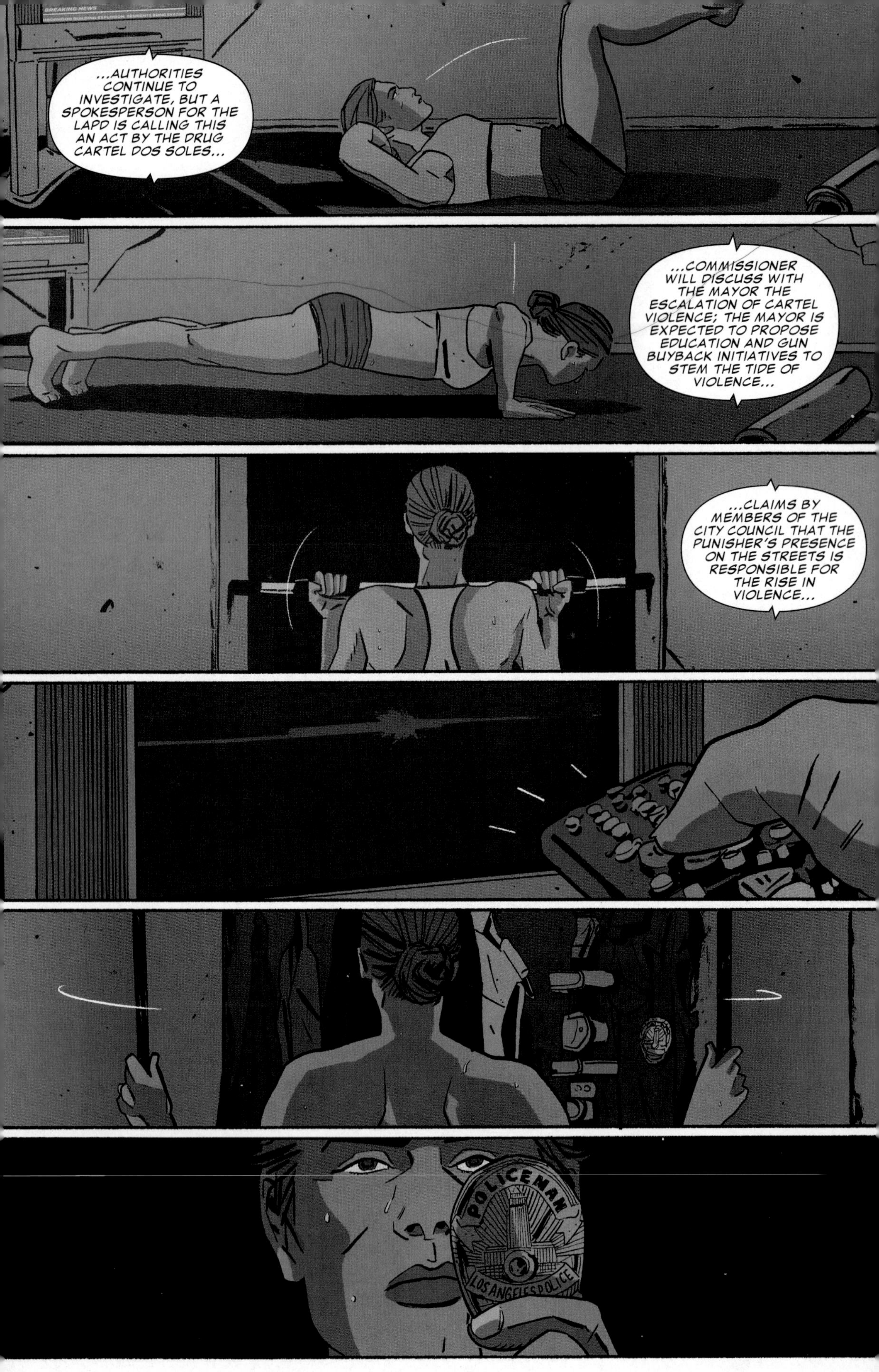
BREAKING NEWS
...AUTHORITIES CONTINUE TO INVESTIGATE, BUT A SPOKESPERSON FOR THE LAPD IS CALLING THIS AN ACT BY THE DRUG CARTEL DOS SOLES...
...COMMISSIONER WILL DISCUSS WITH THE MAYOR THE ESCALATION OF CARTEL VIOLENCE; THE MAYOR IS EXPECTED TO PROPOSE EDUCATION AND GUN BUYBACK INITIATIVES TO STEM THE TIDE OF VIOLENCE...
...CLAIMS BY MEMBERS OF THE CITY COUNCIL THAT THE PUNISHER'S PRESENCE ON THE STREETS IS RESPONSIBLE FOR THE RISE IN VIOLENCE...
POLICEMAN
LOS ANGELES POLICE

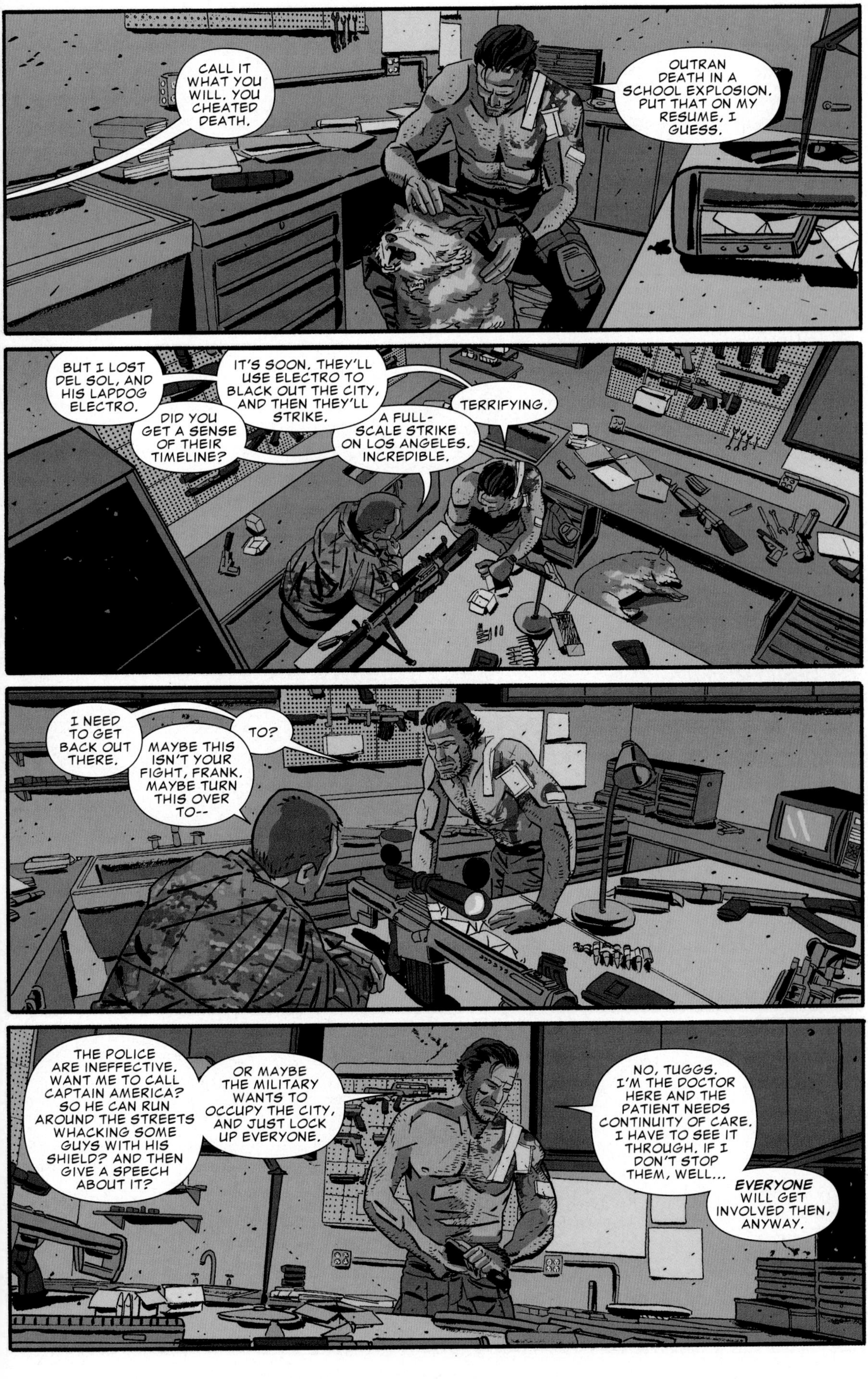
CALL IT WHAT YOU WILL. YOU CHEATED DEATH.
OUTRAN DEATH IN A SCHOOL EXPLOSION. PUT THAT ON MY RESUME, I GUESS.
BUT I LOST DEL SOL, AND HIS LAPDOG ELECTRO.
DID YOU GET A SENSE OF THEIR TIMELINE?
IT'S SOON. THEY'LL USE ELECTRO TO BLACK OUT THE CITY, AND THEN THEY'LL STRIKE.
A FULL-SCALE STRIKE ON LOS ANGELES. INCREDIBLE.
TERRIFYING.
I NEED TO GET BACK OUT THERE.
TO?
MAYBE THIS ISN'T YOUR FIGHT, FRANK. MAYBE TURN THIS OVER TO--
THE POLICE ARE INEFFECTIVE. WANT ME TO CALL CAPTAIN AMERICA? SO HE CAN RUN AROUND THE STREETS WHACKING SOME GUYS WITH HIS SHIELD? AND THEN GIVE A SPEECH ABOUT IT?
OR MAYBE THE MILITARY WANTS TO OCCUPY THE CITY, AND JUST LOCK UP EVERYONE.
NO, TUGGS. I'M THE DOCTOR HERE AND THE PATIENT NEEDS CONTINUITY OF CARE. I HAVE TO SEE IT THROUGH. IF I DON'T STOP THEM, WELL...
EVERYONE WILL GET INVOLVED THEN, ANYWAY.

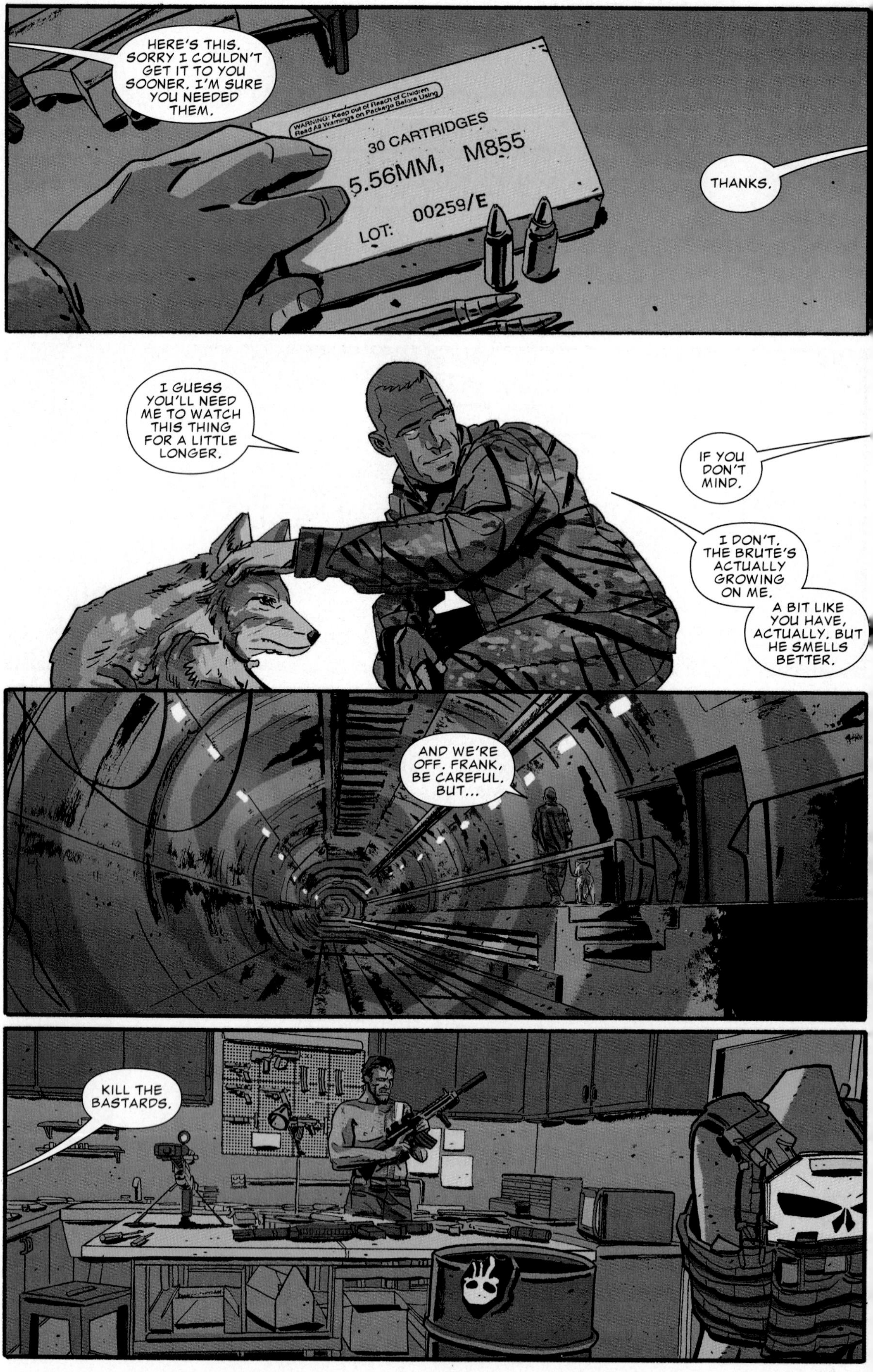
HERE'S THIS. SORRY I COULDN'T GET IT TO YOU SOONER. I'M SURE YOU NEEDED THEM.
WARNING: Keep out of Reach of Children Read All Warnings on Package Before Using
30 CARTRIDGES
5.56MM, M855
LOT: 00259/E
THANKS.
I GUESS YOU'LL NEED ME TO WATCH THIS THING FOR A LITTLE LONGER.
IF YOU DON'T MIND.
I DON'T. THE BRUTE'S ACTUALLY GROWING ON ME.
A BIT LIKE YOU HAVE, ACTUALLY. BUT HE SMELLS BETTER.
AND WE'RE OFF. FRANK, BE CAREFUL. BUT...
KILL THE BASTARDS.

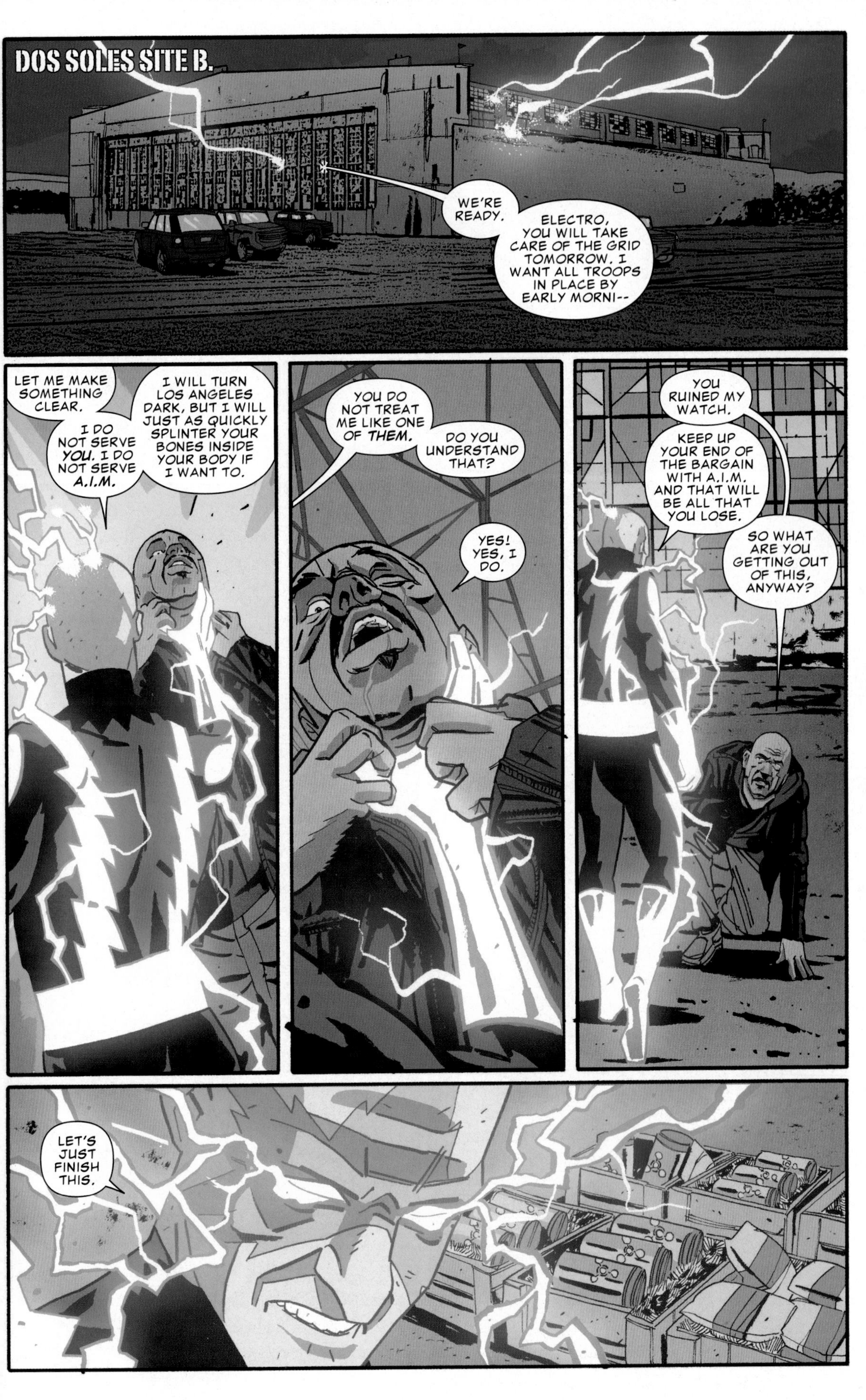
DOS SOLES SITE B.
WE'RE READY.
ELECTRO, YOU WILL TAKE CARE OF THE GRID TOMORROW. I WANT ALL TROOPS IN PLACE BY EARLY MORNI--
LET ME MAKE SOMETHING CLEAR.
I DO NOT SERVE *YOU.* I DO NOT SERVE *A.I.M.*
I WILL TURN LOS ANGELES DARK, BUT I WILL JUST AS QUICKLY SPLINTER YOUR BONES INSIDE YOUR BODY IF I WANT TO.
YOU DO NOT TREAT ME LIKE ONE OF ***THEM.***
DO YOU UNDERSTAND THAT?
YES! YES, I DO.
YOU RUINED MY WATCH.
KEEP UP YOUR END OF THE BARGAIN WITH A.I.M. AND THAT WILL BE ALL THAT YOU LOSE.
SO WHAT ARE YOU GETTING OUT OF THIS, ANYWAY?
LET'S JUST FINISH THIS.

...YES, IF YOU CAN PUSH THROUGH THE SHOCK, YOU'LL FIND THAT YOU WANT TO SEE YOUR LIFE THROUGH.

BECAUSE YOU WANT, MORE THAN ANYTHING, MORE THAN DEATH...

...TO COMPLETELY EXTERMINATE THE KINDS OF BASTARDS WHO TOOK YOUR LIFE AWAY, TO WIPE THEM OFF THE PLANET,

YOU WANT TO EMASCULATE EVIL.

WHAT THE--

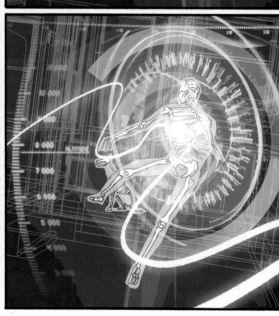

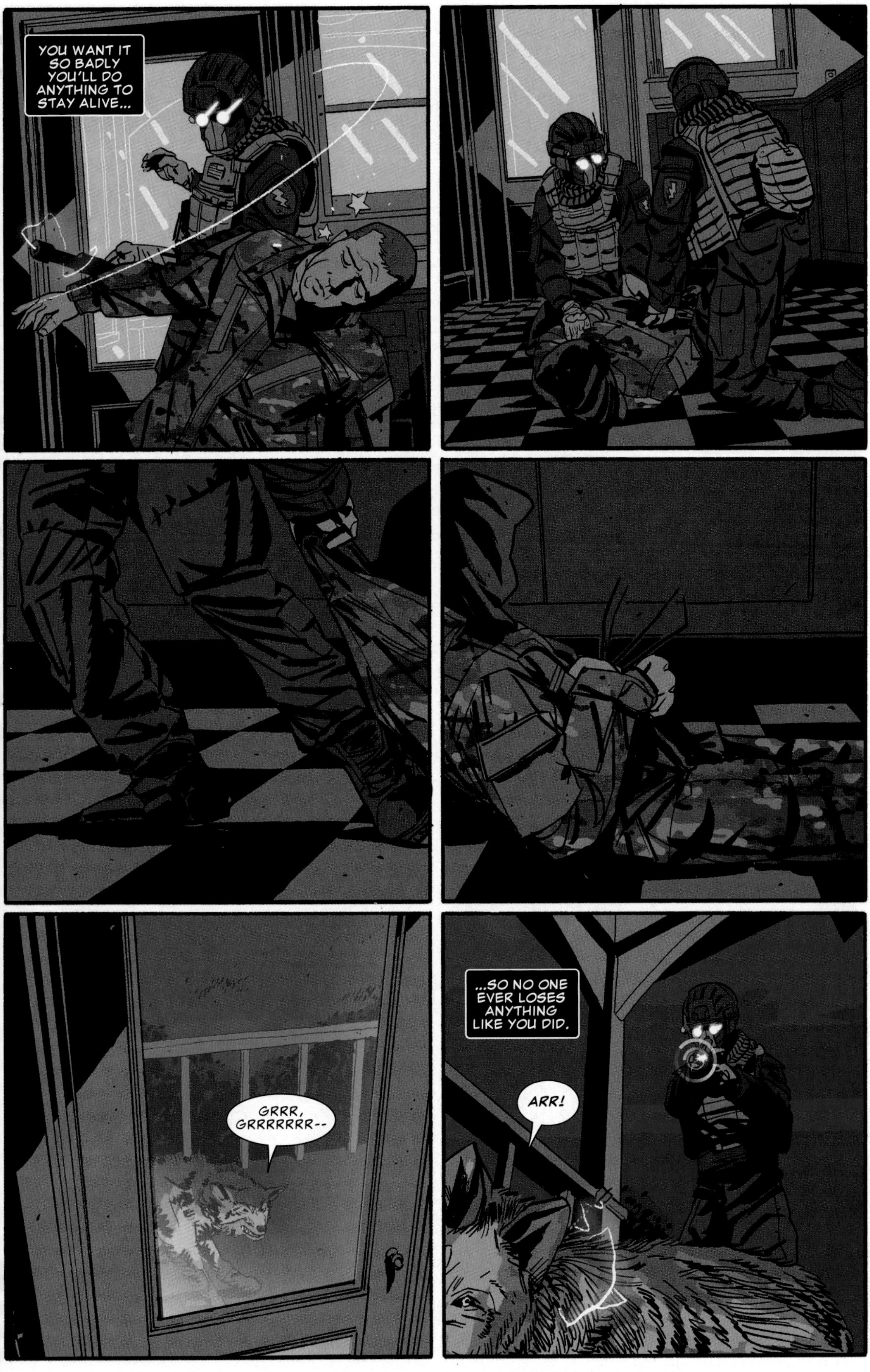
YOU WANT IT SO BADLY YOU'LL DO ANYTHING TO STAY ALIVE...
GRRR, GRRRRRRR--
...SO NO ONE EVER LOSES ANYTHING LIKE YOU DID.
ARR!

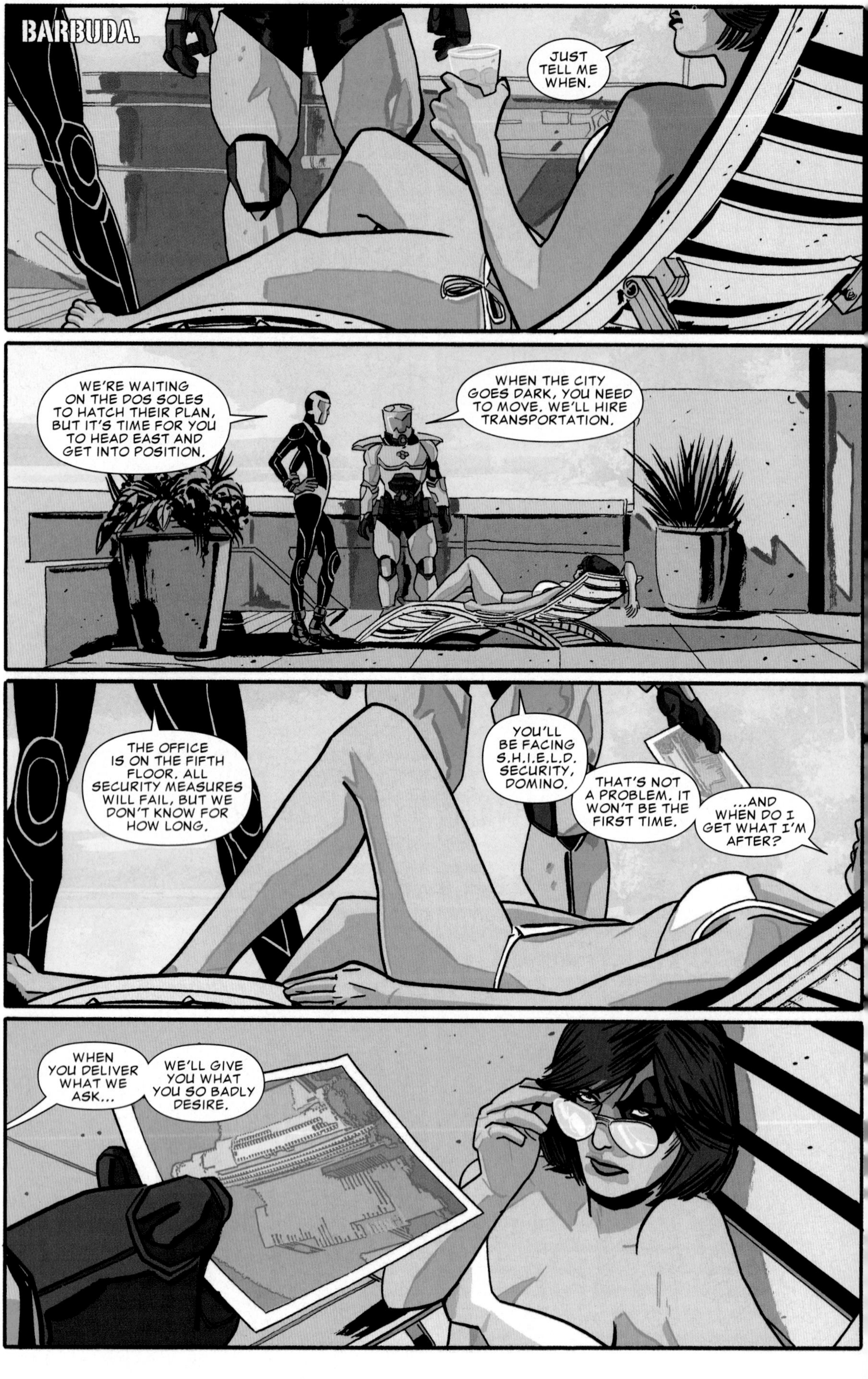
BARBUDA.
JUST TELL ME WHEN.
WE'RE WAITING ON THE DOS SOLES TO HATCH THEIR PLAN, BUT IT'S TIME FOR YOU TO HEAD EAST AND GET INTO POSITION.
WHEN THE CITY GOES DARK, YOU NEED TO MOVE. WE'LL HIRE TRANSPORTATION.
THE OFFICE IS ON THE FIFTH FLOOR. ALL SECURITY MEASURES WILL FAIL, BUT WE DON'T KNOW FOR HOW LONG.
YOU'LL BE FACING S.H.I.E.L.D. SECURITY, DOMINO.
THAT'S NOT A PROBLEM. IT WON'T BE THE FIRST TIME.
...AND WHEN DO I GET WHAT I'M AFTER?
WHEN YOU DELIVER WHAT WE ASK...
WE'LL GIVE YOU WHAT YOU SO BADLY DESIRE.

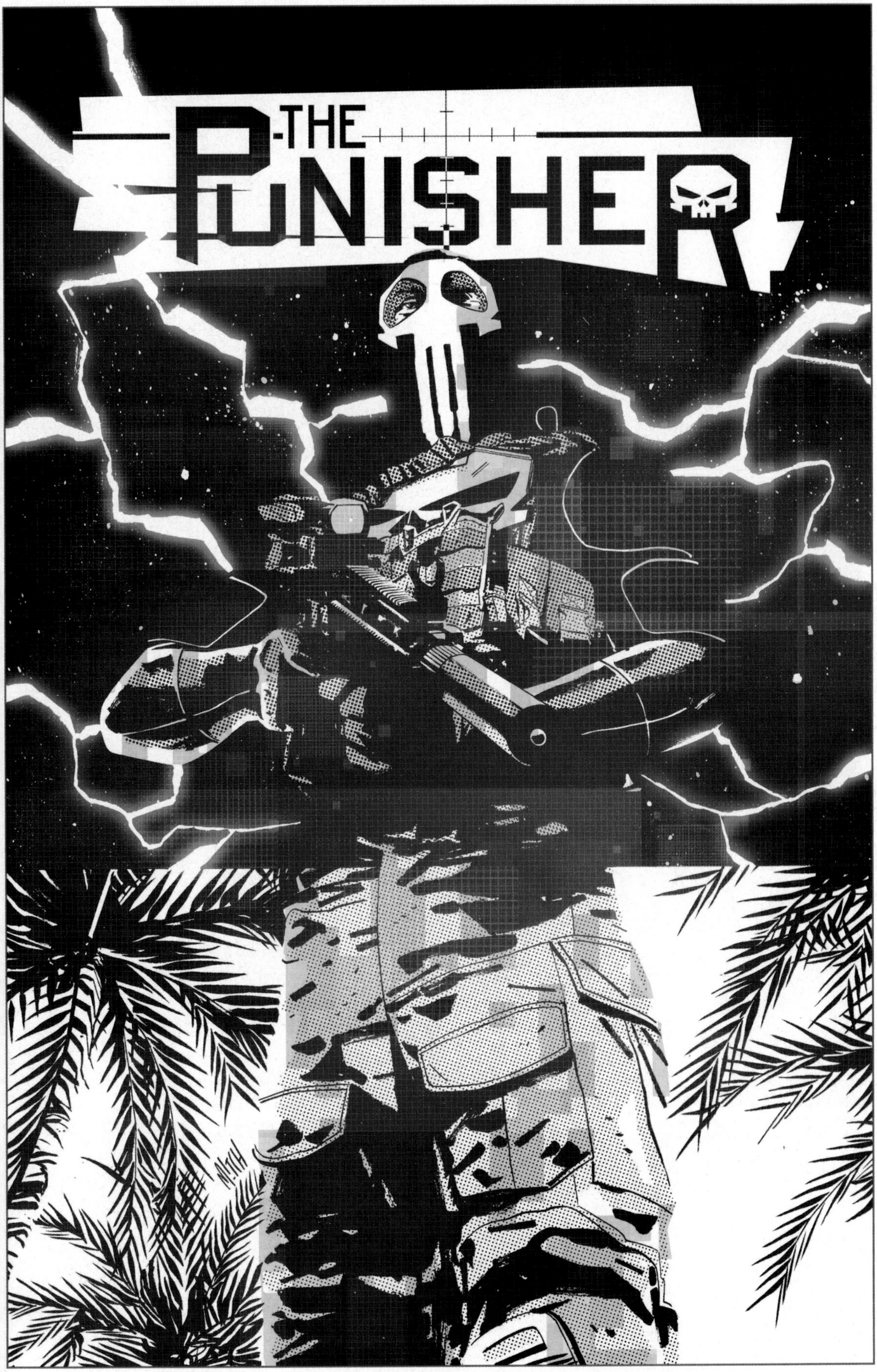
THE PUNISHER

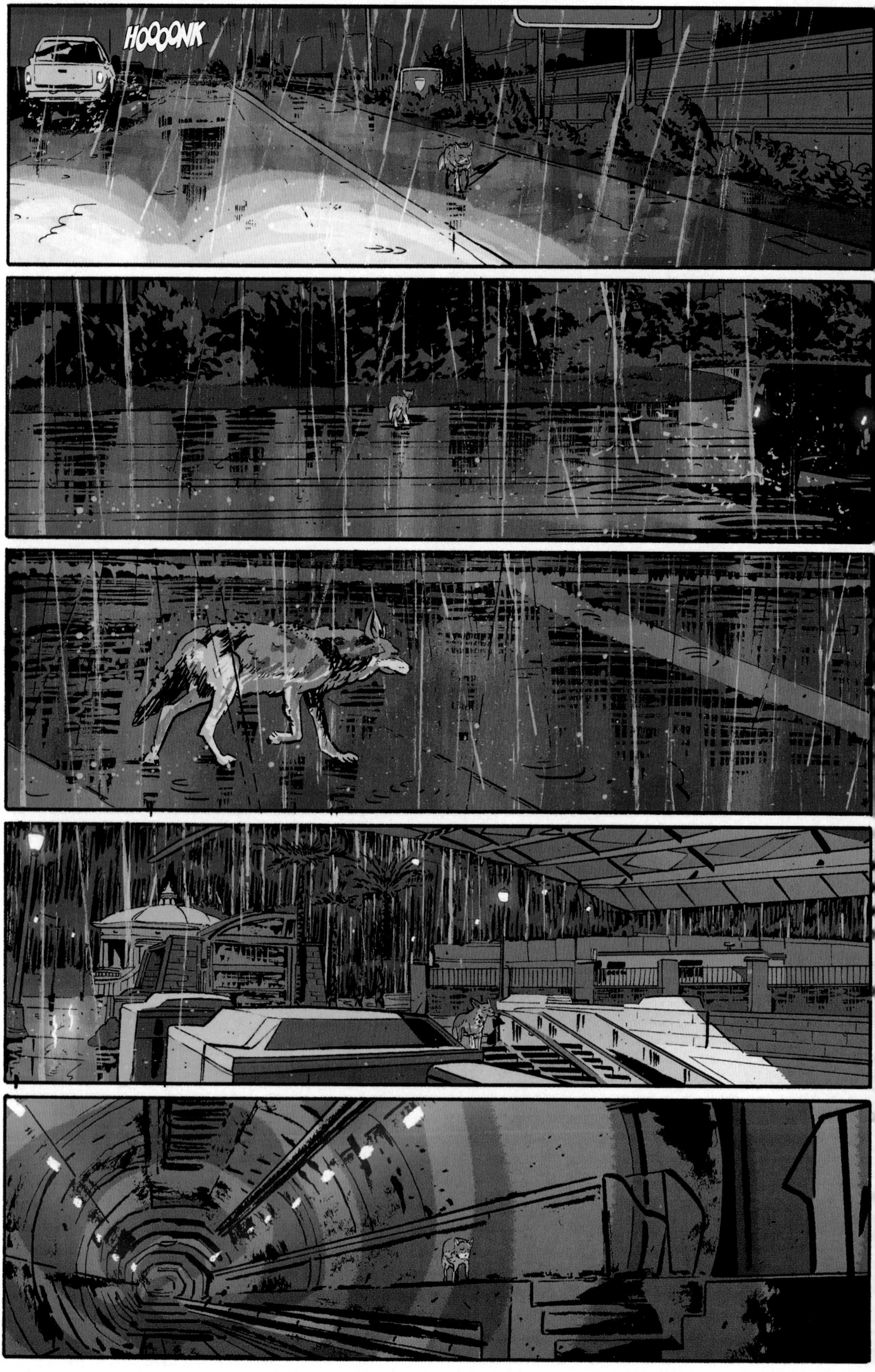
HOOOONK

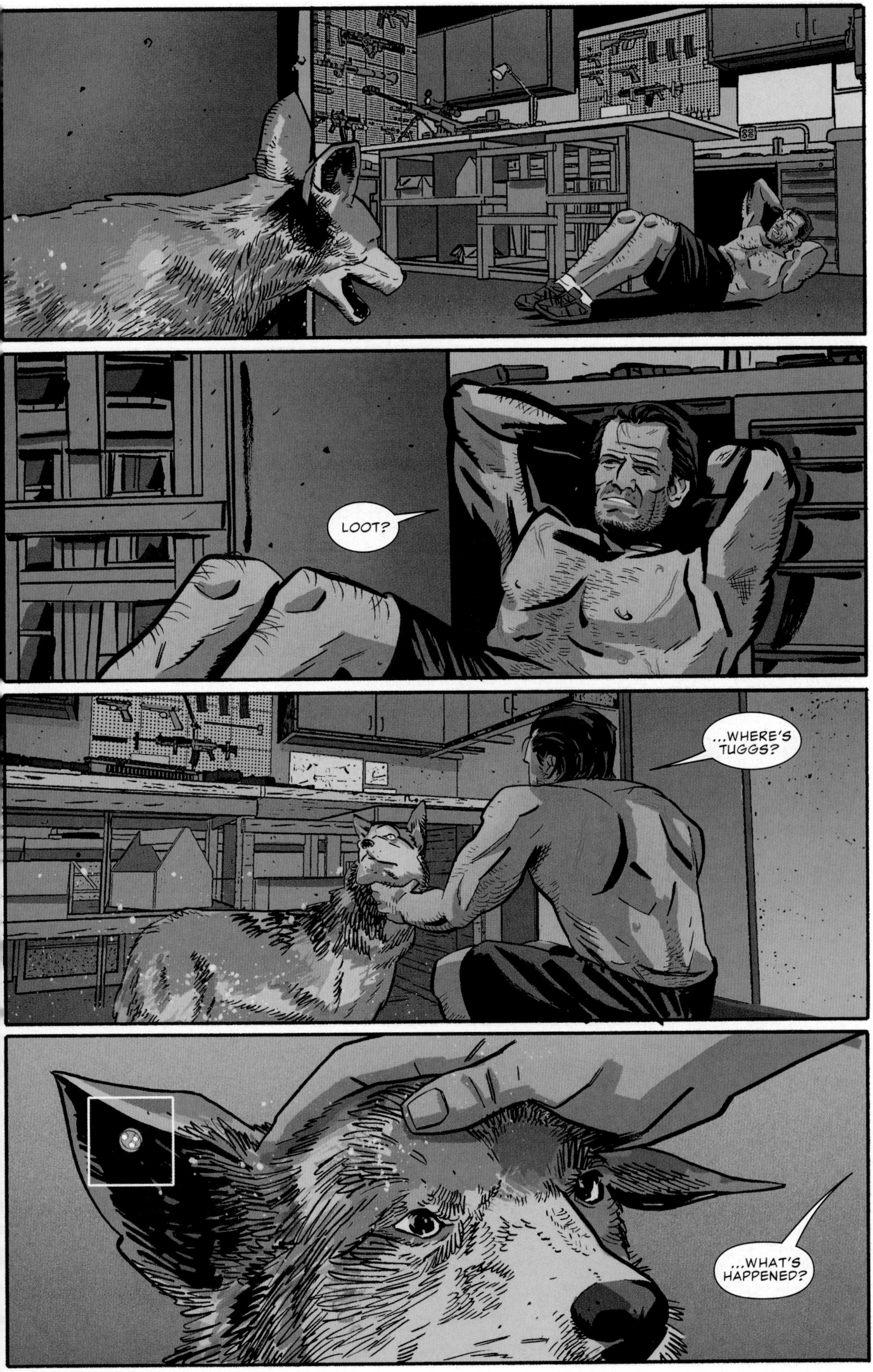
LOOT?
...WHERE'S TUGGS?
...WHAT'S HAPPENED?

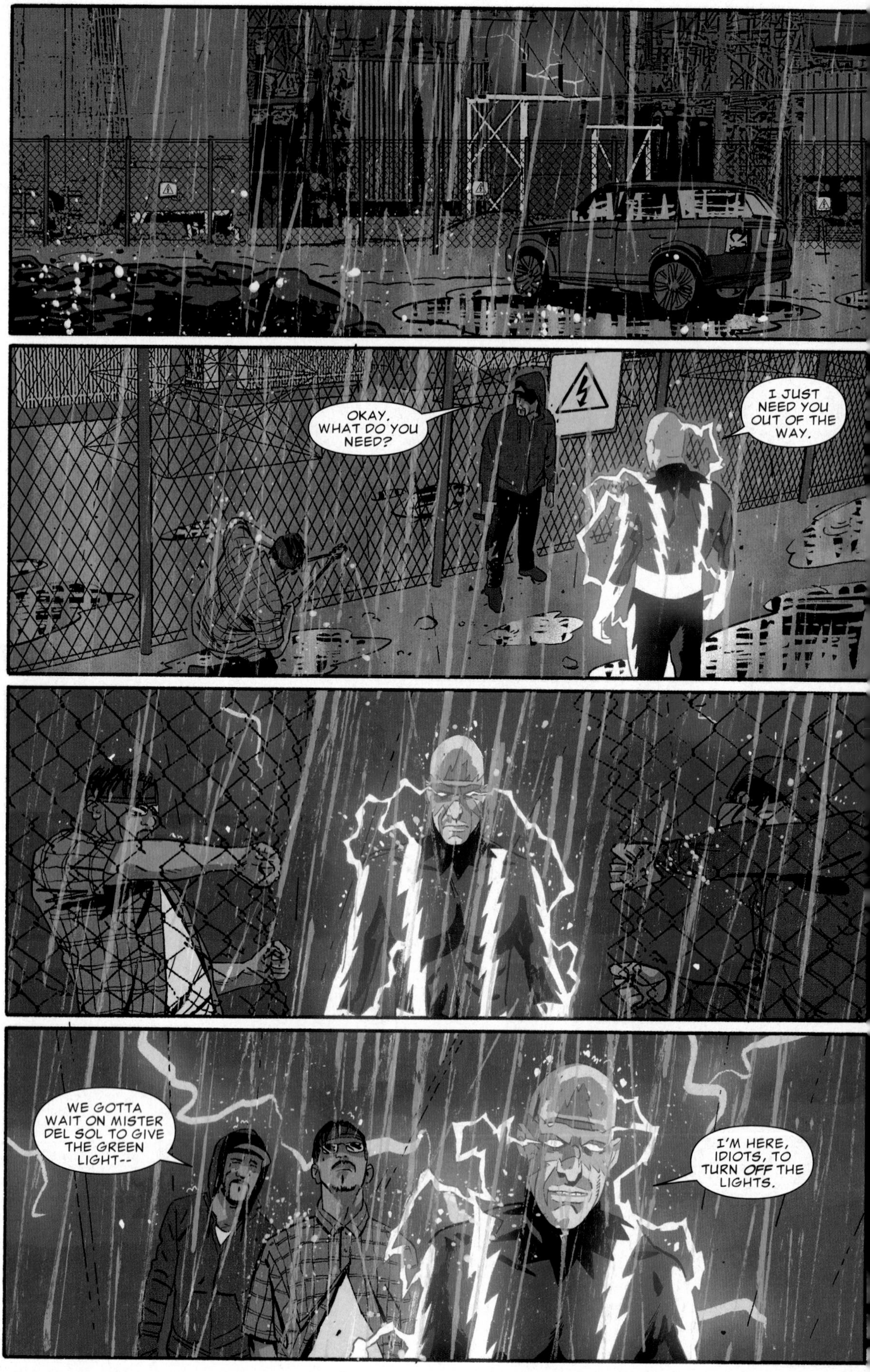
OKAY. WHAT DO YOU NEED?
I JUST NEED YOU OUT OF THE WAY.
WE GOTTA WAIT ON MISTER DEL SOL TO GIVE THE GREEN LIGHT--
I'M HERE, IDIOTS, TO TURN OFF THE LIGHTS.

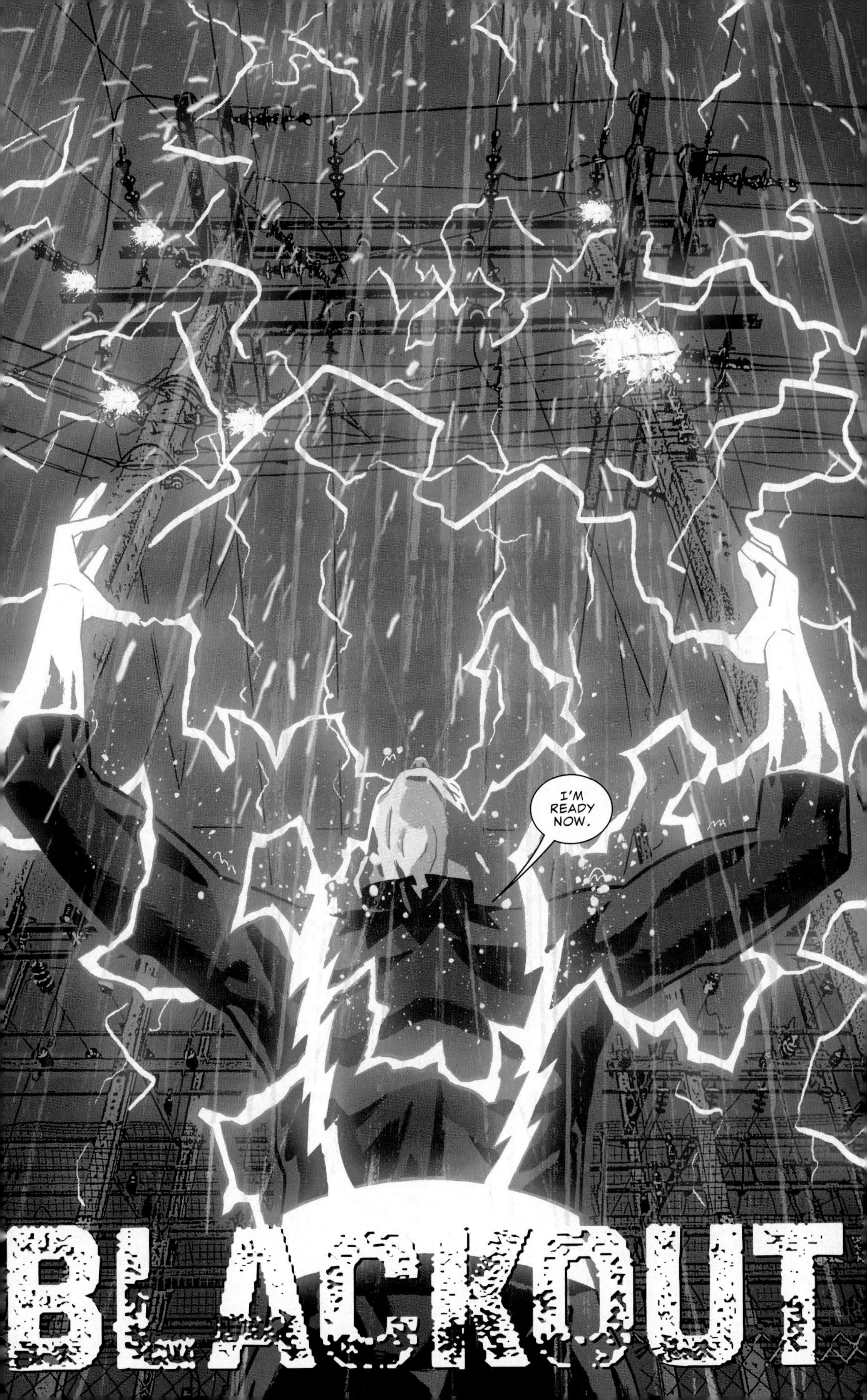
I'M READY NOW.
BLACKOUT

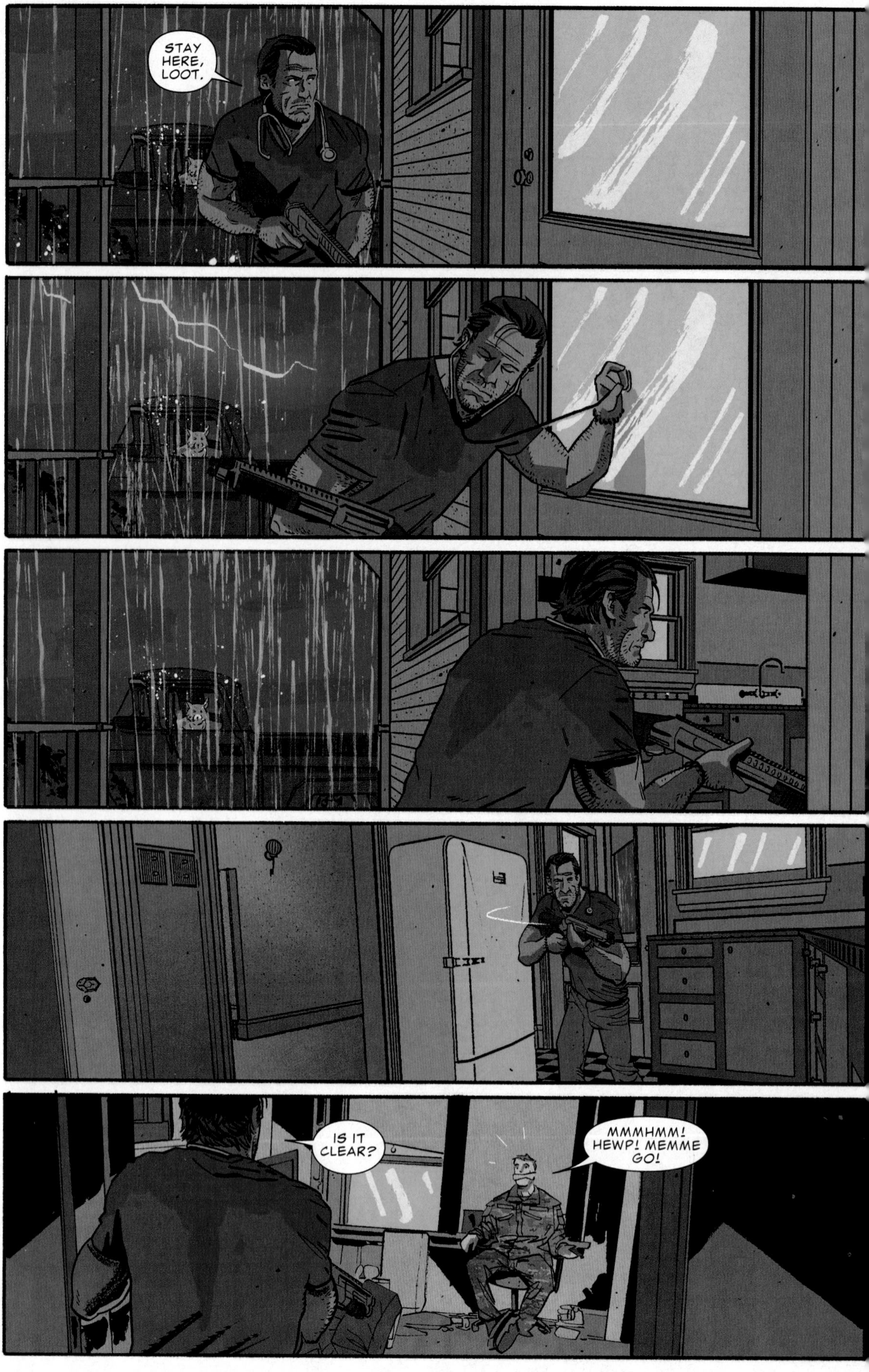
STAY HERE, LOOT.
IS IT CLEAR?
MMMHMM! HEWP! MEMME GO!

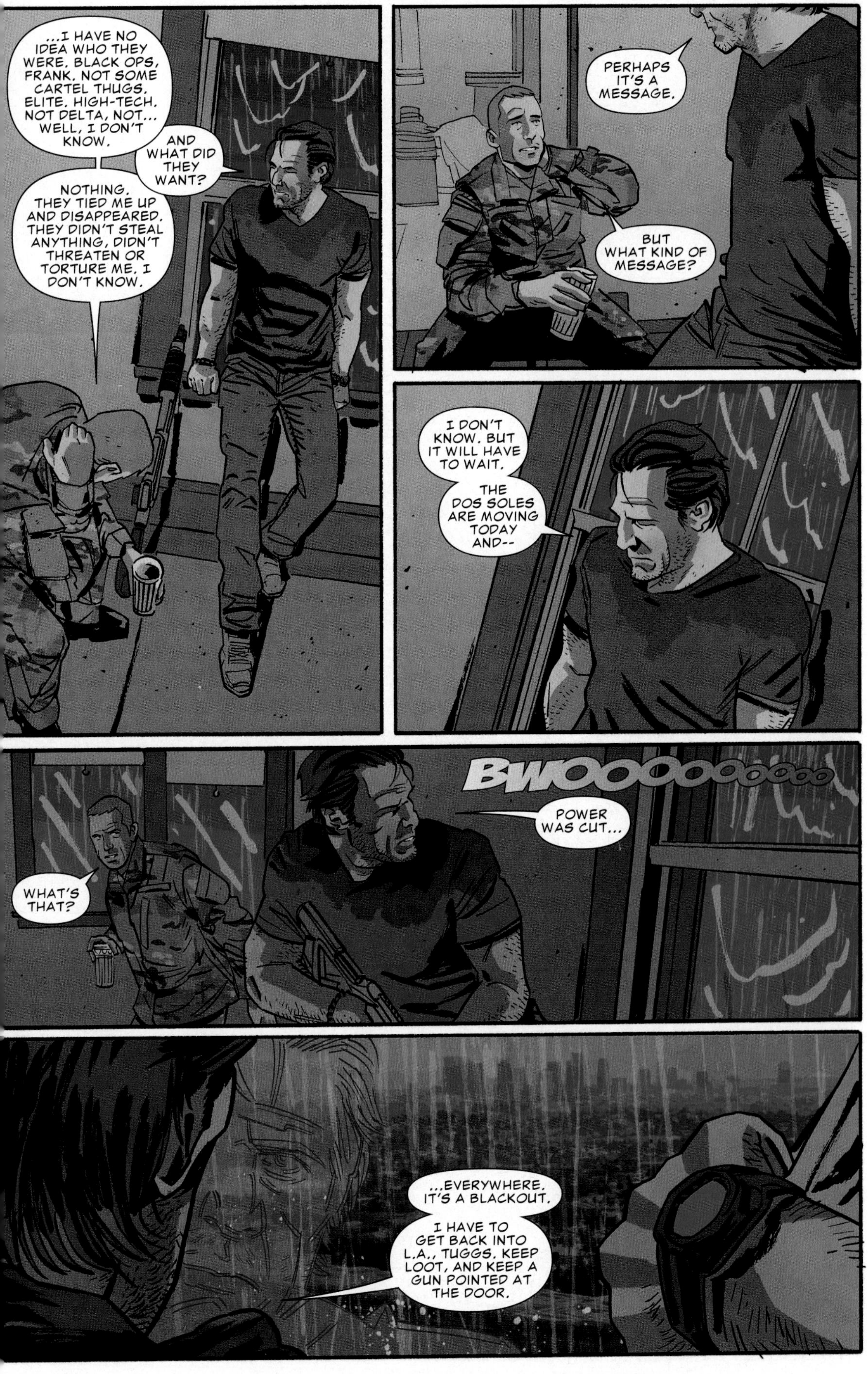
...I HAVE NO IDEA WHO THEY WERE. BLACK OPS, FRANK. NOT SOME CARTEL THUGS. ELITE. HIGH-TECH. NOT DELTA, NOT... WELL, I DON'T KNOW.
AND WHAT DID THEY WANT?
NOTHING. THEY TIED ME UP AND DISAPPEARED. THEY DIDN'T STEAL ANYTHING, DIDN'T THREATEN OR TORTURE ME. I DON'T KNOW.
PERHAPS IT'S A MESSAGE.
BUT WHAT KIND OF MESSAGE?
I DON'T KNOW. BUT IT WILL HAVE TO WAIT.
THE DOS SOLES ARE MOVING TODAY AND--
BWOOOOOOOOOO
POWER WAS CUT...
WHAT'S THAT?
...EVERYWHERE. IT'S A BLACKOUT.
I HAVE TO GET BACK INTO L.A., TUGGS. KEEP LOOT, AND KEEP A GUN POINTED AT THE DOOR.

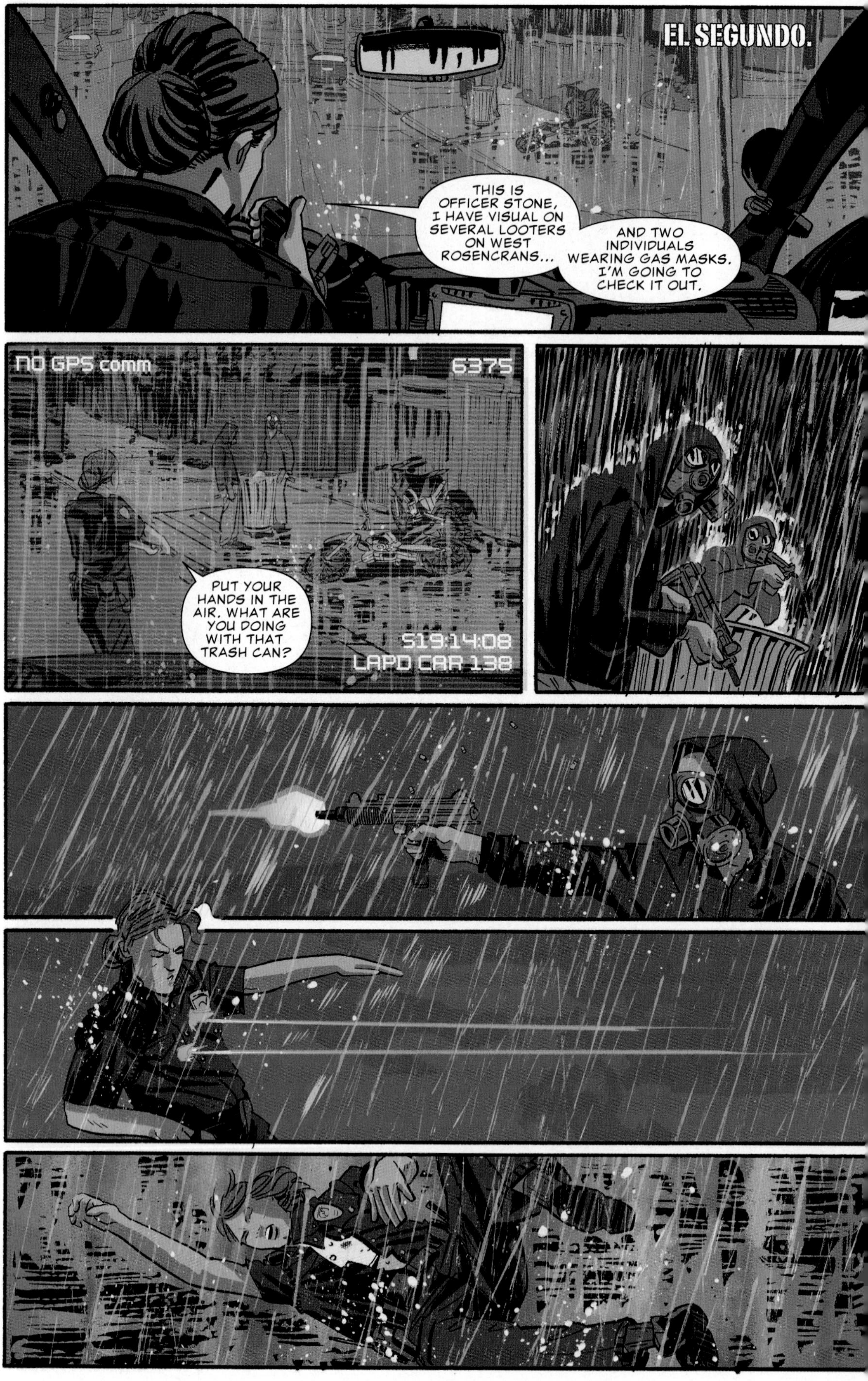
EL SEGUNDO.
THIS IS OFFICER STONE, I HAVE VISUAL ON SEVERAL LOOTERS ON WEST ROSENCRANS...
AND TWO INDIVIDUALS WEARING GAS MASKS. I'M GOING TO CHECK IT OUT.
NO GPS comm
6375
PUT YOUR HANDS IN THE AIR. WHAT ARE YOU DOING WITH THAT TRASH CAN?
S19:14:08
LAPD CAR 138

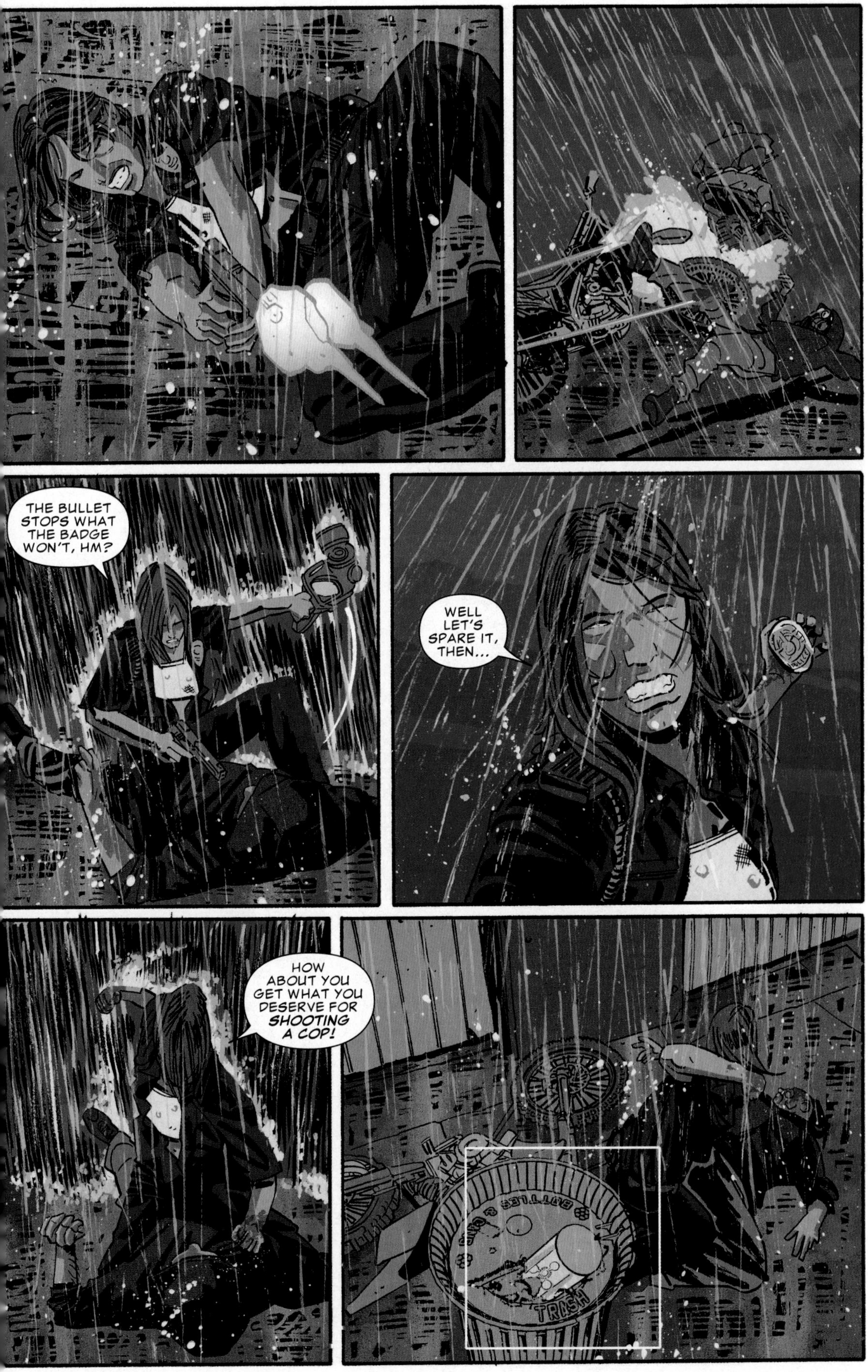
THE BULLET STOPS WHAT THE BADGE WON'T, HM?
WELL LET'S SPARE IT, THEN...
HOW ABOUT YOU GET WHAT YOU DESERVE FOR *SHOOTING* A COP!
TRASH

CAN'T GET THROUGH TO ANYONE.

POWER'S OUT EVERYWHERE, MAYBE A CAR HIT A POWERLINE--

BAM

BAM

SECURE ALL ENTRYWAYS.

OKAY, YOU HAVE YOUR BUILDING READY, SEND IN YOUR PEOPLE, I HAVE A CITY TO ATTACK.

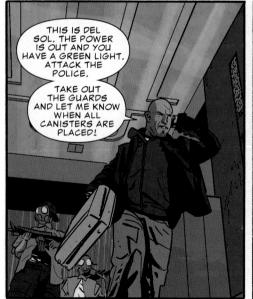

THIS IS DEL SOL. THE POWER IS OUT AND YOU HAVE A GREEN LIGHT. ATTACK THE POLICE.

TAKE OUT THE GUARDS AND LET ME KNOW WHEN ALL CANISTERS ARE PLACED!

I'LL PULL THE TRIGGER, THE CITY WILL CHOKE, AND TWO SONS WILL RISE.

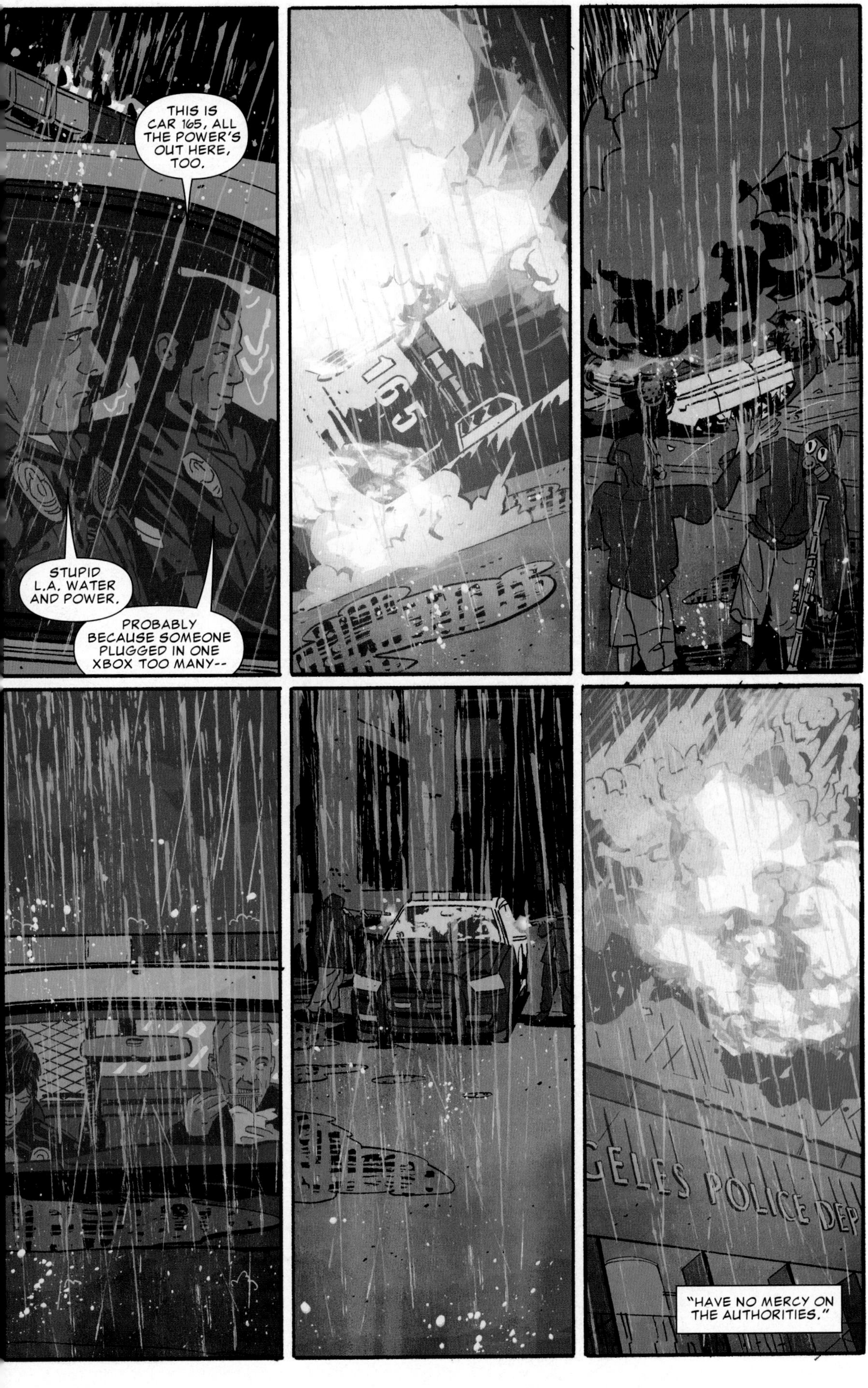
THIS IS CAR 165, ALL THE POWER'S OUT HERE, TOO.
STUPID L.A. WATER AND POWER.
PROBABLY BECAUSE SOMEONE PLUGGED IN ONE XBOX TOO MANY--
165
GELES POLICE DEP
"HAVE NO MERCY ON THE AUTHORITIES."

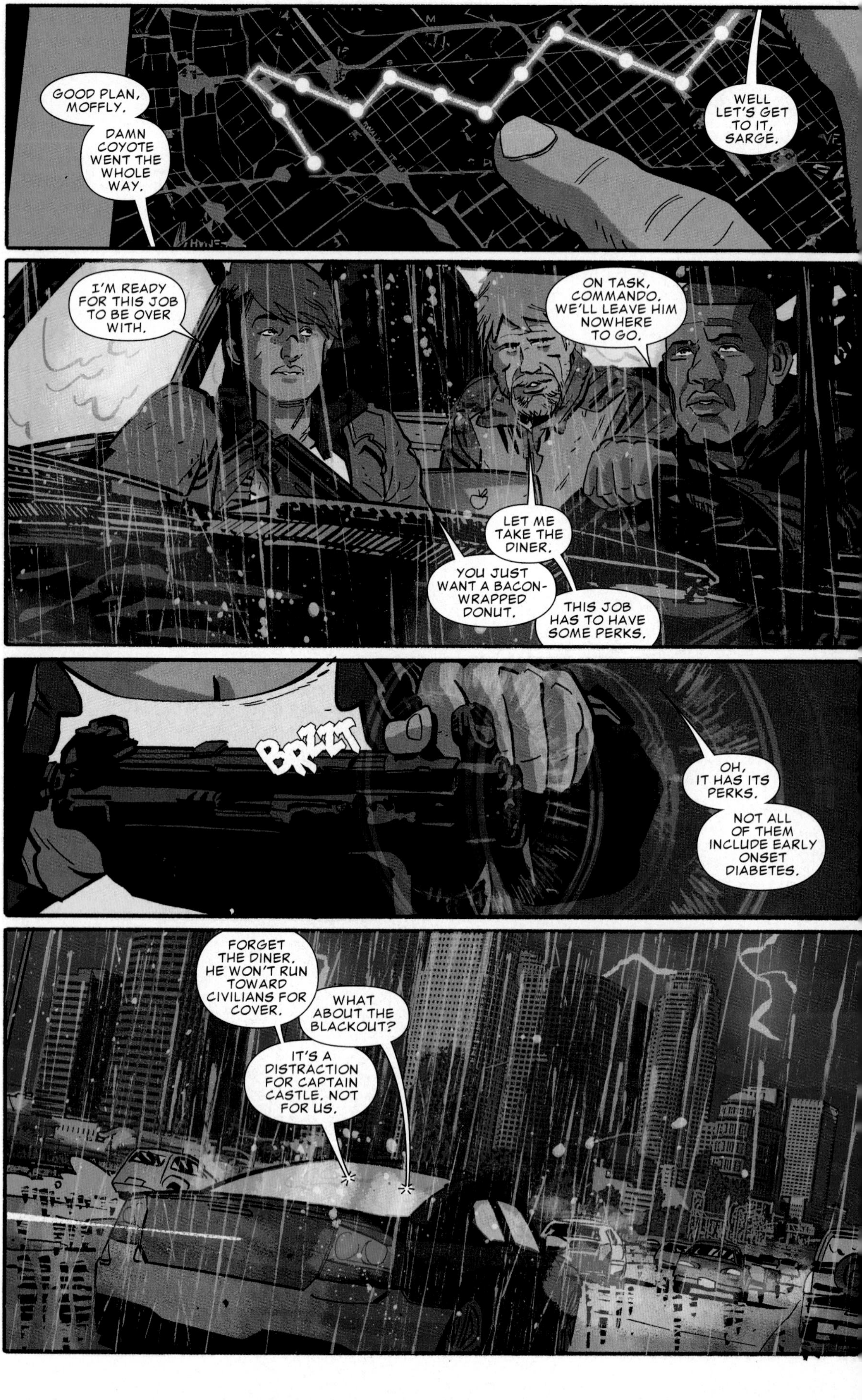
GOOD PLAN, MOFFLY.
DAMN COYOTE WENT THE WHOLE WAY.
WELL LET'S GET TO IT, SARGE.
I'M READY FOR THIS JOB TO BE OVER WITH.
ON TASK, COMMANDO. WE'LL LEAVE HIM NOWHERE TO GO.
LET ME TAKE THE DINER.
YOU JUST WANT A BACON-WRAPPED DONUT.
THIS JOB HAS TO HAVE SOME PERKS.
BRZZZT
OH, IT HAS ITS PERKS.
NOT ALL OF THEM INCLUDE EARLY ONSET DIABETES.
FORGET THE DINER. HE WON'T RUN TOWARD CIVILIANS FOR COVER.
WHAT ABOUT THE BLACKOUT?
IT'S A DISTRACTION FOR CAPTAIN CASTLE. NOT FOR US.

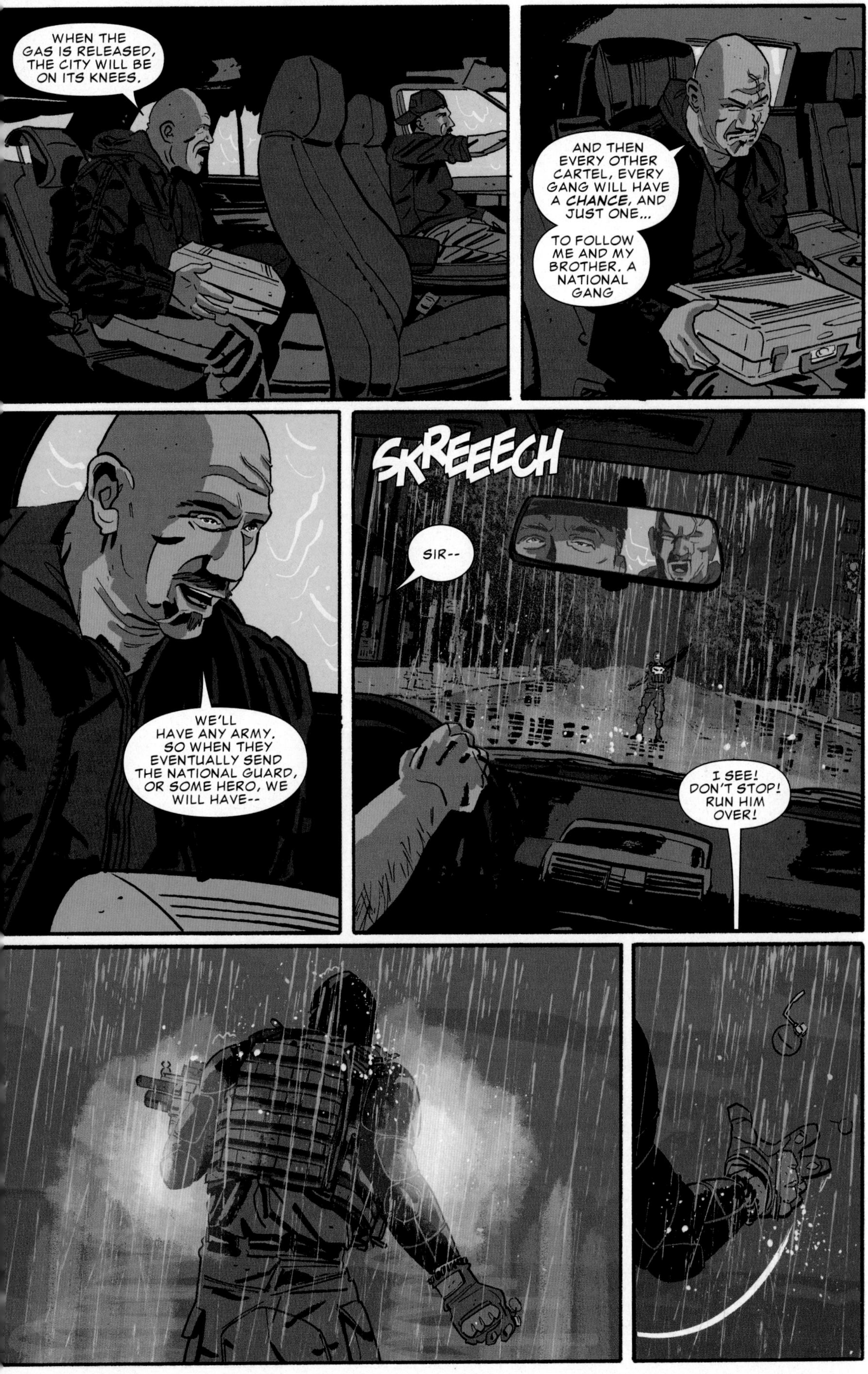
WHEN THE GAS IS RELEASED, THE CITY WILL BE ON ITS KNEES.
AND THEN EVERY OTHER CARTEL, EVERY GANG WILL HAVE A *CHANCE*, AND JUST ONE...
TO FOLLOW ME AND MY BROTHER. A NATIONAL GANG
WE'LL HAVE ANY ARMY. SO WHEN THEY EVENTUALLY SEND THE NATIONAL GUARD, OR SOME HERO, WE WILL HAVE--
SKREEEECH
SIR--
I SEE! DON'T STOP! RUN HIM OVER!

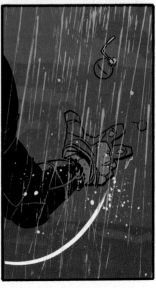

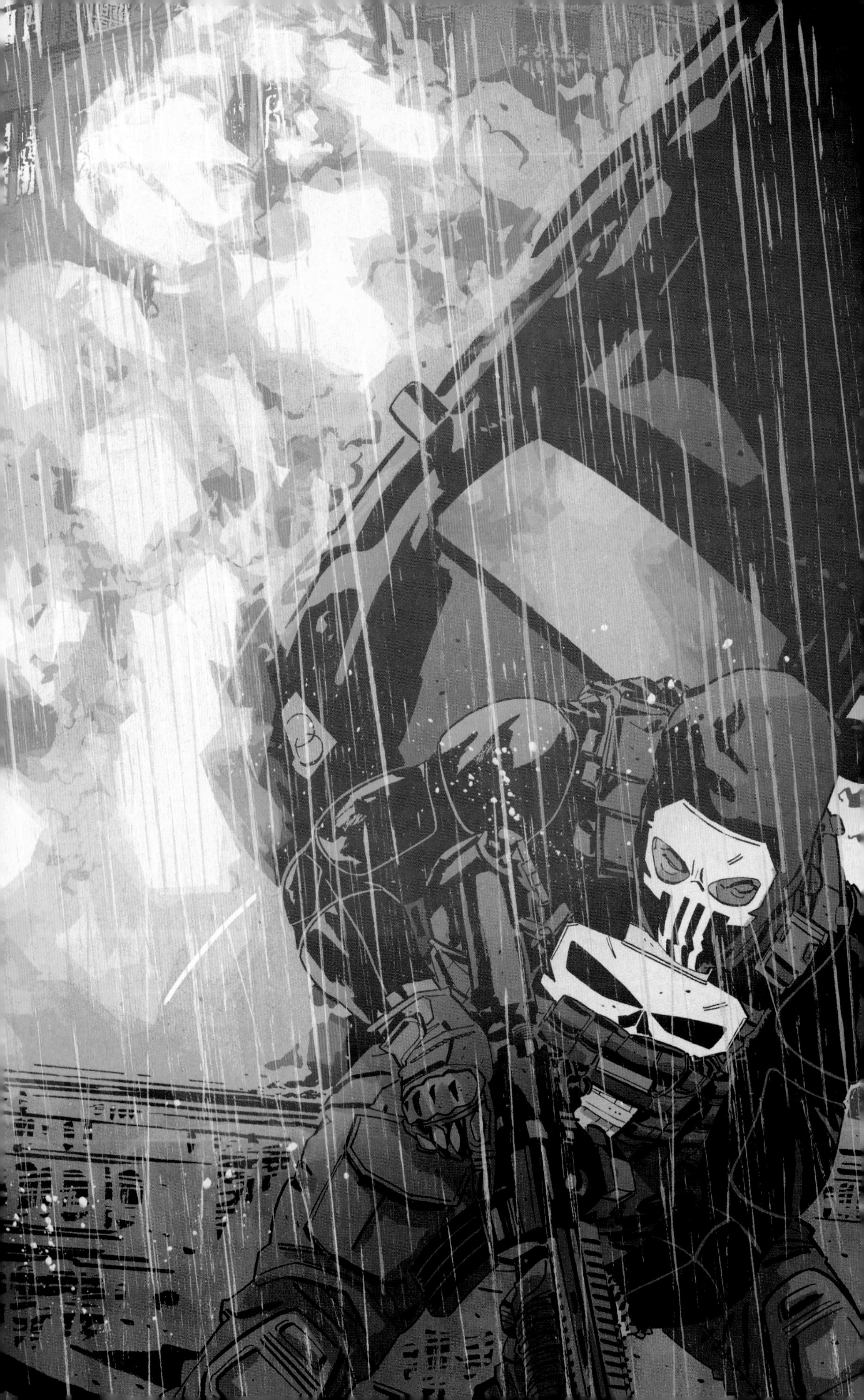

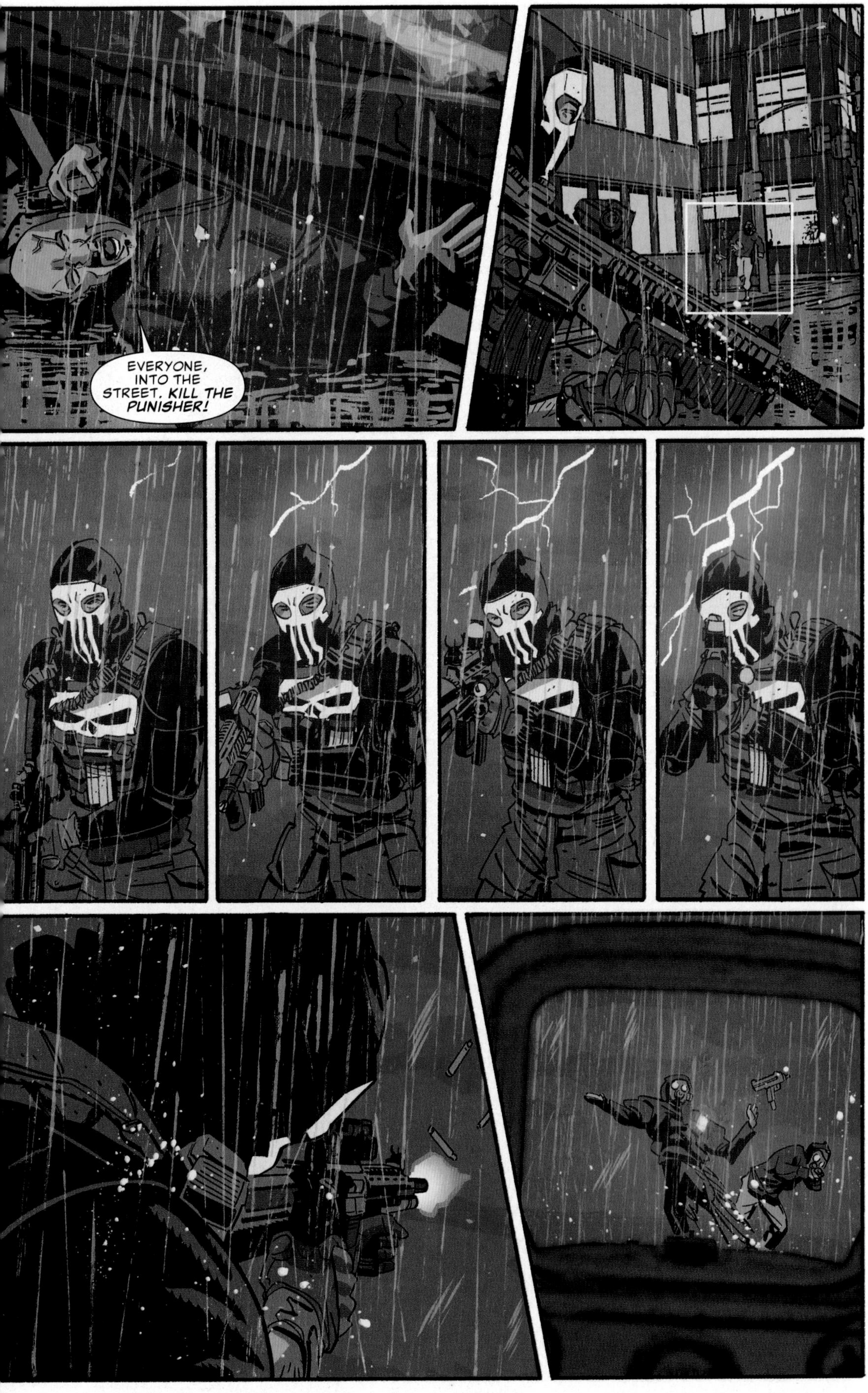
EVERYONE, INTO THE STREET. KILL THE PUNISHER!

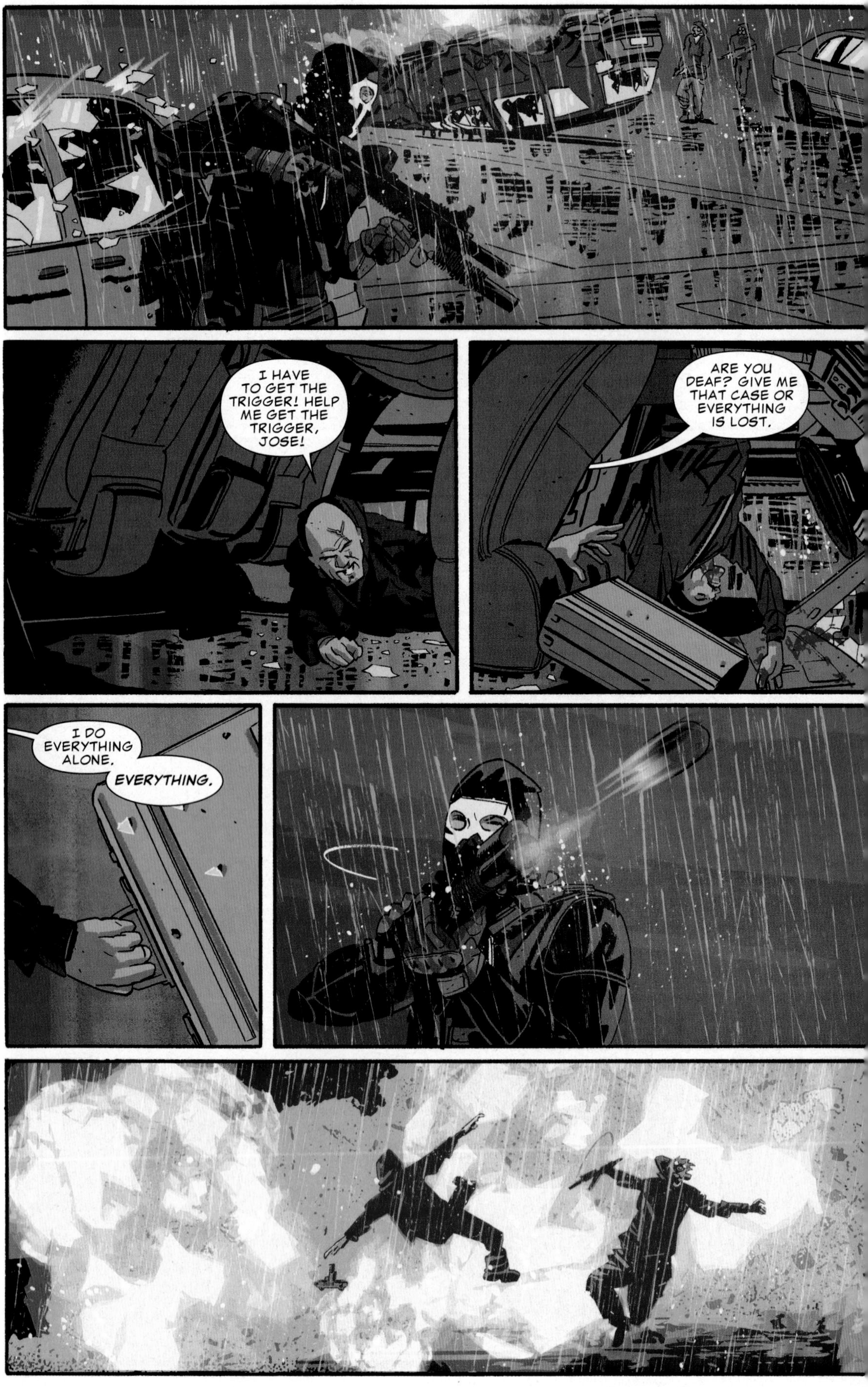
I HAVE TO GET THE TRIGGER! HELP ME GET THE TRIGGER, JOSE!
ARE YOU DEAF? GIVE ME THAT CASE OR EVERYTHING IS LOST.
I DO EVERYTHING ALONE.
EVERYTHING.

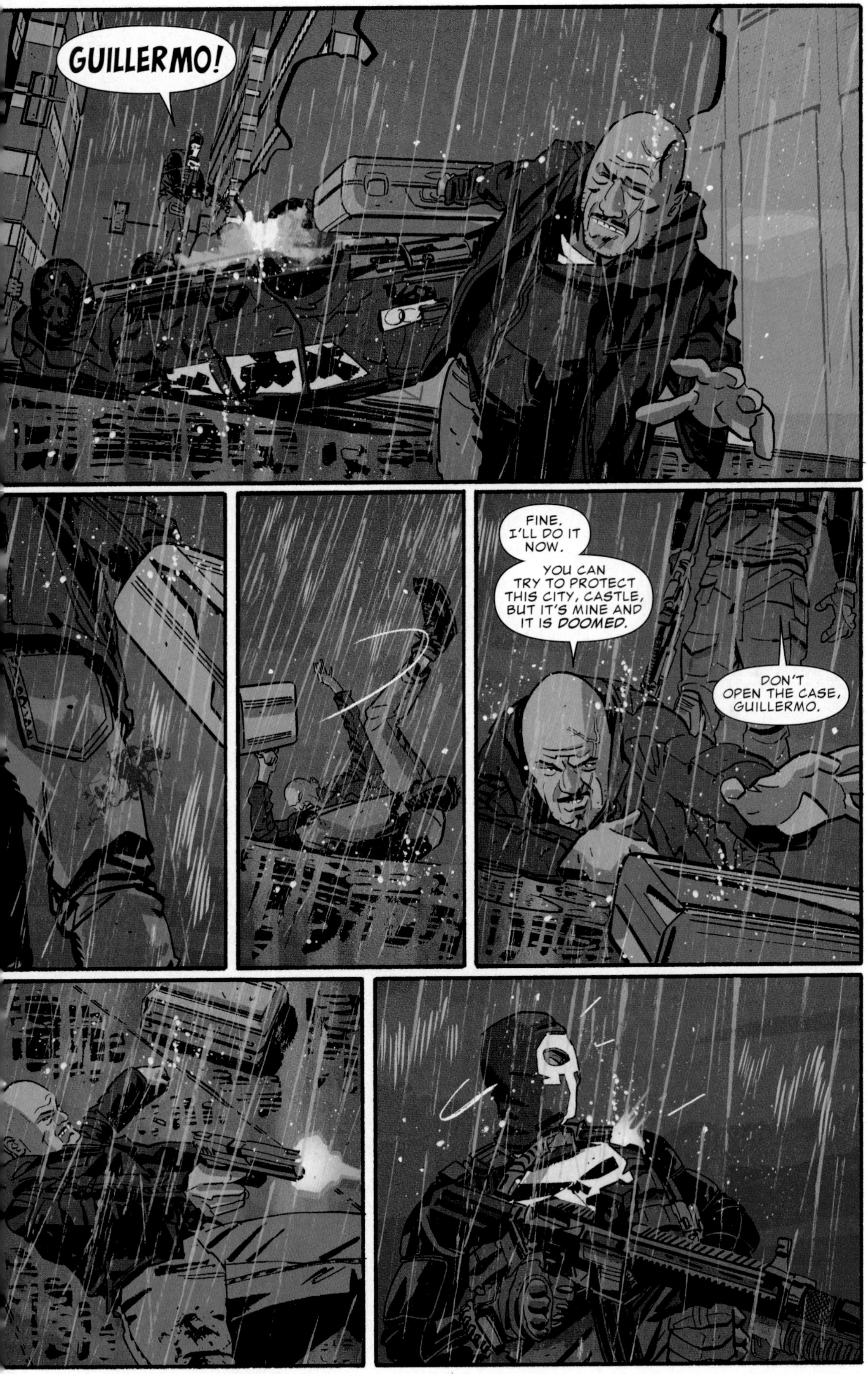
GUILLERMO!
FINE. I'LL DO IT NOW.
YOU CAN TRY TO PROTECT THIS CITY, CASTLE, BUT IT'S MINE AND IT IS DOOMED.
DON'T OPEN THE CASE, GUILLERMO.

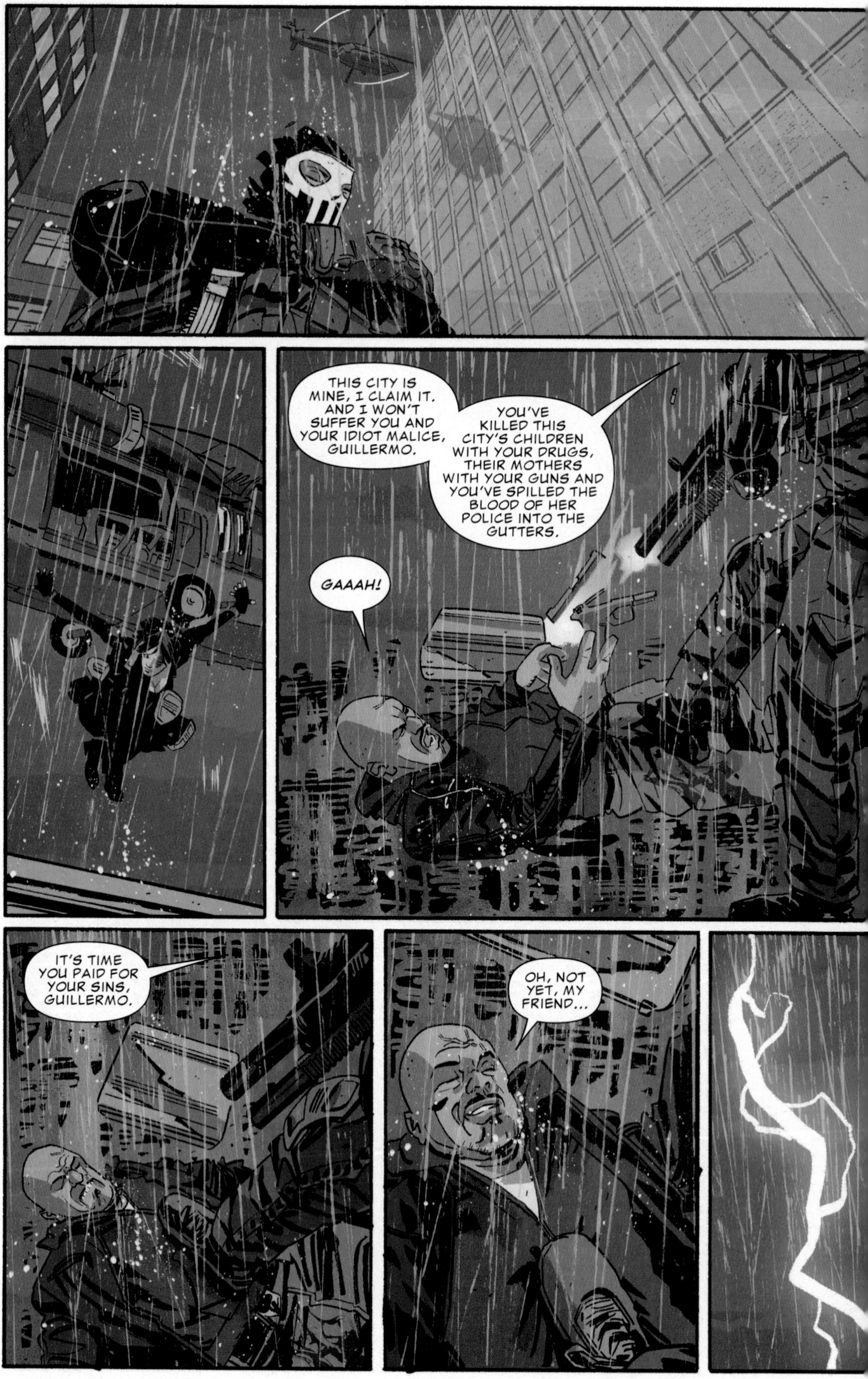
THIS CITY IS MINE, I CLAIM IT. AND I WON'T SUFFER YOU AND YOUR IDIOT MALICE, GUILLERMO.
YOU'VE KILLED THIS CITY'S CHILDREN WITH YOUR DRUGS, THEIR MOTHERS WITH YOUR GUNS AND YOU'VE SPILLED THE BLOOD OF HER POLICE INTO THE GUTTERS.
GAAAH!
IT'S TIME YOU PAID FOR YOUR SINS, GUILLERMO.
OH, NOT YET, MY FRIEND...

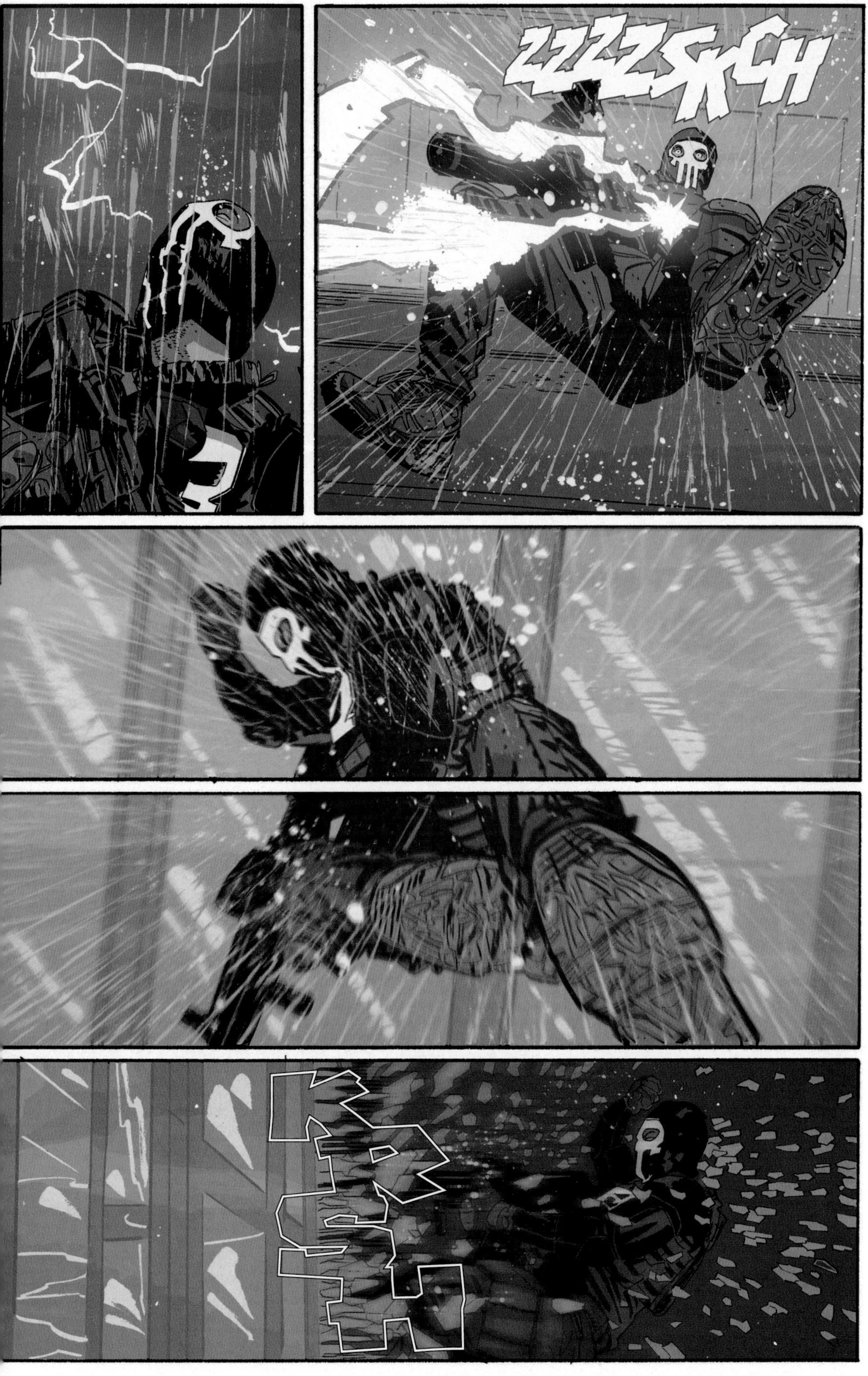
ZZZZSKCH
KRSH

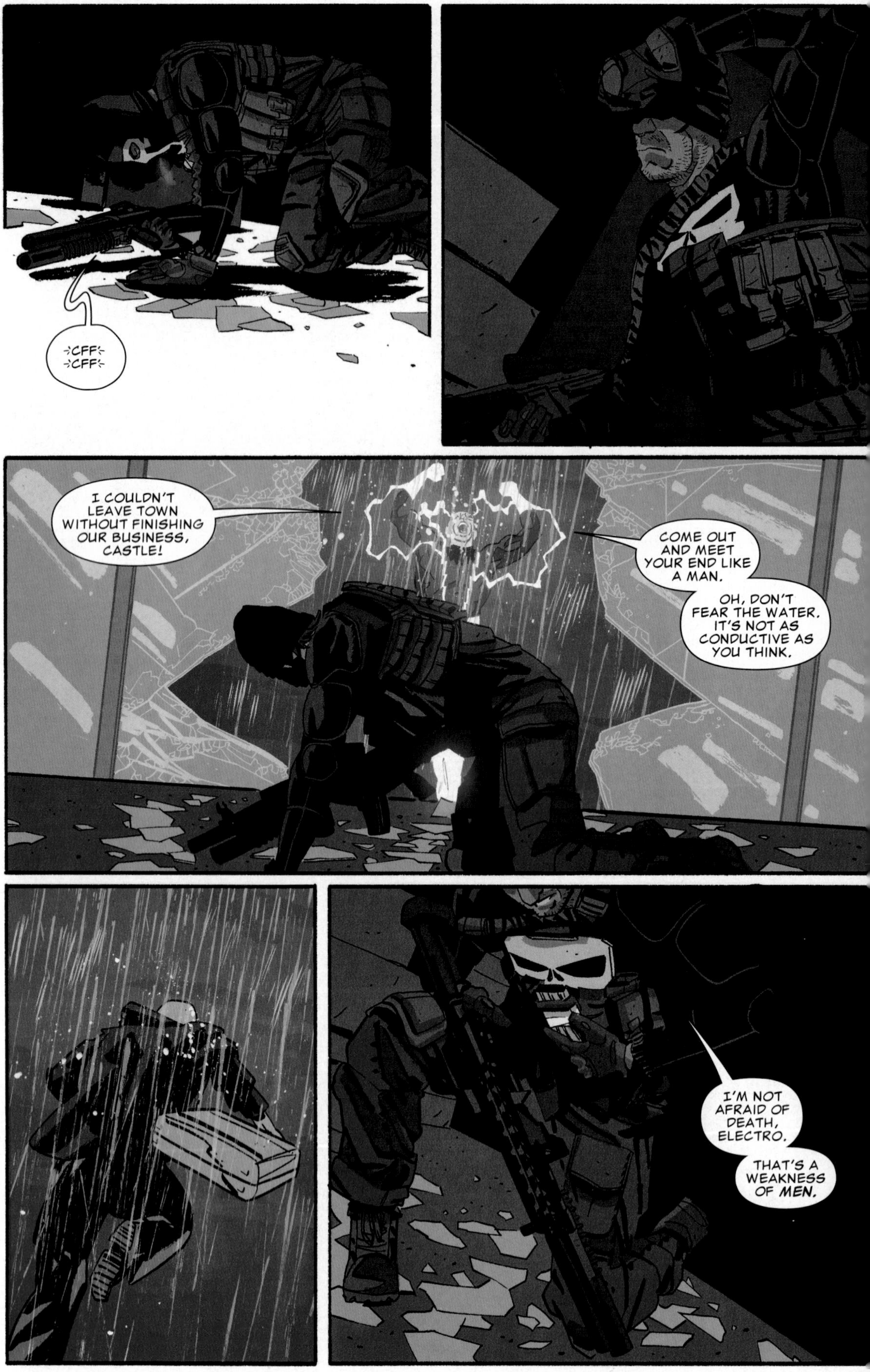
CFF CFF
I COULDN'T LEAVE TOWN WITHOUT FINISHING OUR BUSINESS, CASTLE!
COME OUT AND MEET YOUR END LIKE A MAN.
OH, DON'T FEAR THE WATER. IT'S NOT AS CONDUCTIVE AS YOU THINK.
I'M NOT AFRAID OF DEATH, ELECTRO.
THAT'S A WEAKNESS OF MEN.

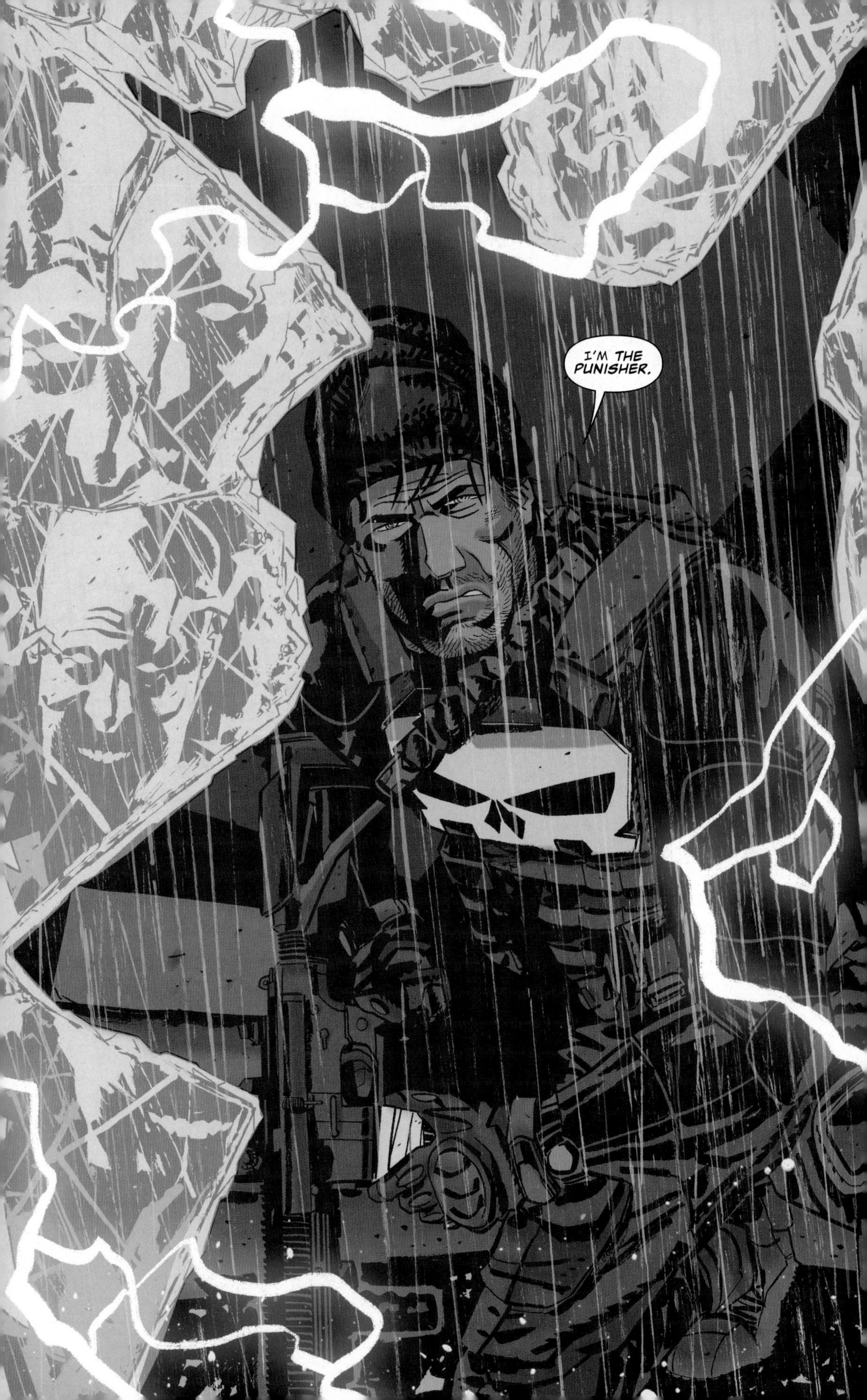
I'M THE PUNISHER.

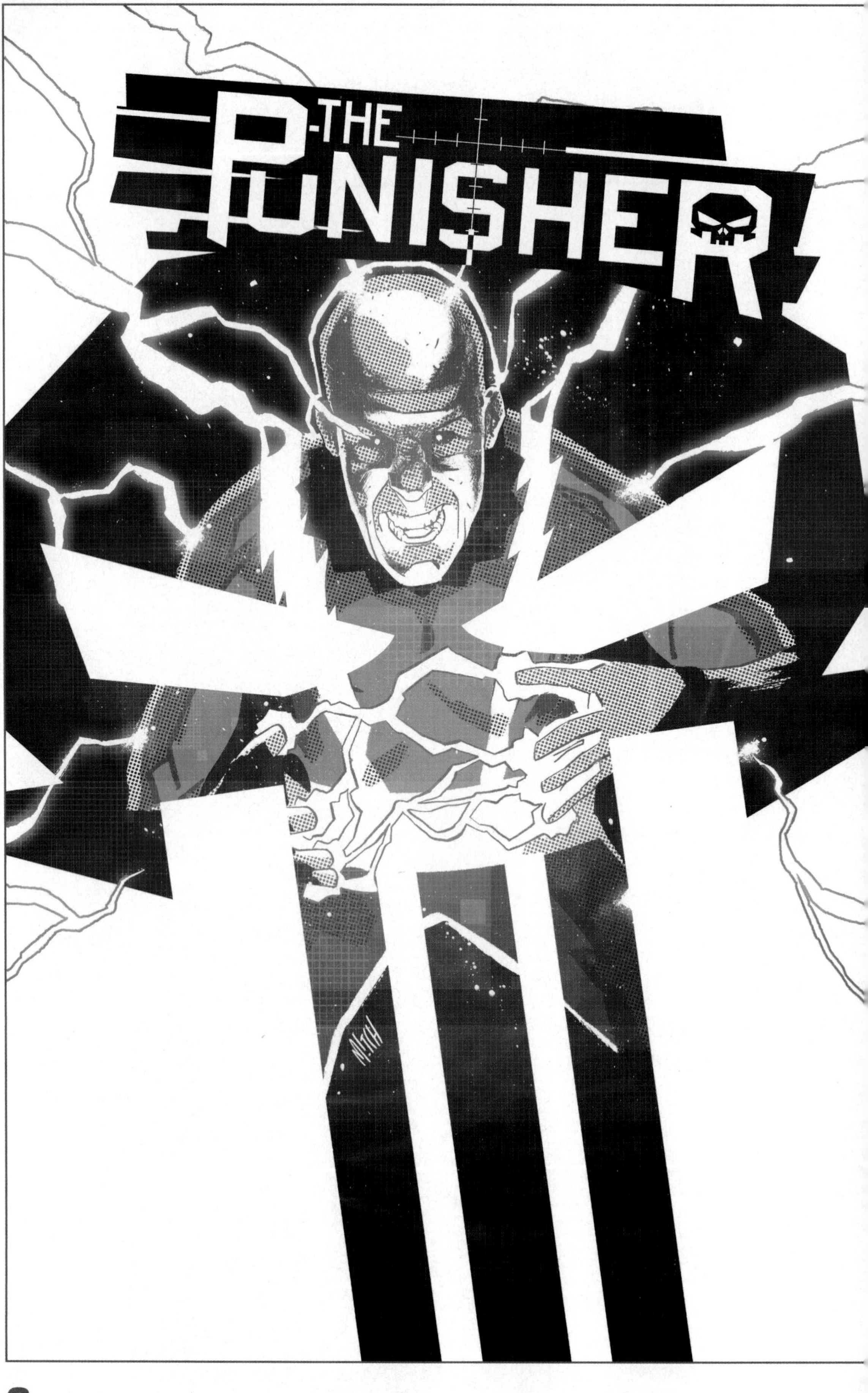
THE
PUNISHER

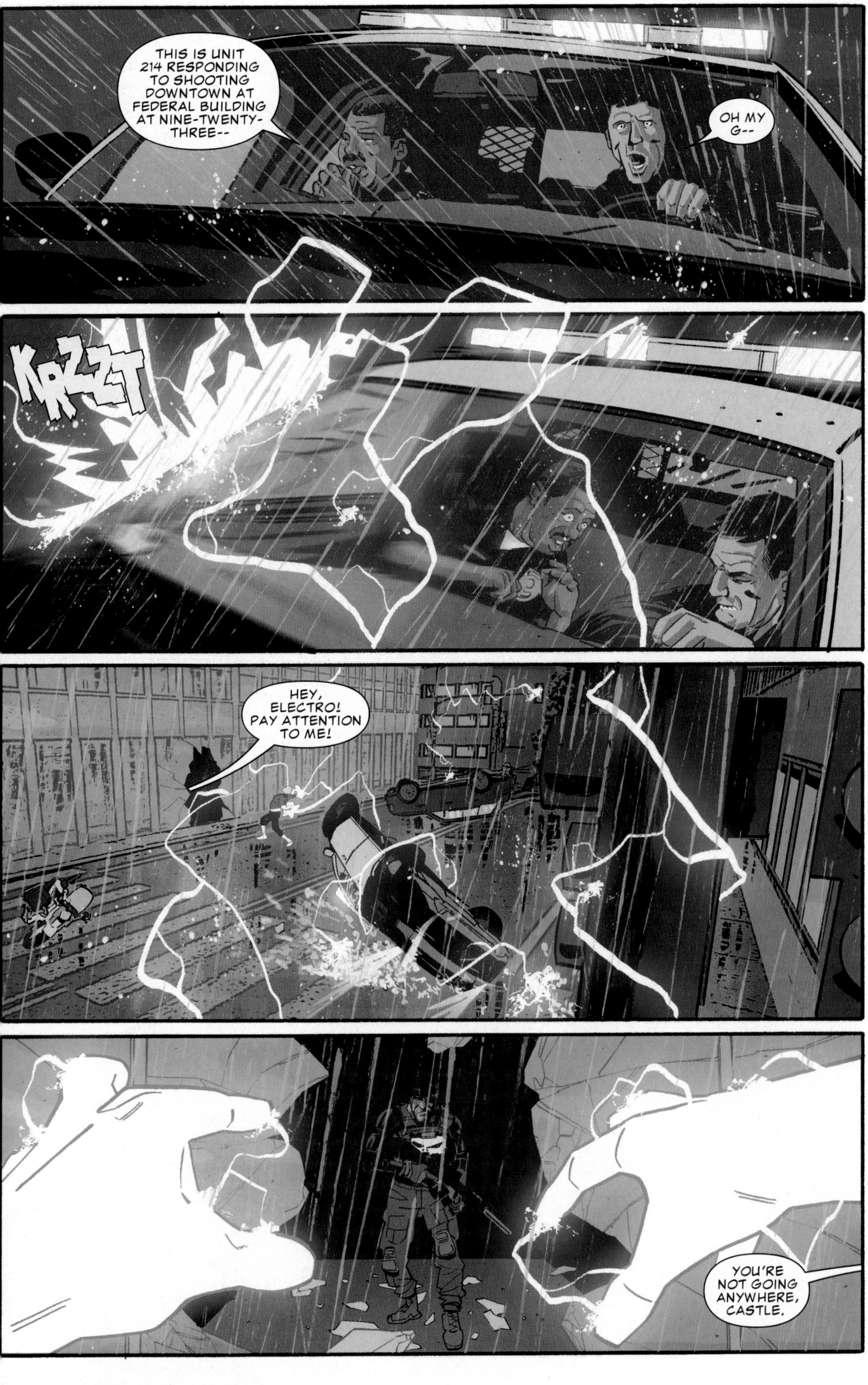
THIS IS UNIT 214 RESPONDING TO SHOOTING DOWNTOWN AT FEDERAL BUILDING AT NINE-TWENTY-THREE--
OH MY G--
KRZZT
HEY, ELECTRO! PAY ATTENTION TO ME!
YOU'RE NOT GOING ANYWHERE, CASTLE.

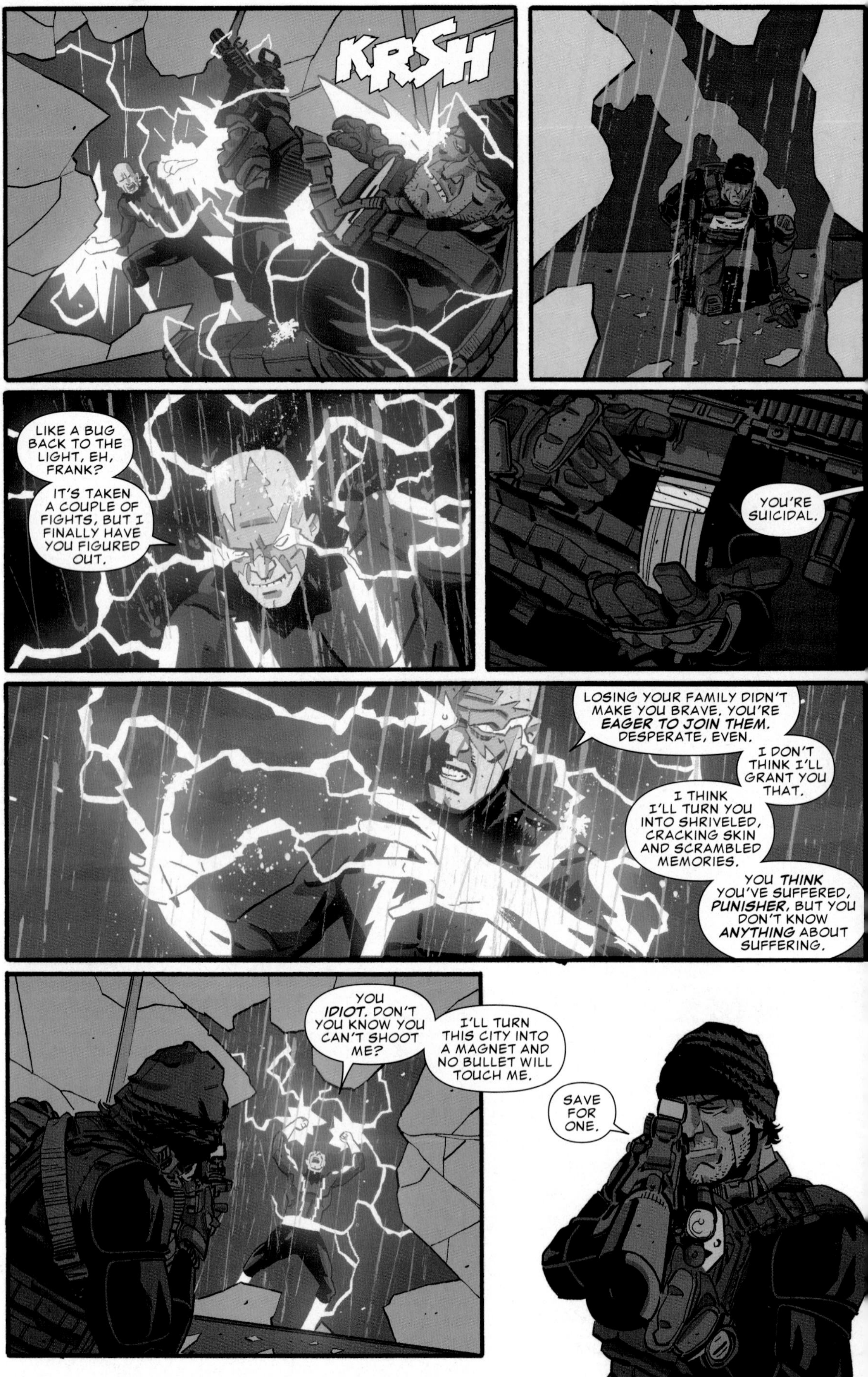
KRSH
LIKE A BUG BACK TO THE LIGHT, EH, FRANK?
IT'S TAKEN A COUPLE OF FIGHTS, BUT I FINALLY HAVE YOU FIGURED OUT.
YOU'RE SUICIDAL.
LOSING YOUR FAMILY DIDN'T MAKE YOU BRAVE. YOU'RE EAGER TO JOIN THEM. DESPERATE, EVEN.
I DON'T THINK I'LL GRANT YOU THAT.
I THINK I'LL TURN YOU INTO SHRIVELED, CRACKING SKIN AND SCRAMBLED MEMORIES.
YOU THINK YOU'VE SUFFERED, PUNISHER, BUT YOU DON'T KNOW ANYTHING ABOUT SUFFERING.
YOU IDIOT. DON'T YOU KNOW YOU CAN'T SHOOT ME?
I'LL TURN THIS CITY INTO A MAGNET AND NO BULLET WILL TOUCH ME.
SAVE FOR ONE.

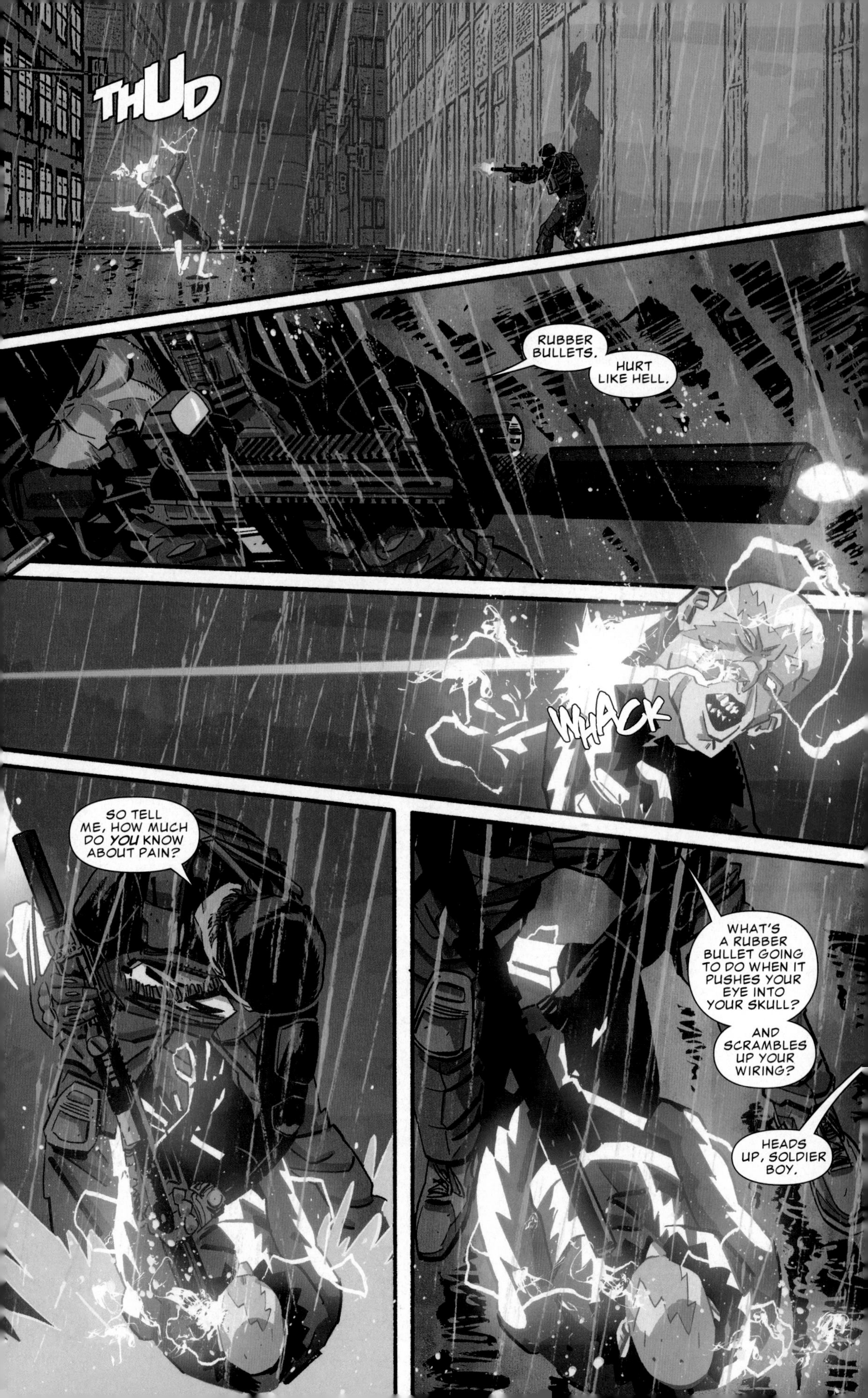
THUD
RUBBER BULLETS.
HURT LIKE HELL.
WHACK
SO TELL ME, HOW MUCH DO *YOU* KNOW ABOUT PAIN?
WHAT'S A RUBBER BULLET GOING TO DO WHEN IT PUSHES YOUR EYE INTO YOUR SKULL?
AND SCRAMBLES UP YOUR WIRING?
HEADS UP, SOLDIER BOY.

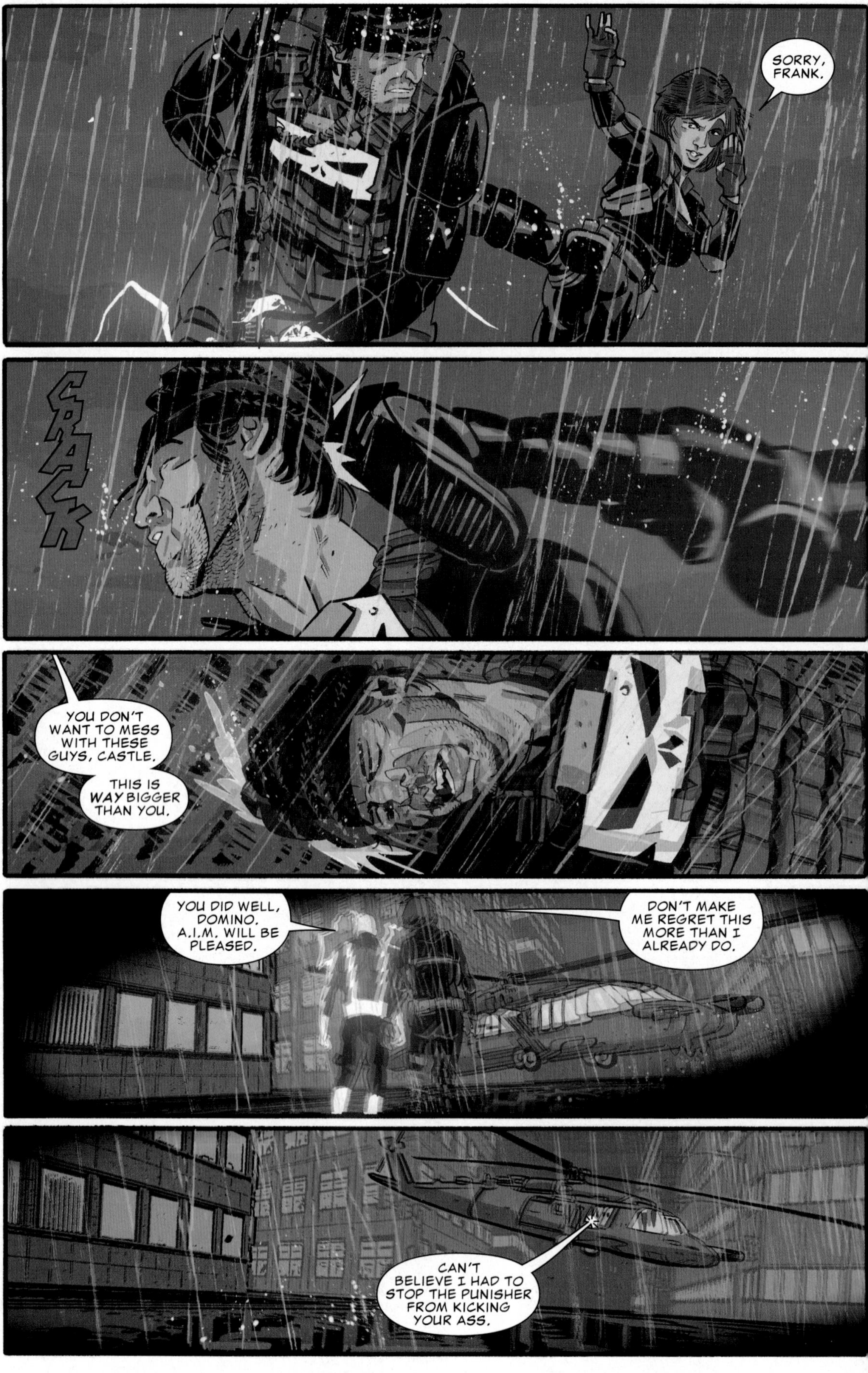
SORRY, FRANK.
CRACK
YOU DON'T WANT TO MESS WITH THESE GUYS, CASTLE.
THIS IS WAY BIGGER THAN YOU.
YOU DID WELL, DOMINO. A.I.M. WILL BE PLEASED.
DON'T MAKE ME REGRET THIS MORE THAN I ALREADY DO.
CAN'T BELIEVE I HAD TO STOP THE PUNISHER FROM KICKING YOUR ASS.

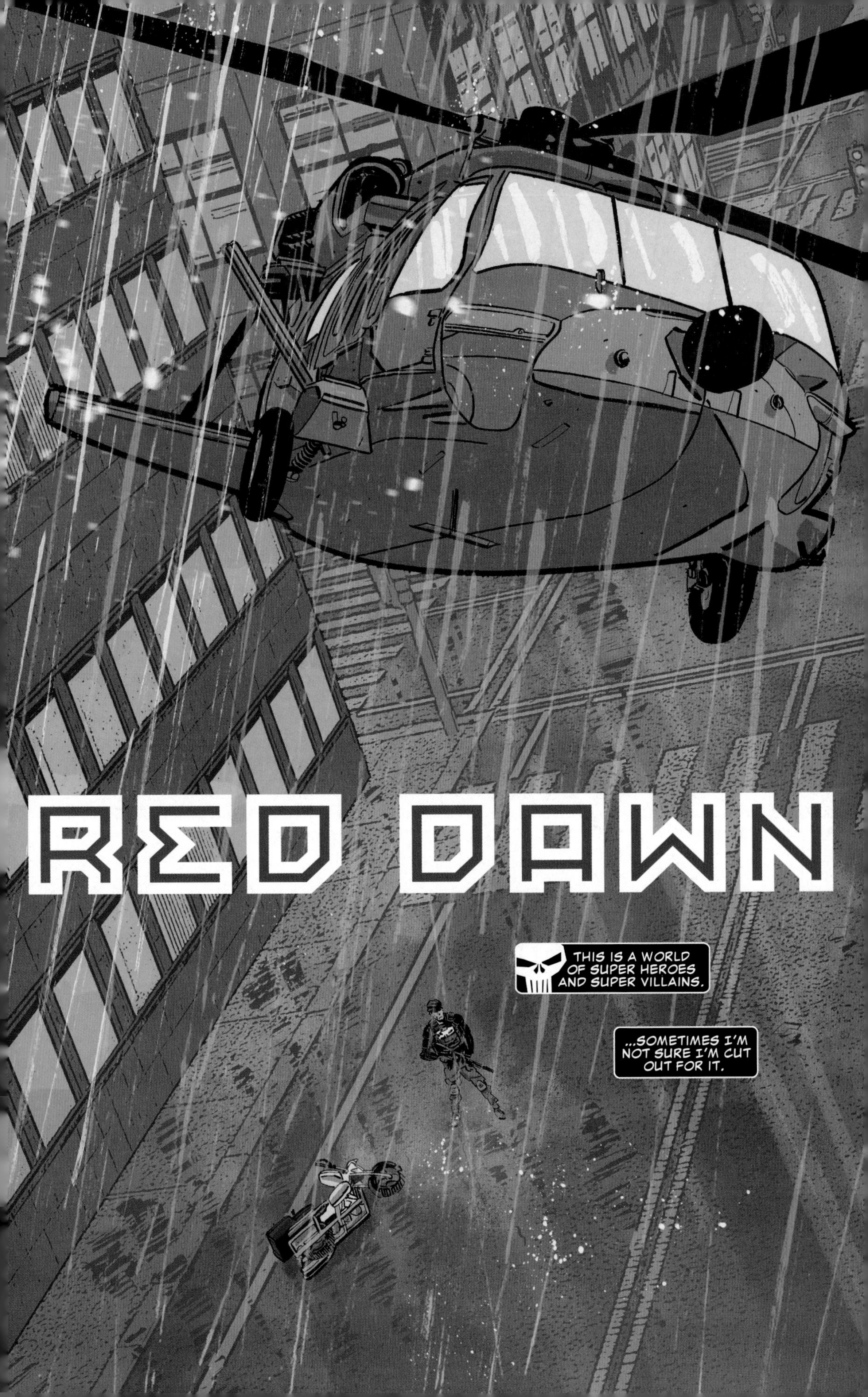
RED DAWN
THIS IS A WORLD OF SUPER HEROES AND SUPER VILLAINS.
...SOMETIMES I'M NOT SURE I'M CUT OUT FOR IT.

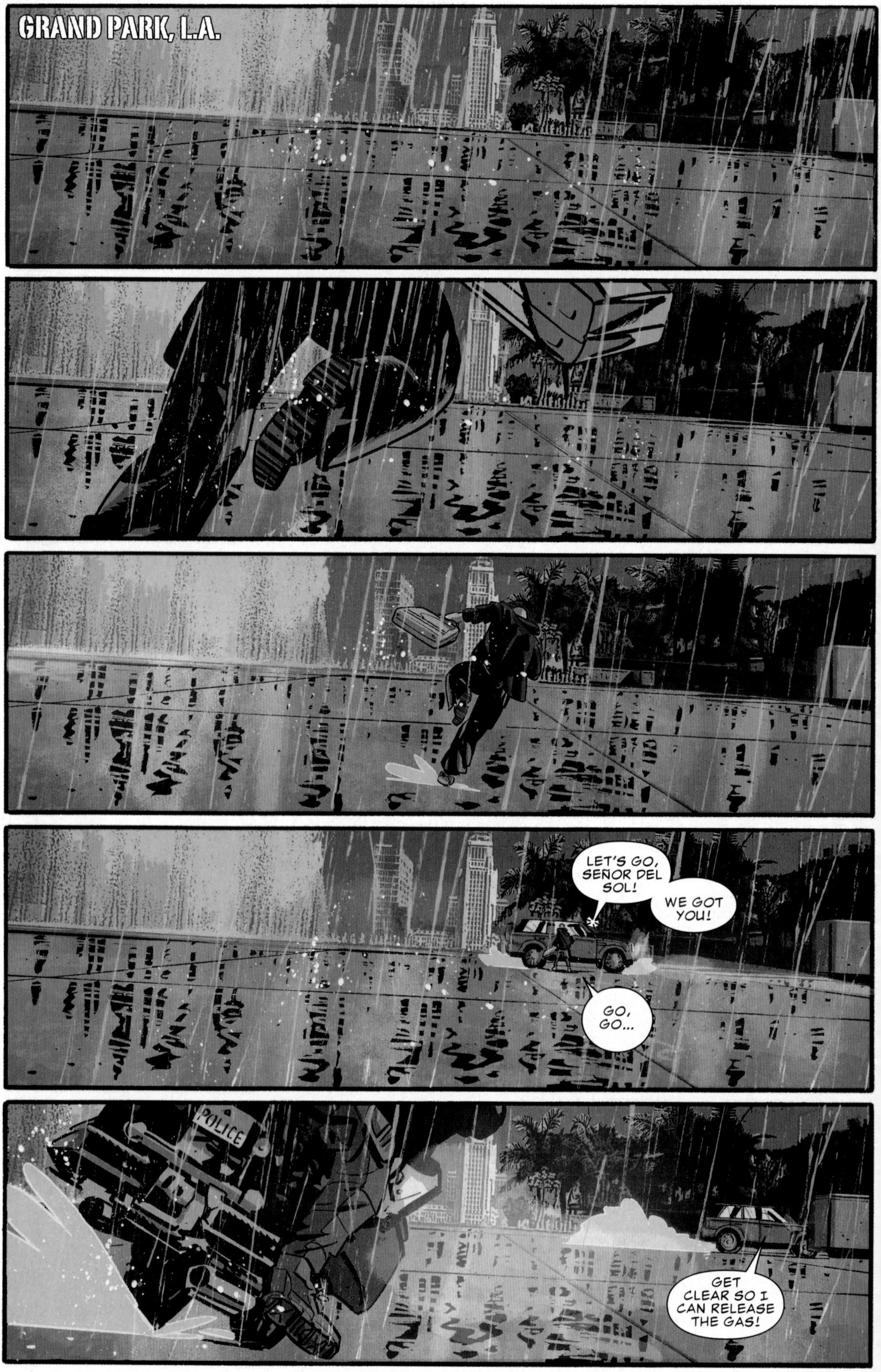
GRAND PARK, L.A.
LET'S GO, SEÑOR DEL SOL!
WE GOT YOU!
GO, GO...
POLICE
GET CLEAR SO I CAN RELEASE THE GAS!

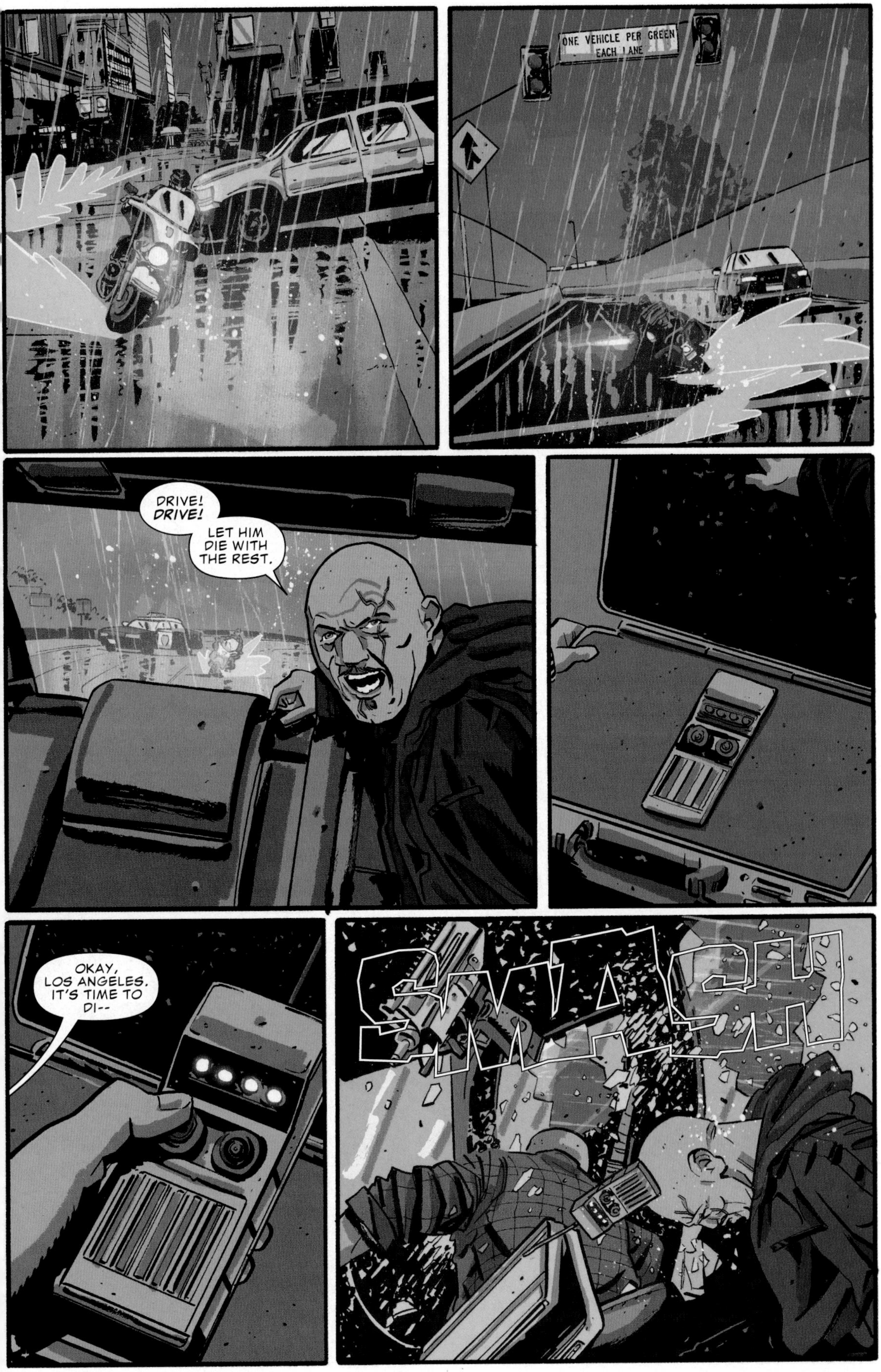
ONE VEHICLE PER GREEN
EACH LANE
DRIVE! DRIVE!
LET HIM DIE WITH THE REST.
OKAY, LOS ANGELES. IT'S TIME TO DI--
SMASH

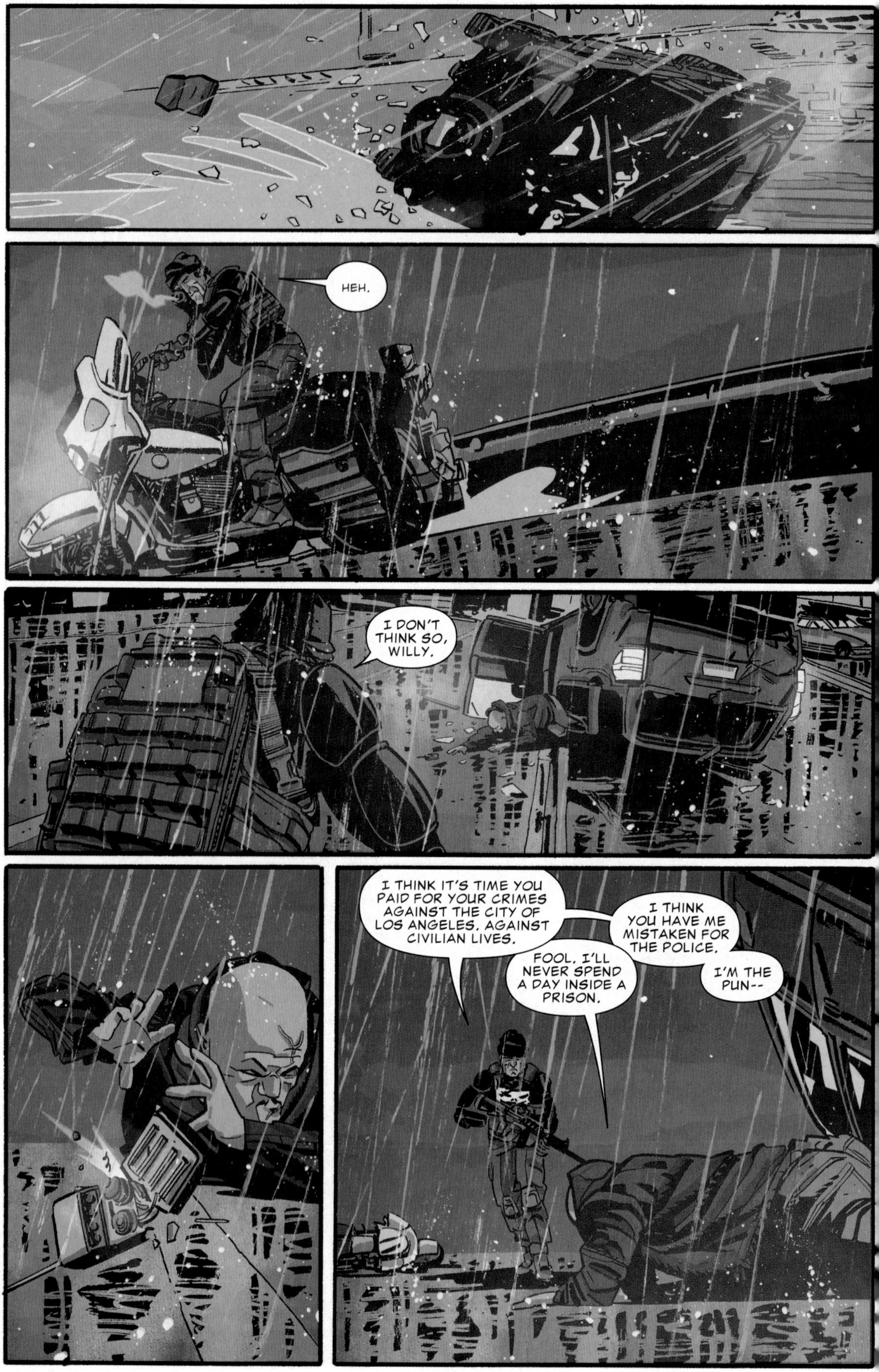
HEH.
I DON'T THINK SO, WILLY.
I THINK IT'S TIME YOU PAID FOR YOUR CRIMES AGAINST THE CITY OF LOS ANGELES. AGAINST CIVILIAN LIVES.
FOOL. I'LL NEVER SPEND A DAY INSIDE A PRISON.
I THINK YOU HAVE ME MISTAKEN FOR THE POLICE.
I'M THE PUN--

BOOM
SOUTH

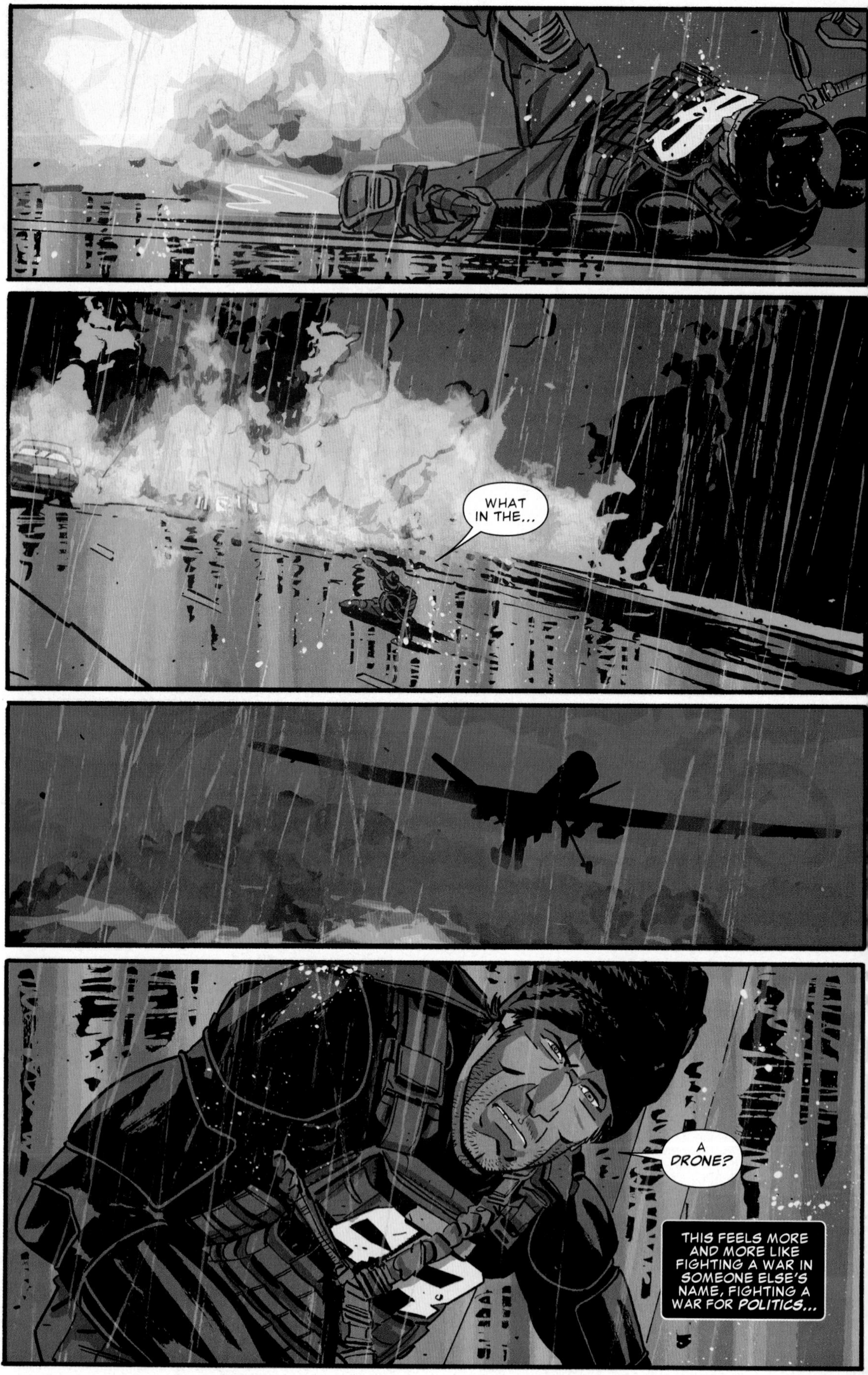
WHAT IN THE...
A DRONE?
THIS FEELS MORE AND MORE LIKE FIGHTING A WAR IN SOMEONE ELSE'S NAME, FIGHTING A WAR FOR POLITICS...

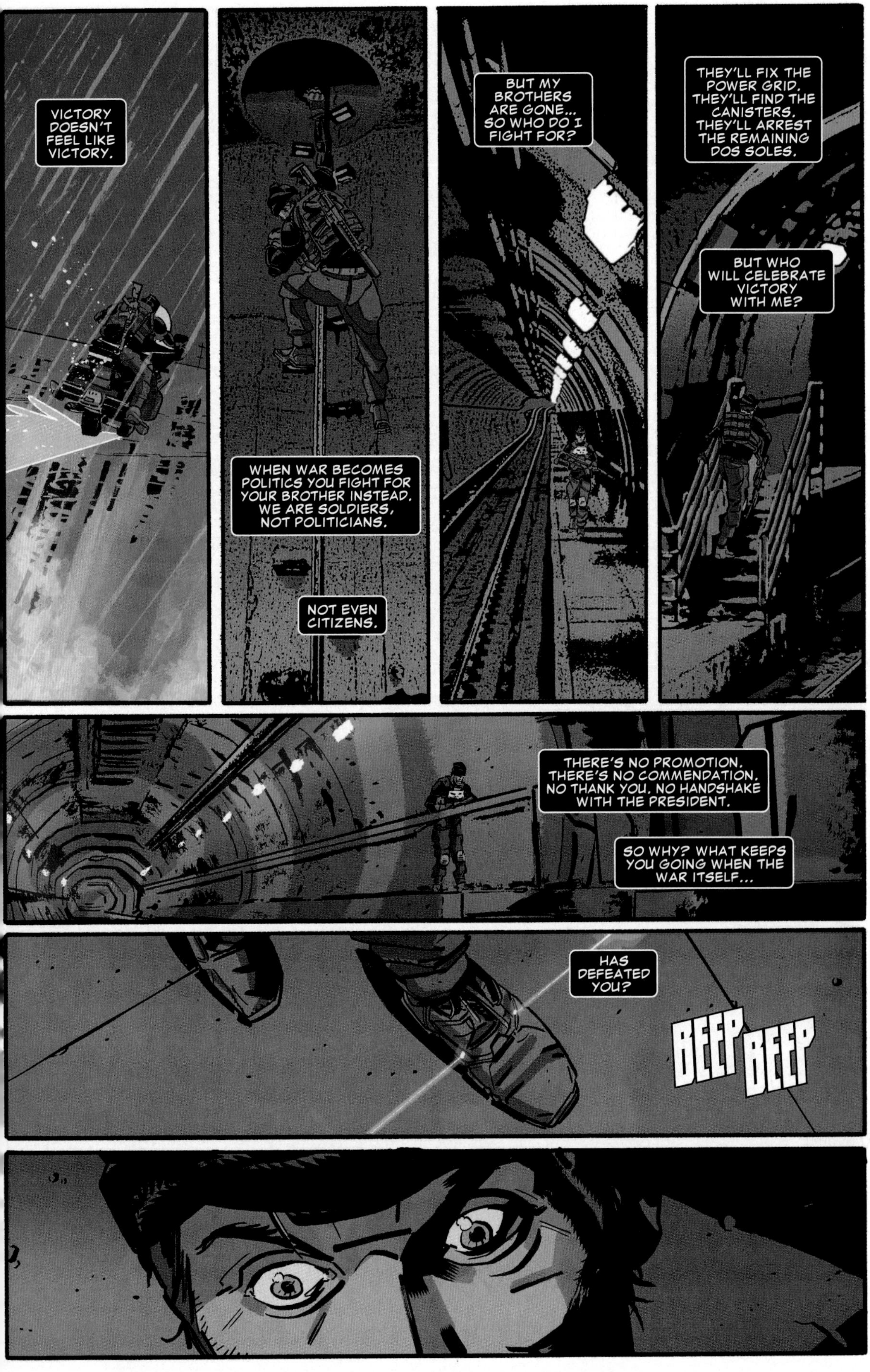
VICTORY DOESN'T FEEL LIKE VICTORY.
WHEN WAR BECOMES POLITICS YOU FIGHT FOR YOUR BROTHER INSTEAD. WE ARE SOLDIERS, NOT POLITICIANS.
NOT EVEN CITIZENS.
BUT MY BROTHERS ARE GONE... SO WHO DO I FIGHT FOR?
THEY'LL FIX THE POWER GRID. THEY'LL FIND THE CANISTERS. THEY'LL ARREST THE REMAINING DOS SOLES.
BUT WHO WILL CELEBRATE VICTORY WITH ME?
THERE'S NO PROMOTION. THERE'S NO COMMENDATION. NO THANK YOU. NO HANDSHAKE WITH THE PRESIDENT.
SO WHY? WHAT KEEPS YOU GOING WHEN THE WAR ITSELF...
HAS DEFEATED YOU?
BEEP BEEP

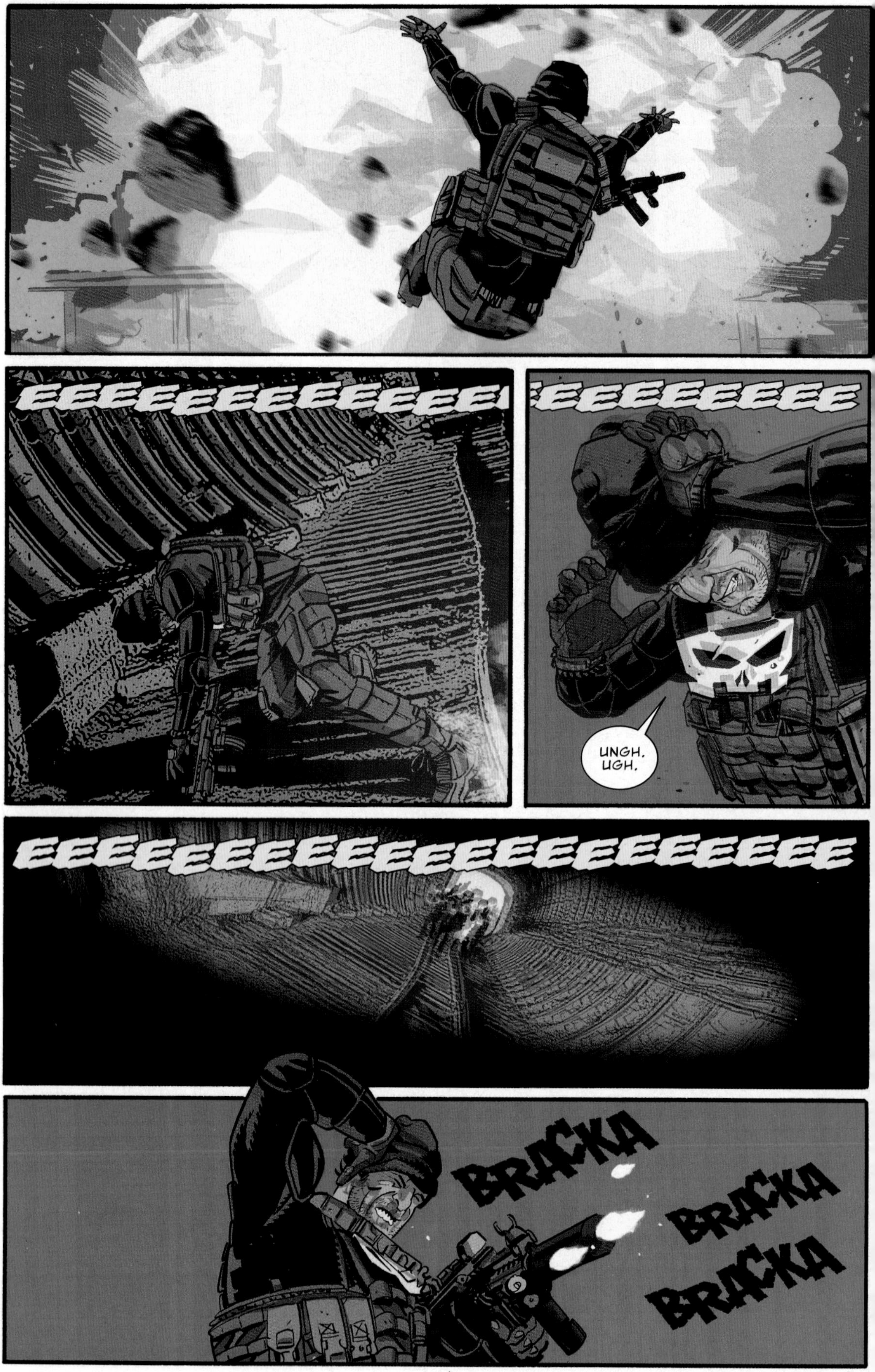

EEEEEEEEEEEEEEE
EEEEEEEEEEEE
UNGH. UGH.
EEEEEEEEEEEEEEEEEEEEEEEE
BRACKA
BRACKA
BRACKA

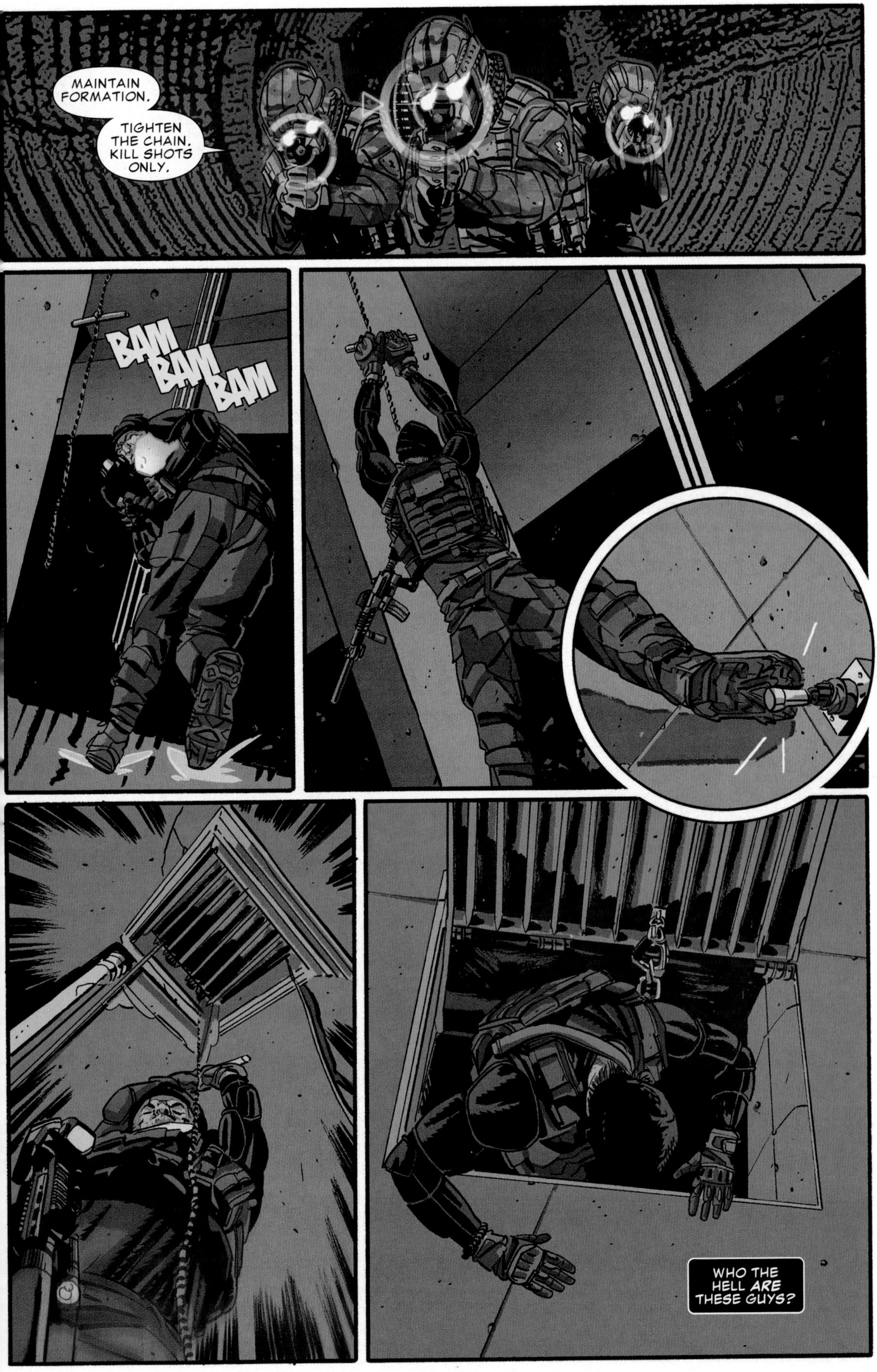
MAINTAIN FORMATION.
TIGHTEN THE CHAIN. KILL SHOTS ONLY.
BAM BAM BAM
WHO THE HELL *ARE* THESE GUYS?

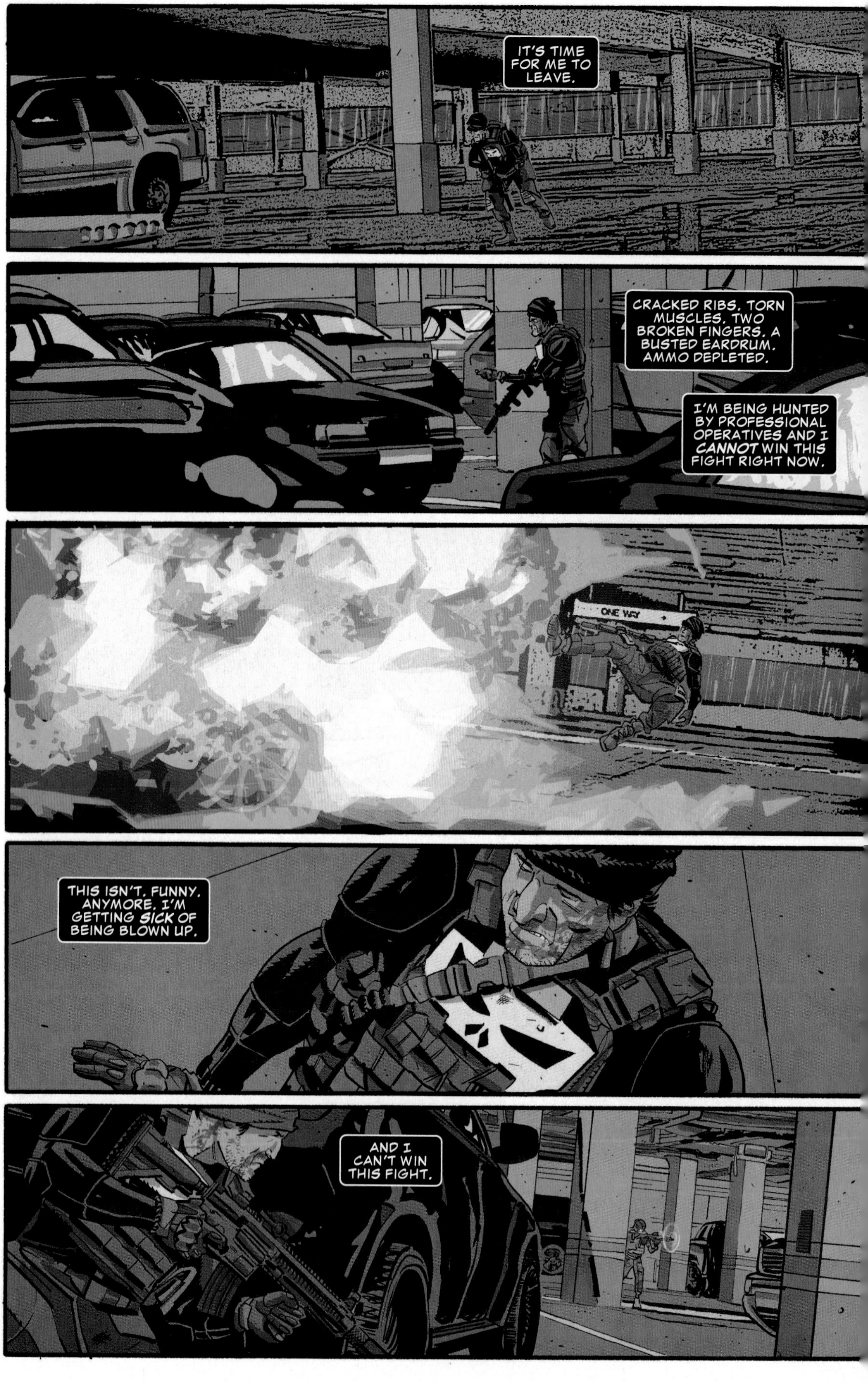
IT'S TIME FOR ME TO LEAVE.
CRACKED RIBS. TORN MUSCLES. TWO BROKEN FINGERS. A BUSTED EARDRUM. AMMO DEPLETED.
I'M BEING HUNTED BY PROFESSIONAL OPERATIVES AND I CANNOT WIN THIS FIGHT RIGHT NOW.
ONE WAY
THIS ISN'T. FUNNY. ANYMORE. I'M GETTING SICK OF BEING BLOWN UP.
AND I CAN'T WIN THIS FIGHT.

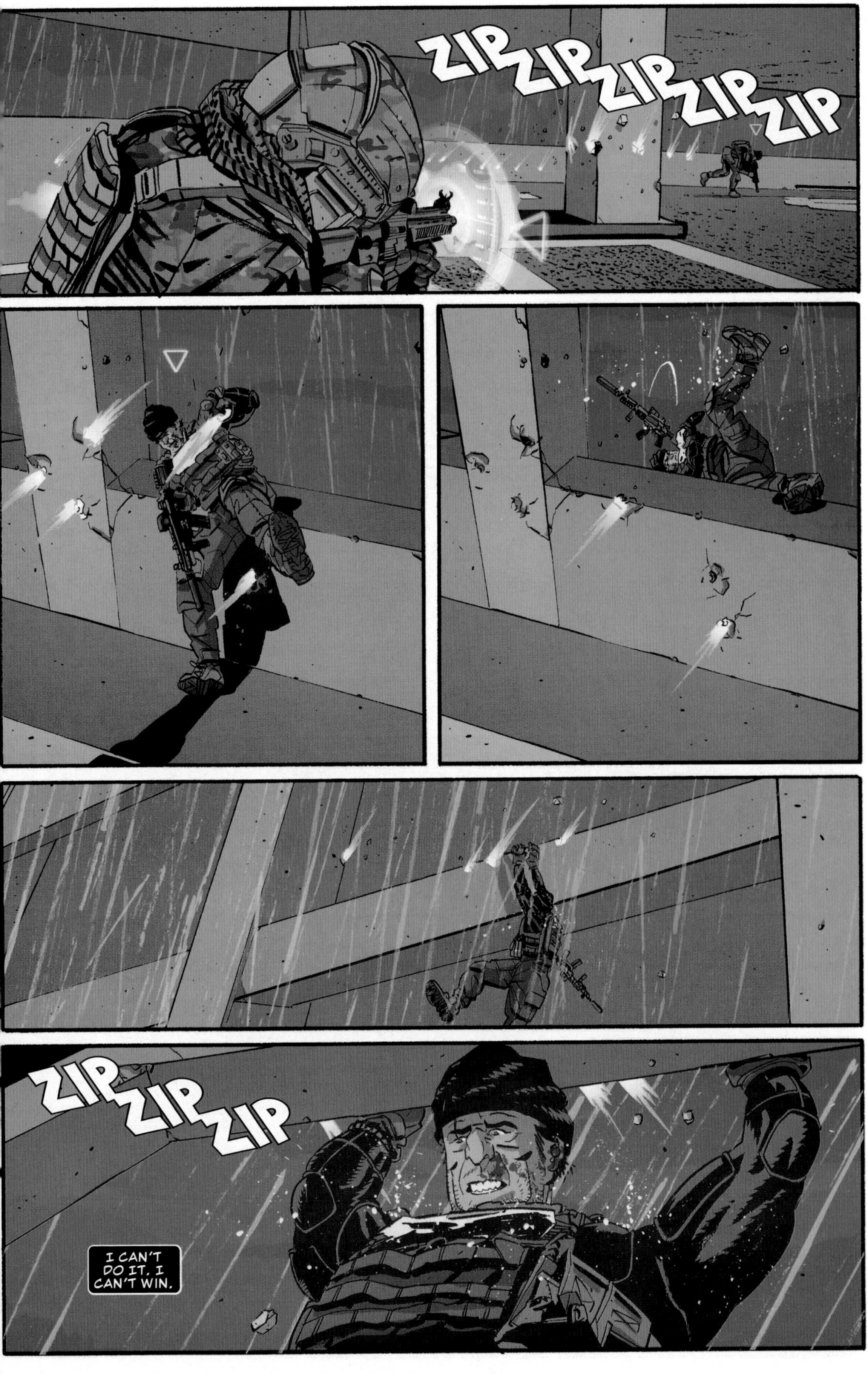
ZIP ZIP ZIP ZIP ZIP
ZIP ZIP ZIP
I CAN'T DO IT. I CAN'T WIN.

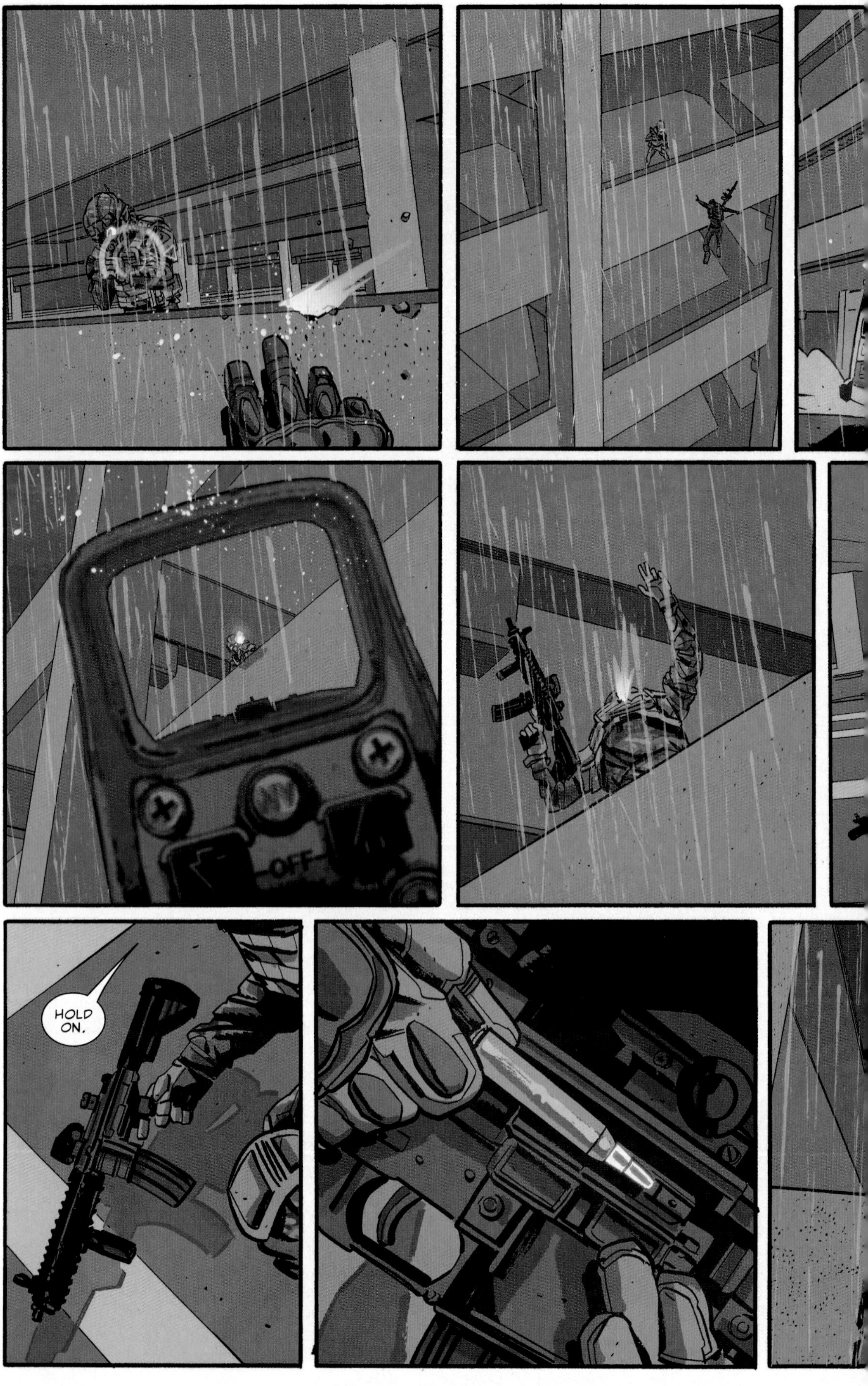
HOLD ON.

YOU OKAY, COMMANDO?

FINE. GET ME UP.

ROGER, BUT HE'S GETTING AWAY.

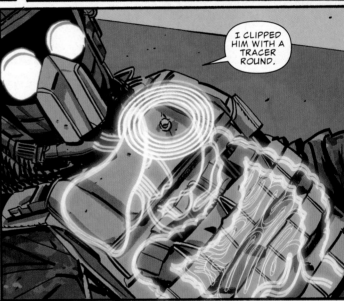

I CLIPPED HIM WITH A TRACER ROUND.

HAVEN'T BEEN KNOCKED ON MY ASS IN A FIGHT IN A LONG TIME.

OH, I DON'T THINK SO, SIDEWINDER.

MAYBE YOU'RE GETTING SLOW, RUBY RED.

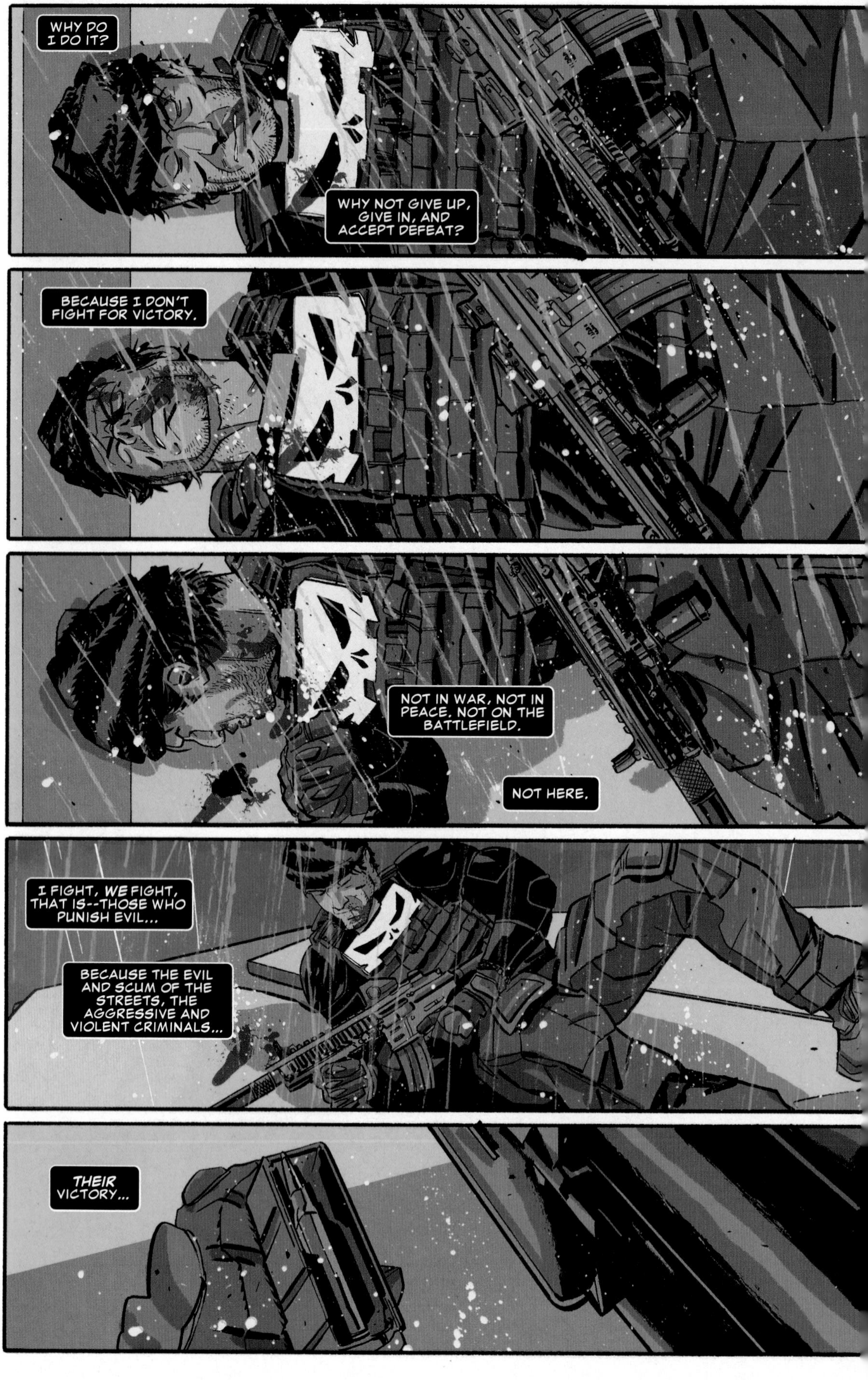
WHY DO I DO IT?
WHY NOT GIVE UP, GIVE IN, AND ACCEPT DEFEAT?
BECAUSE I DON'T FIGHT FOR VICTORY.
NOT IN WAR, NOT IN PEACE. NOT ON THE BATTLEFIELD.
NOT HERE.
I FIGHT, WE FIGHT, THAT IS--THOSE WHO PUNISH EVIL...
BECAUSE THE EVIL AND SCUM OF THE STREETS, THE AGGRESSIVE AND VIOLENT CRIMINALS...
THEIR VICTORY...

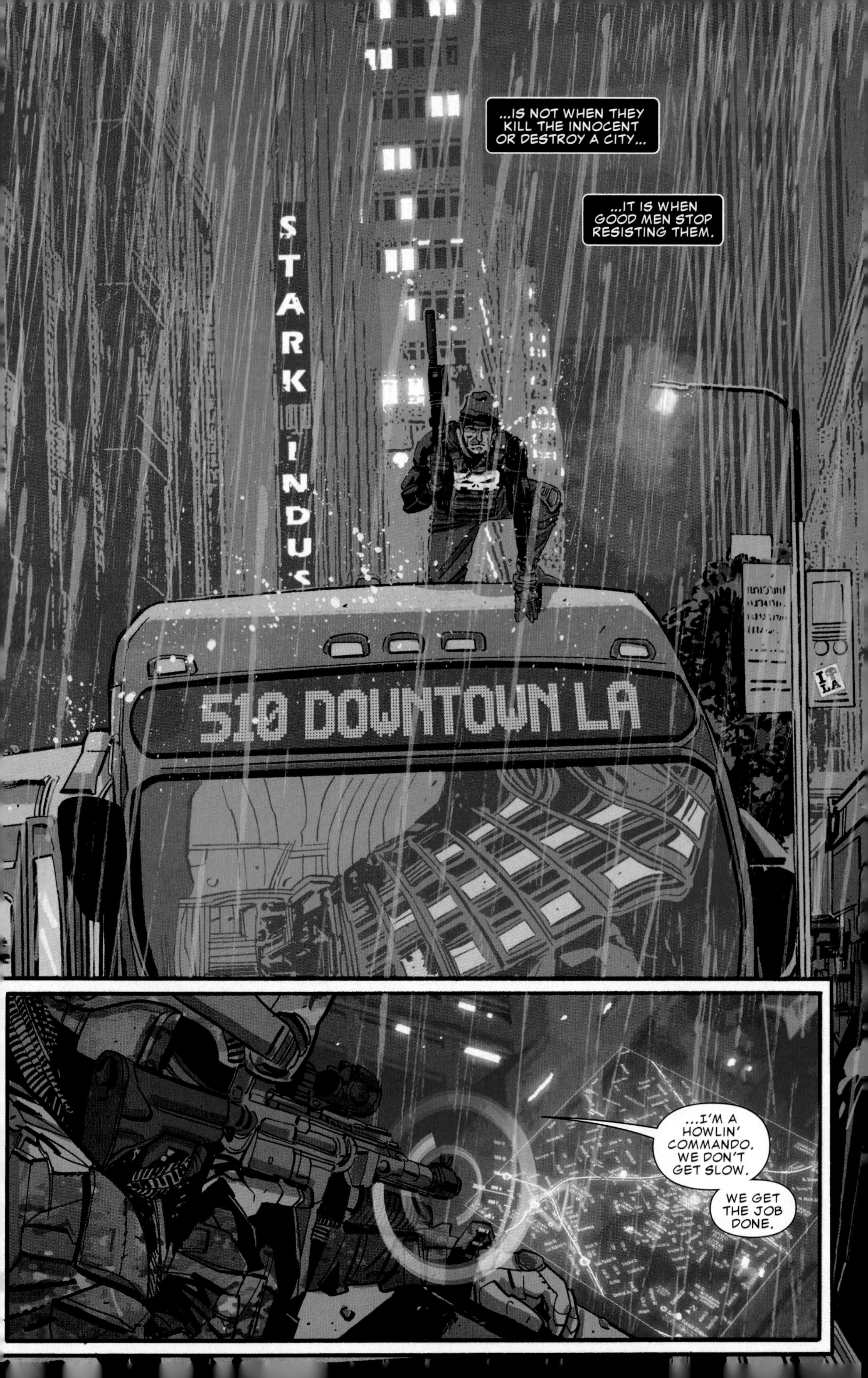
...IS NOT WHEN THEY KILL THE INNOCENT OR DESTROY A CITY...
...IT IS WHEN GOOD MEN STOP RESISTING THEM.
STARK INDUS
510 DOWNTOWN LA
...I'M A HOWLIN' COMMANDO. WE DON'T GET SLOW.
WE GET THE JOB DONE.

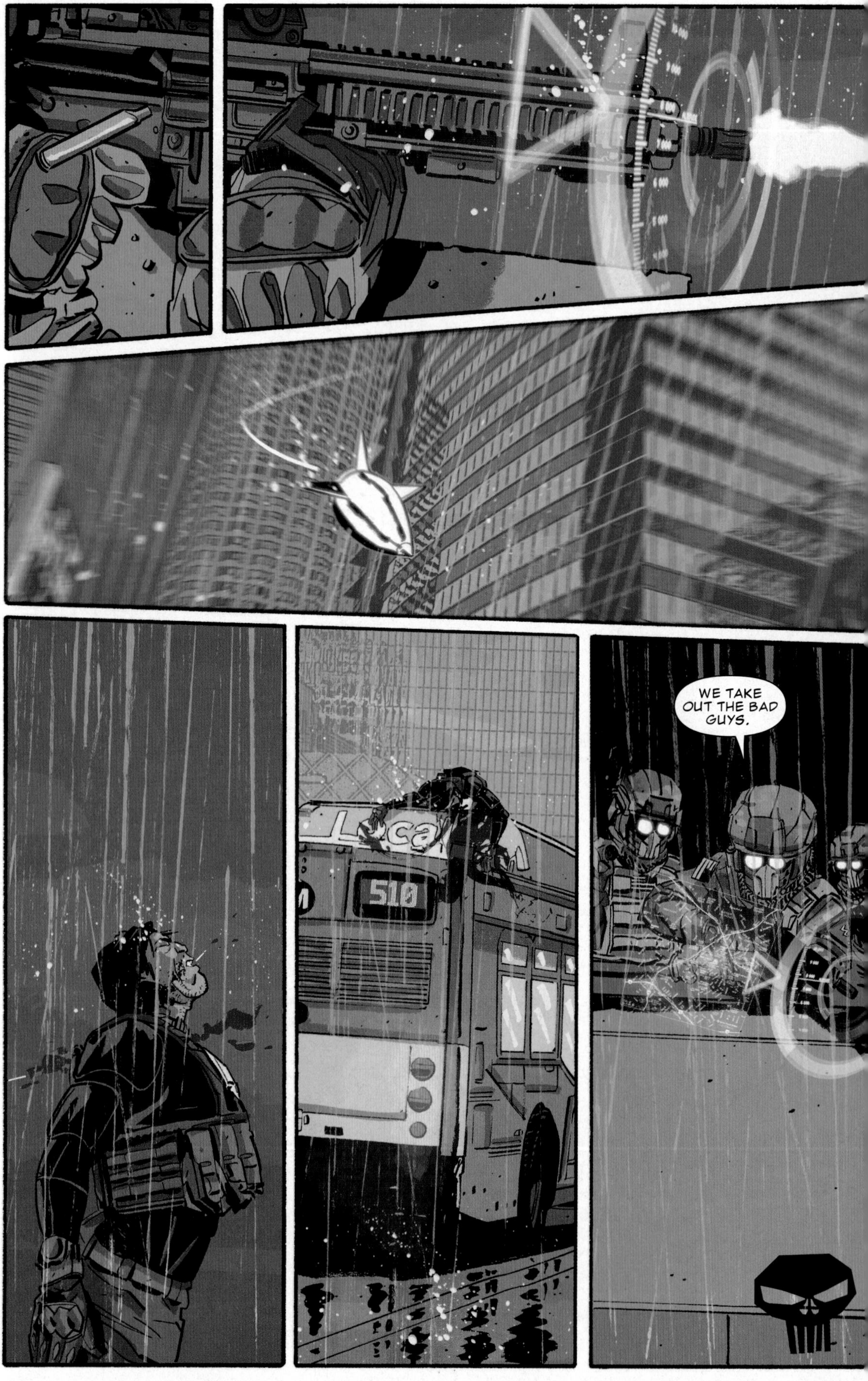
WE TAKE OUT THE BAD GUYS.

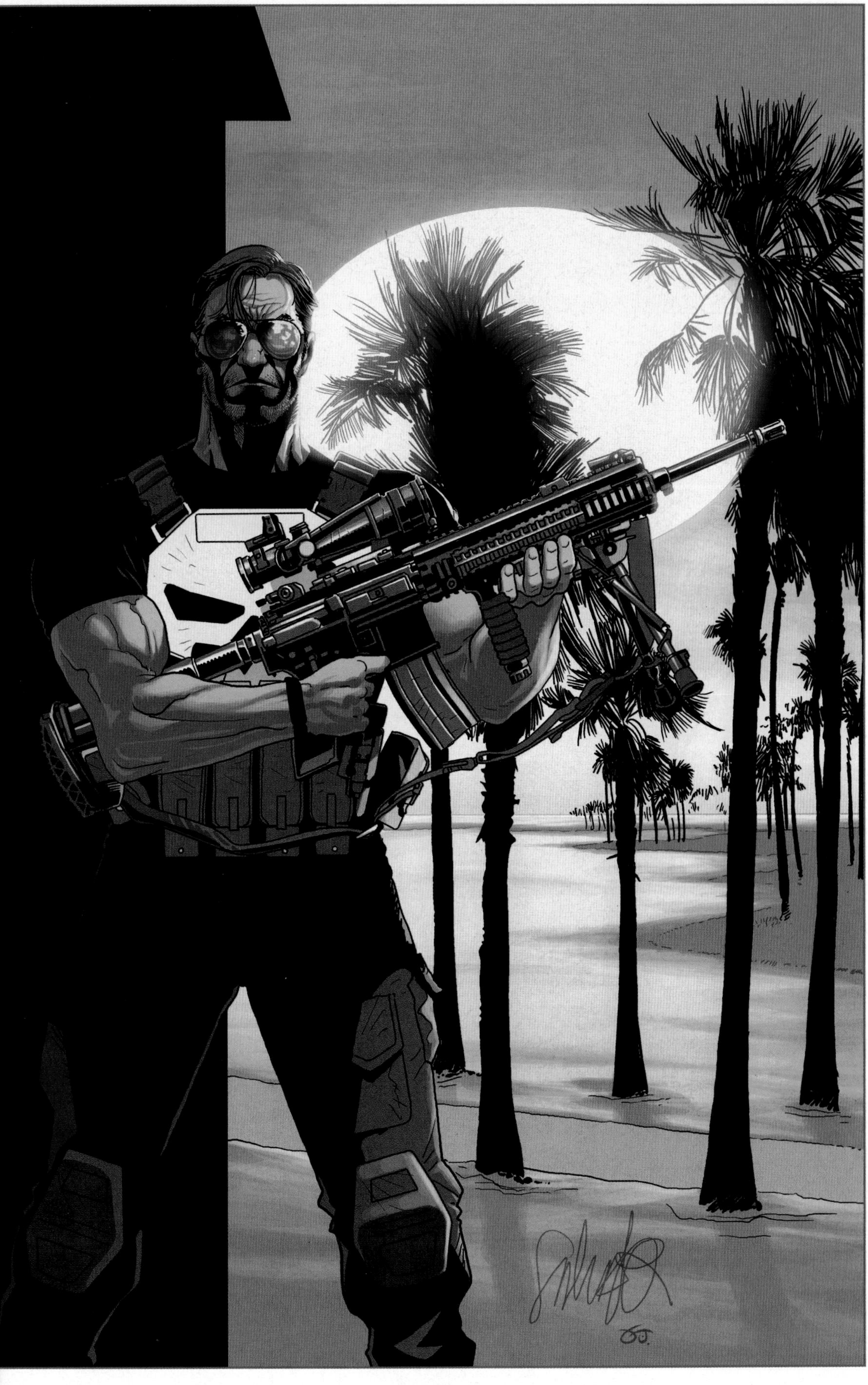

PUNISHER #1 VARIANT BY SALVADOR LARROCA & FRANK MARTIN

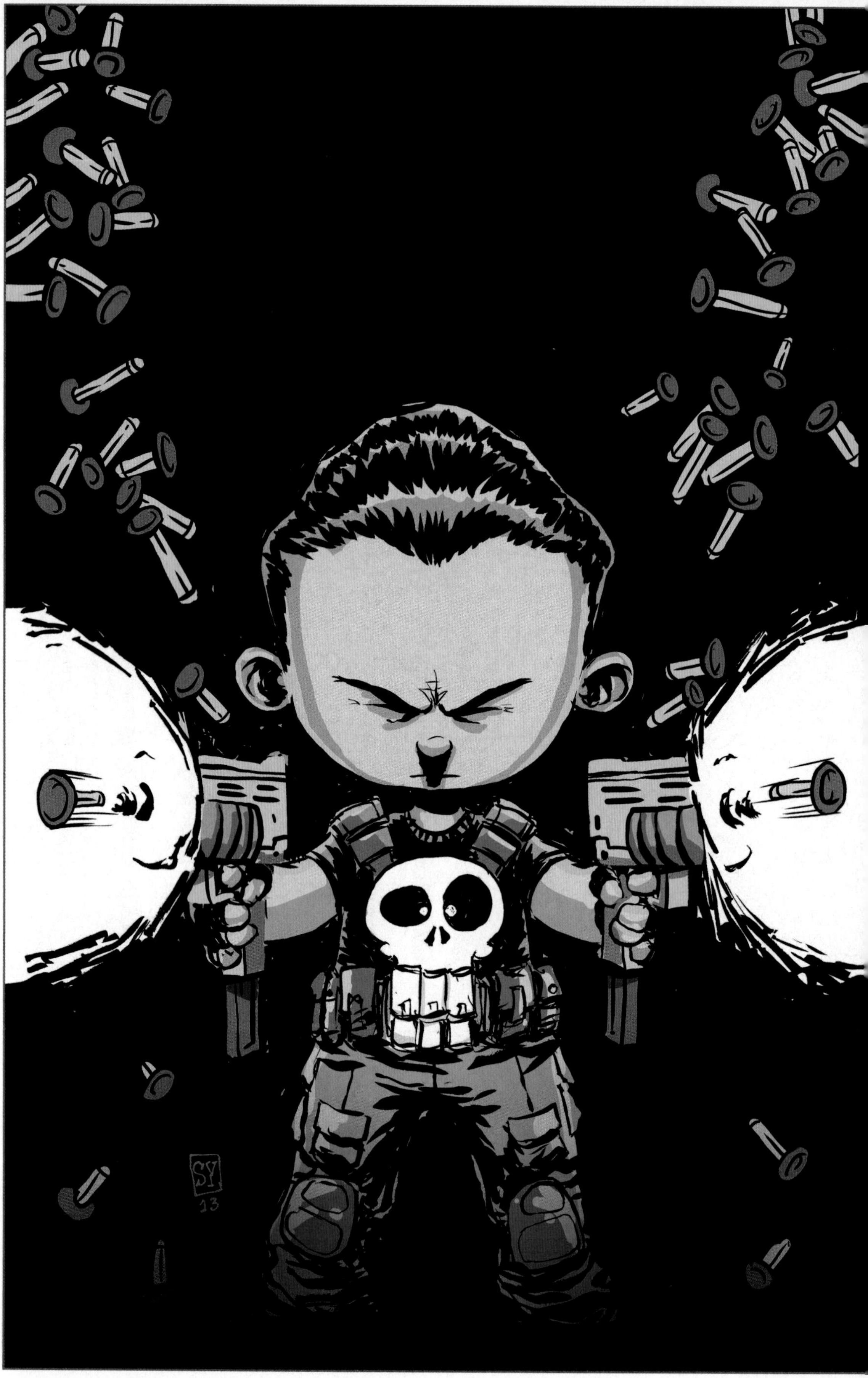
SY
13

PUNISHER #1 VARIANT BY SKOTTIE YOUNG

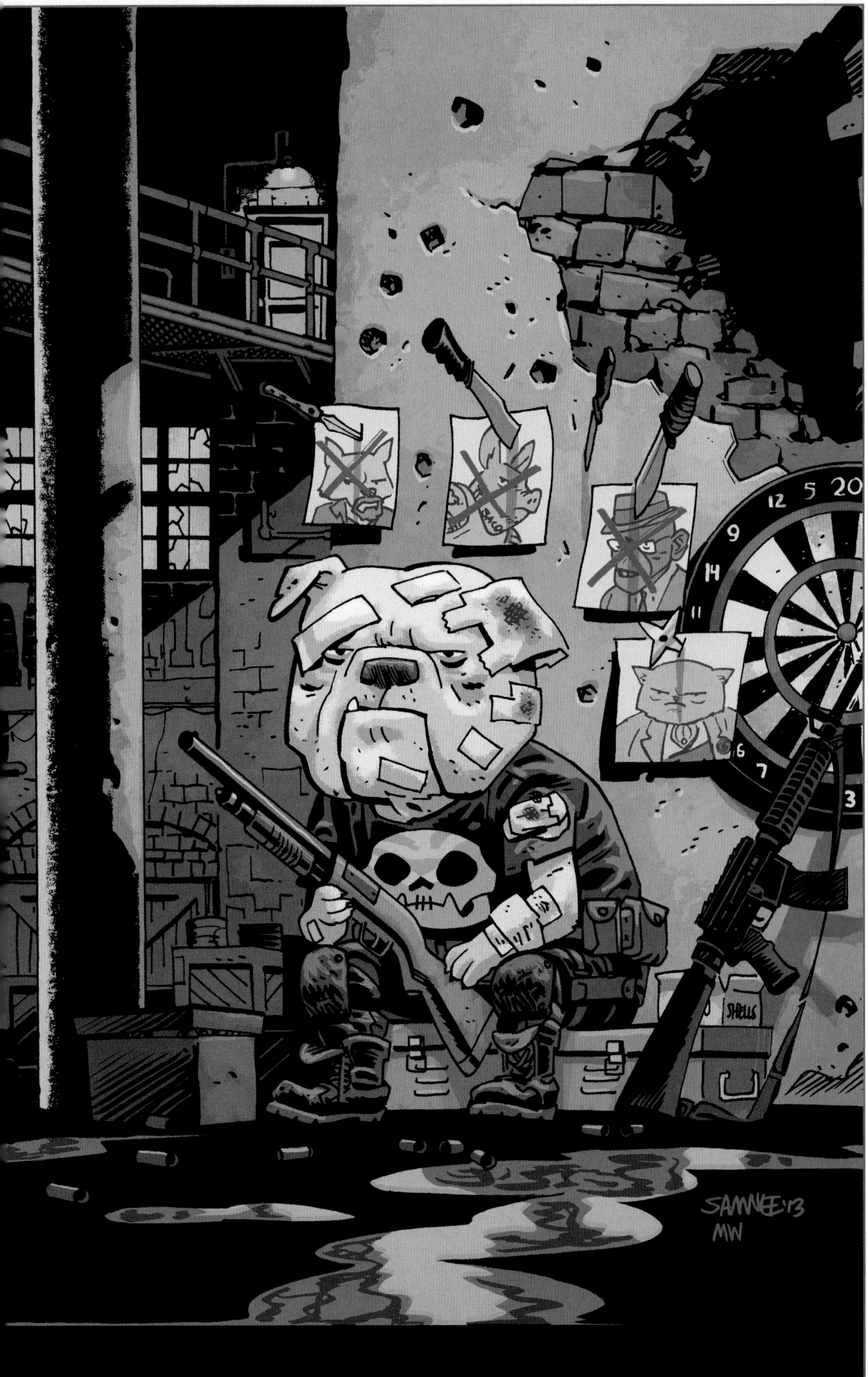
SHELLS
SAMNEE '13
MW

PUNISHER #1 ANIMAL VARIANT BY CHRIS SAMNEE & MATT WILSON

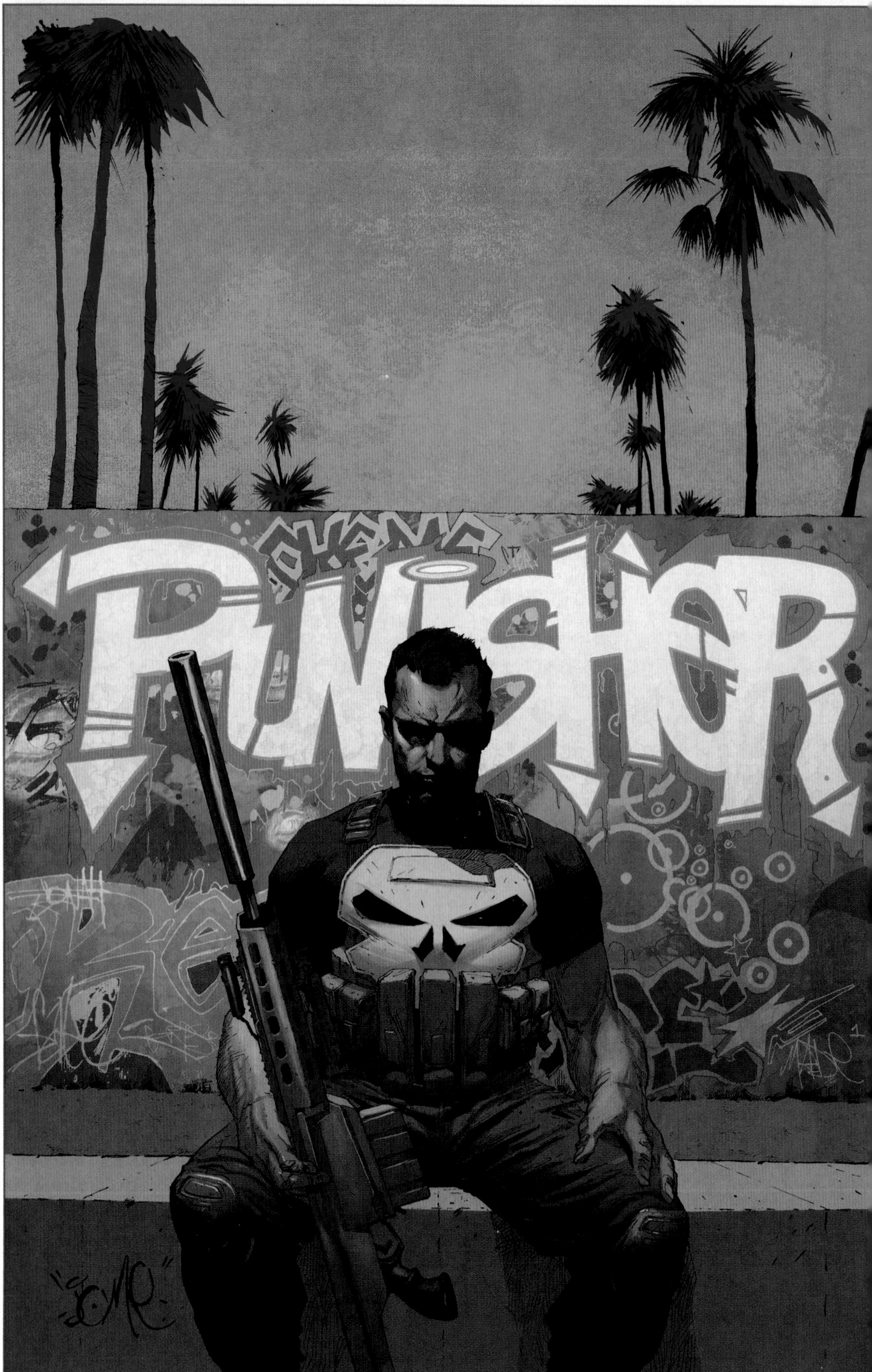

PUNISHER #2 VARIANT BY JEROME OPEÑA & FRANK MARTIN

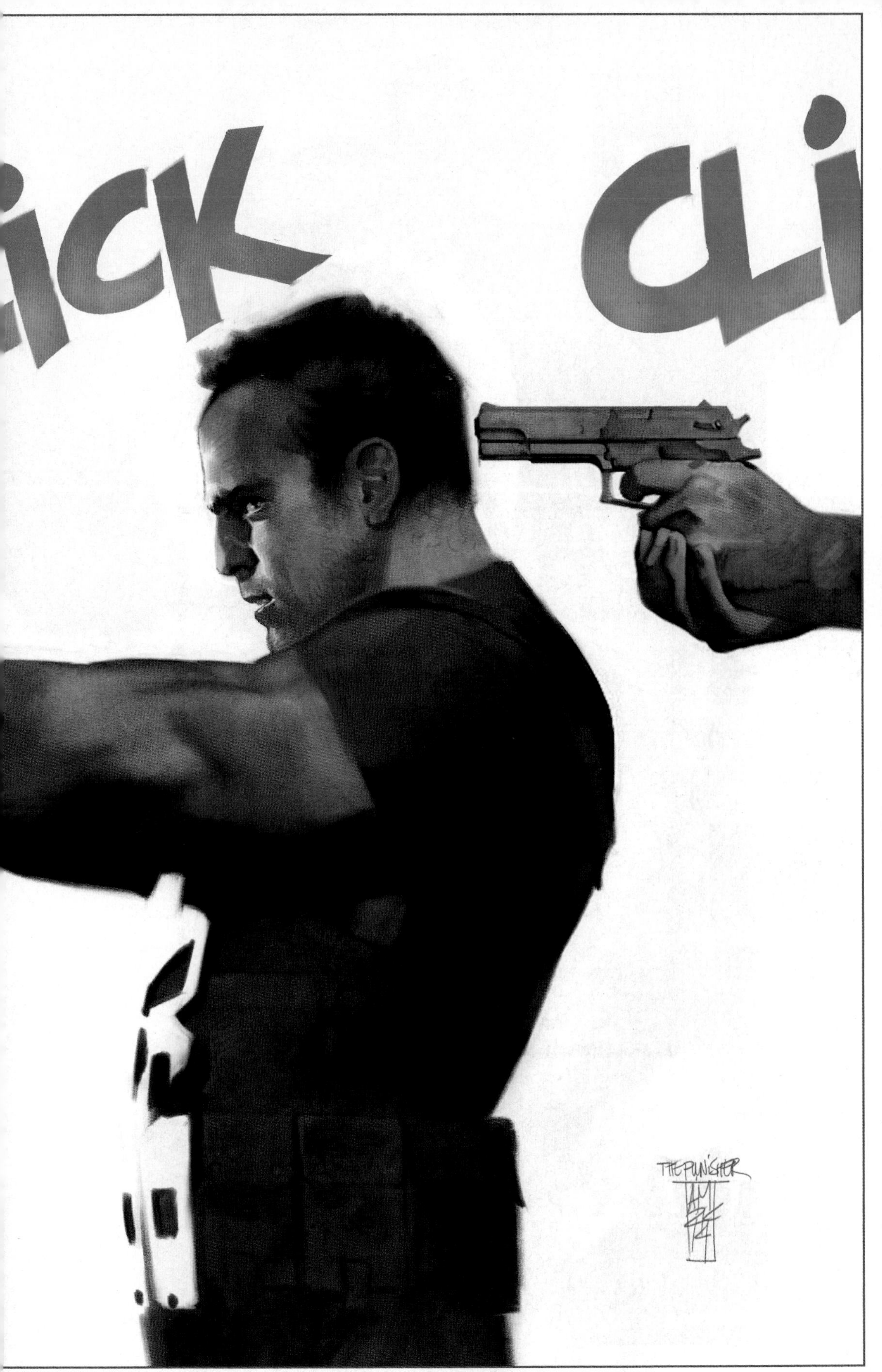
ICK
CLI
THE PUNISHER

PUNISHER #3 VARIANT BY ALEX MALEEV

PUNISHER CHARACTER SKETCH BY MITCH GERADS

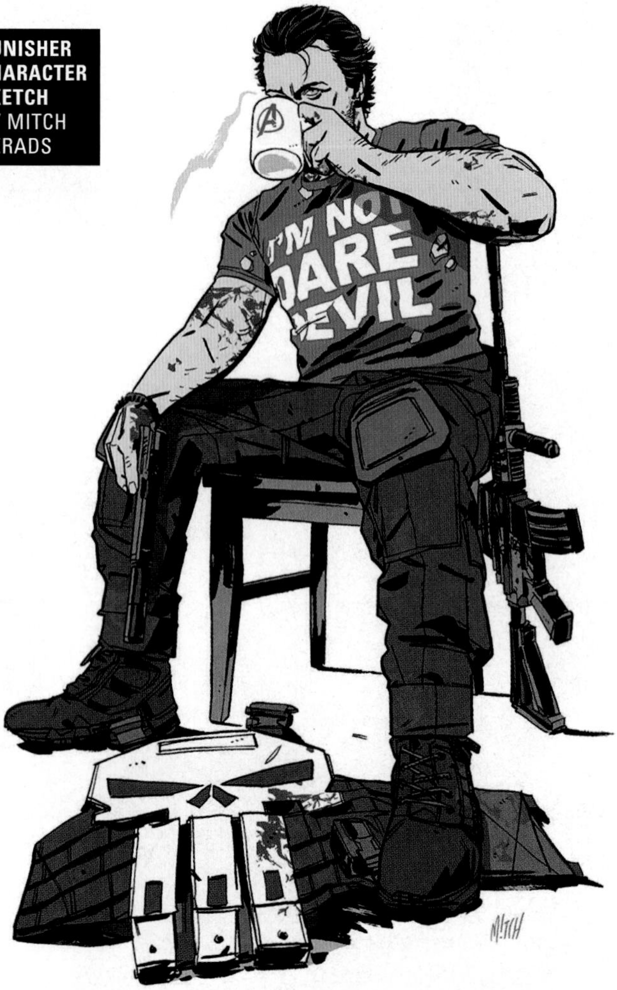
MITCH

PUNISHER ADAPTIVE VEST SYSTEM BY MITCH GERADS

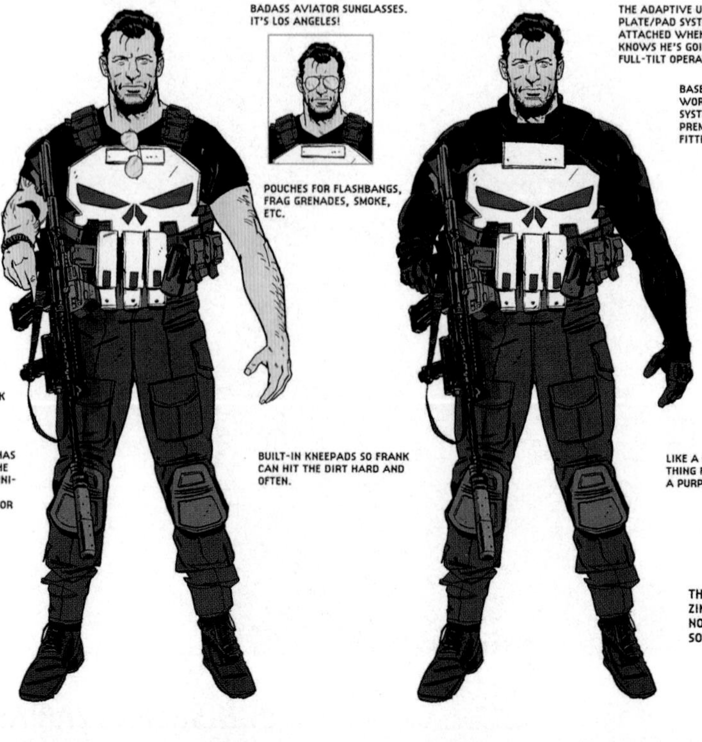
THE PUNISHER COSTUME IS ADAPTIVE FOR THE SITUATION WITH THE PLATE CARRIER/VEST AS THE CONSTANT CORE.
BIG BOLD SKULL CUSTOM BUILT INTO THE PLATE CARRIER.
THE THREE-TIER MAGAZINE POUCH DOUBLES AS THE SKULL "TEETH".
EVERY BIT OF GEAR FRANK WEARS IS BASED ON ACTUAL MODERN SPECIAL OPERATIONS KIT AND OUTFITTING.
SIDEARM MAG-CLIPPED TO THE PLATE CARRIER.
POUCH ATTACHED TO THE BACK OF THE PLATE CARRIER FOR MISC. ITEMS.
THE PLATE CARRIER/VEST HAS THE ESSENTIALS OF WHAT HE NEEDS, BUT KEPT FAIRLY MINIMAL IN CASE HE NEEDS TO THROW A JACKET ON TOP FOR CONCEALMENT.
BADASS AVIATOR SUNGLASSES. IT'S LOS ANGELES!
POUCHES FOR FLASHBANGS, FRAG GRENADES, SMOKE, ETC.
BUILT-IN KNEEPADS SO FRANK CAN HIT THE DIRT HARD AND OFTEN.
THE ADAPTIVE UPPER-BODY PLATE/PAD SYSTEM IS ATTACHED WHEN FRANK KNOWS HE'S GOING INTO A FULL-TILT OPERATION.
BASED OFF AN ACTUAL REAL-WORLD, STILL IN-DEVELOPMENT KIT SYSTEM FROM CRYE PRECISION. THE PREMIER SPECIAL OPERATIONS OUTFITTER. (INSIDER COOL!)
HARD-KNUCKLED TACTICAL GLOVES FOR WHEN FRANK GETS A LITTLE MORE...HANDS-ON.
LIKE A REAL SOLDIER, EVERYTHING FRANK IS WEARING HAS A PURPOSE.
THIS BOOK IS THE "HANS ZIMMER SCORED" PUNISHER, NOT THE "SLIPKNOT SOUNDTRACK" PUNISHER.
- MITCH

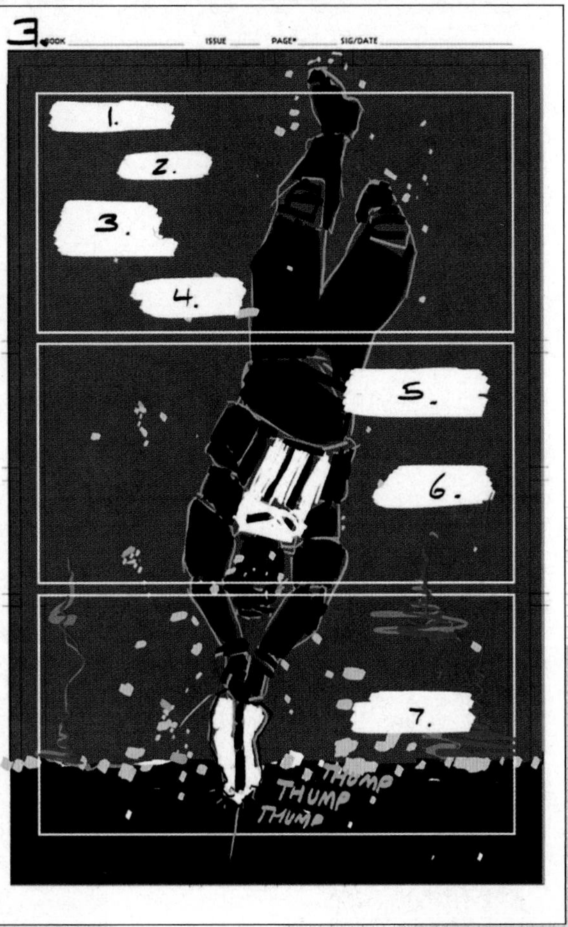
3.
1.
2.
3.
4.
5.
6.
7.
THUMP
THUMP
THUMP

PUNISHER #1
PAGE 03 LAYOUTS
BY MITCH GERADS

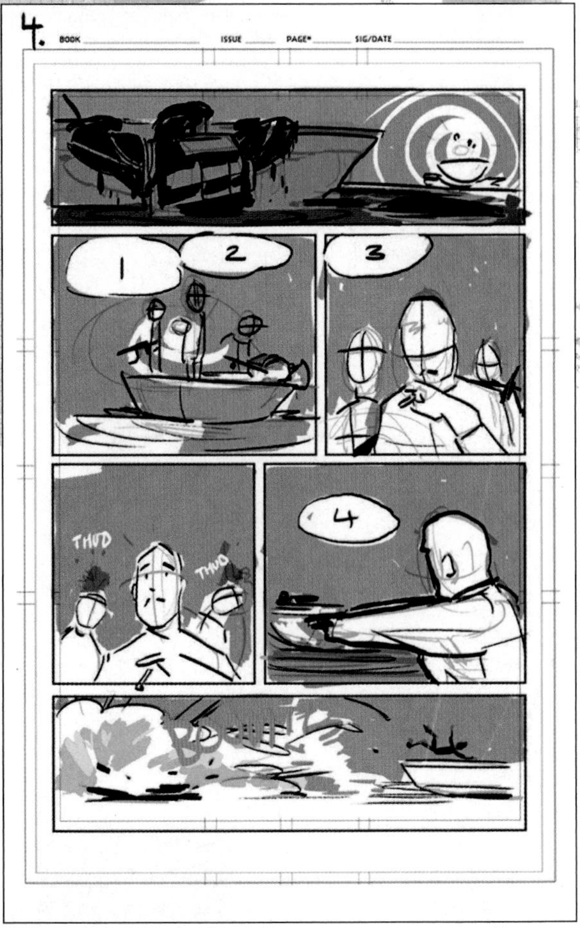
4.
1
2
3
THUD
THUD
4

PUNISHER #1
PAGE 04 LAYOUTS
BY MITCH GERADS

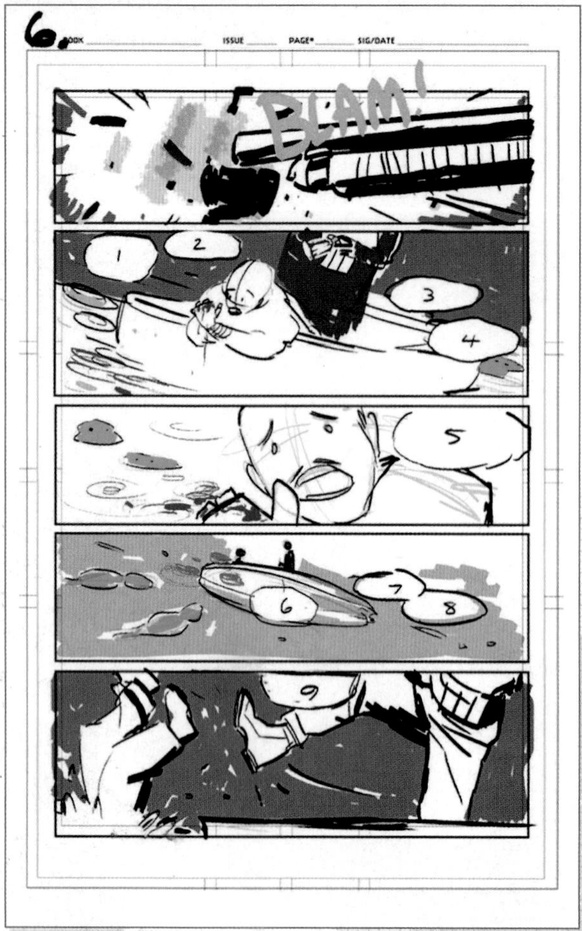
6.
BLAM!

PUNISHER #1
PAGE 06 LAYOUTS
BY MITCH GERADS

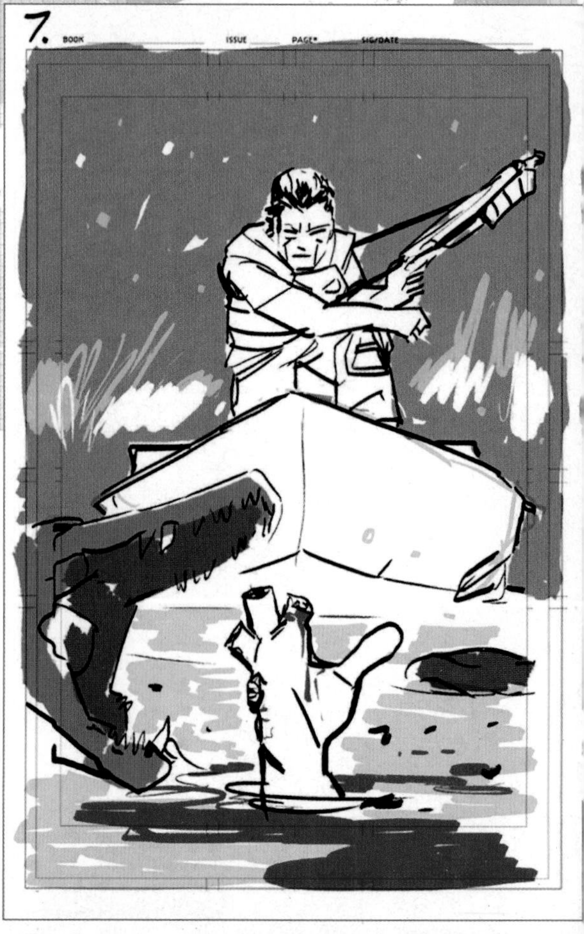
7.

PUNISHER #1
PAGE 07 LAYOUTS
BY MITCH GERADS